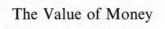

The Value of Money

The Value of Money

Ethics and the World of Finance

Catherine Cowley

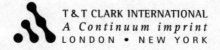

T&T CLARK INTERNATIONAL
A Continuum imprint
LONDON • NEW YORK

Published by T&T Clark
A Continuum imprint
The Tower Building, 11 York Road, London SE1 7NX
80 Maiden Lane, Suite 704, New York, NY 10038

www.tandtclark.com

British Library Cataloguing-in-Publication Data
A catalogue record for this book is available from the British Library

Typeset by YHT Ltd, London
Printed on acid-free paper in Great Britain by
MPG Books Ltd, Bodmin, Cornwall

ISBN 0567030903 (hardback)

Contents

BIS	Bank for International Settlements
FSA	Financial Services Authority
HLI(s)	Highly Leveraged Institution(s)
IMF	International Monetary Fund
LTCM	Long Term Capital Management
OECD	Organisation for Economic Cooperation and Development
OTC	over-the-counter
SEC	Securities and Exchange Commission
VaR	Value-at-Risk

Chapter 1

INTRODUCTION

In the sixteenth century Giovanni Botero wrote a forerunner to Adam
Smith's *Wealth of Nations* with his *The Cause of the Greatness of Cities*.
Like Smith, he wanted to analyse what it was that led some places to
wealth and others to miss out. He describes two City Republics in Italy
which stood in contrast to each other; Venice, where private citizens were
fairly wealthy but the state was extremely wealthy, and Genoa, whose
citizens had enormous private wealth in a relatively impoverished state.[1]
The reason for this, although he did not spell it out in great detail, was
that Venetians traded in goods and Genoese in money. Why this simple
fact should have led to such different states of affairs, and its relevance for
today, is the subject of this book. I shall be looking at how money shapes
our world, our understanding of value, our relationships and the influence
of finance on the economy.

Overview

We cannot, however, jump straight into finance; there are a number of
important preliminaries to be discussed first. The finance sector exists
within a context – the free market with its ideology of neoclassical economics. Trying to discuss finance without some clarity about what that
context means would be like trying to discuss football without knowing
that two teams, a ball and a set of rules are involved: not very illumi-
nating. I shall also be putting morality and the global economy into the
mix, aware that for some people morality and finance, or morality and the
global economy, are mutually exclusive concepts. Finally, issues will be
examined from both a Christian and an economics perspective. The
Christian perspective will be strongly, but not exclusively, Catholic;
drawing on the wide range of Catholic social teaching, and from theologians from different traditions.

For many Christians, the mention of economics causes a glazed

---

1. Giovanni Botero, *A Treatise Concerning the Causes of the Magnificencie and Greatnes of
Cities*, 1606.

expression to settle in; for many economists, the mention of theology seems wholly inappropriate to the issues at hand. I hope to prevent the glazing over by making the economics and finance accessible, and to demonstrate the relevance of theology – without, I hope, irritating the purists too much. Understanding a new subject is always demanding. The extensive use of unfamiliar terms and the fiendishly complex nature of some financial dealings can seem an impenetrable barrier. But I believe that understanding the finance sector (at least in general terms) is a moral demand of our time – otherwise it operates within an unchallengeable mystique. Only with such understanding can the necessary conversation between society as a whole and the sector be had. Because I want to address very different groups who may well not be experts in both fields, I shall not be engaging in those detailed internecine debates which might normally be expected. To spell out all the possibilities would double the length of this book and probably cause many readers to take to the hills rather than continue. Finally, both sides of this debate (economists and theologians) often use their particular approach simply to define the other approach as inadequate. This is never fruitful and will not be the method I use.

If there is to be a true dialogue between equal partners, it is important that each one is heard in its own terms, that is, that each 'voice' is respected. Following this brief overview I will explain the approach I am adopting. This allows the distinctive 'voice' of business to be heard and helps to highlight aspects which have been neglected by mainstream business ethics, including the issue of the 'positioning' of business within society. Some influential economists have asserted that there is no legitimate place for a specific business ethics. I will need to show that this assertion is mistaken if the rest of my argument is to stand up.

Following this chapter, I will present the conversation partners. The next chapter will examine and test the adequacy of the ethical claims of the market from within its own frame of reference. These claims are of justice, efficiency and freedom. In Chapter 3 I will examine two major assumptions which underpin the neoclassical model. These are the disjunction between value and fact, and self-interested rationality. Key questions here will be whether these assumptions adequately account for central elements of what it is to be human and what they do to the complex social interdependency within which business operates. Chapters 4 and 5 will take these two questions and examine them from a Christian point of view; Chapter 4 will present an alternative account of what it is to be human and Chapter 5 will examine the social interdependency.

Having established something of the context, I will then begin the discussion on the finance sector. Chapter 6 looks at the most fundamental distinction between the finance sector and business in general. That distinction arises from what the sector trades in, that is, money. I will be examining how the symbolic reality of money, in and of itself, has become the underlying phenomenon which drives the finance sector, and with it the process of globalization. Chapter 7 will show that the very nature of the sector requires specific attention which it has not adequately received from mainstream business ethics. Several specific characteristics of the sector have been overlooked due to the micro-focus usually adopted. Many of the ethical issues of the sector identified in this chapter, and explored in the remaining chapters, arise not from the actions or intentions of individuals or individual firms, but from the operation of financial markets as a whole. It is necessary, therefore, to consider both systemic factors and individual actions in any adequate ethics of the sector.

A Bottom-up Approach

I want to begin with a small, but important clarification. I shall often be referring to 'business ethics' as a shorthand way of referring to ethical reflection on economic activity and 'mainstream business ethics' as a way of referring to the dominant approach in that discipline. This approach takes as normative the North American business model. As will become apparent, I disagree with the most common methodology of the discipline (what I refer to as the micro-focus) as well as with its framework of the North American business model with its reliance on a particular view of economics.

The approach I have adopted for the next two chapters is one which is open to broader considerations than those often examined. In part it can be characterized as dialectical in the Aristotelian sense – that is, eliciting truth by beginning with prevailing opinion. Aristotle began his investigation into justice by asking 'What do citizens say is just?'[2] In other words, he surveyed the beliefs, opinions and theories of his contemporaries. Analogously, one could say that I begin by asking 'What does the market say is its ethical justification?'

So although it is usual practice in works concerning business ethics,[3] this preliminary section will not begin with a survey of ethical theories – utilitarian, deontological ethics, contractarianism and so on. Such an approach obscures the potential distinctiveness of business ethics. It assumes that there is just ethical theory which, if you are a Kantian, you will apply like this or, if an act utilitarian, like that. Ethical theory will not, however, settle highly theoretical questions such as distribution mechanisms or property rights which would need to draw on economic

2. Aristotle, *Nicomachean Ethics*, Book V.
3. For example Tom L. Beauchamp and Norman E. Bowie (eds.), *Ethical Theory and Business*, 7th edn, 2004.

philosophy. Neither can economic philosophy, in its turn, provide the ethical framework to decide which mechanisms or rights are appropriate in any particular situation. This is not to imply that these theories have nothing to offer moral reflection, because clearly they do. Rather, I am suggesting that they are not the place to start. This is not only because this method of reflection results in arguments which many business practitioners regard as, at best, relativistic, and, at worst, irrelevant. It is also because, as MacIntyre has pointed out[4] the moral theories are part of the problem.

During the eighteenth and nineteenth centuries several forms of moral theory developed. These were principally theories of utility or rights. However, as MacIntyre demonstrates, these arguments are incommensurable in moral debate. The concept of rights arose to serve one set of purposes, while that of utility was devised for another.[5] Genuine moral debate cannot take place between one who argues in terms of social utility and one who believes in the priority of rights. They justify moral priorities in different ways. What is considered of legitimate interest will be defined differently depending upon the choice of moral theory. One claim cannot be matched to the other. Hence there is no rational way of deciding which type of claim has priority, nor a way of weighing one claim against the other. All that results is a dialogue of the deaf.

One consequence of this is that liberal societies have no adequate shared morality in which debate can be grounded. Yet society expects its members to resolve often complex moral issues. MacIntyre shows that when there is no common ground for debate and no method to which all parties may appeal, reasoned argument necessarily fails. In so far as moral agents must still reach a resolution of their conflict, power must be resorted to in order to act. In this he is surely correct. The social context of economic activity underlines that the resolution of key economic issues, such as the distribution of income, depends as much on balances of power within society as on the operation of economic 'law'. Power in the business context will be an important theme in all that follows. A further reason for the perceived inadequacy of some moral debate is the neglect of what experience is considered legitimate for moral evaluation. Particularly since the work of Carol Gilligan[6] many authors have identified the importance of ensuring that all voices in the debate are heard as clearly as possible. The purpose of an Aristotelian bottom-up approach is to provide for just such a possibility.

---

4. Alasdair MacIntyre, *After Virtue: A Study in Moral Theory*, 1981.

5. MacIntyre, p. 68.

6. Carol Gilligan, *In a Different Voice: Psychological Theory and Women's Development*, 1982.

Functional Differentiation

A hotly contested question about economic activity is 'who gets to decide what is moral?' One of the reasons why this is a complicated issue is the functional differentiation which is a feature of modern and postmodern society. Pre-modern conceptions of society did not differentiate between the social spheres of family life, economic activity, religion and art (some readers may prefer the term social sectors to social spheres). Contemporary society is characterized by its fragmentation into several relatively autonomous spheres. The inescapable framework for ethical reflection today, therefore, is one in which there can be no presumed unity of moral principles. Indeed, conflict may be inherent in the different expectations of the respective spheres.

Following Weber, society may be roughly divided into two distinct realms. The first is the *Lebenswelt* (life world) which consists of the cultural and moral spheres of society.[7] It provides the shared background of meaning, recognition and support. It is the realm of basic world-views and moral beliefs into which people are born, the content of which is internalized through socialization and education. It is in this sphere that religious belief is located. The second realm consists of a number of highly specialized functional spheres which are no longer in an unbroken unity with the *Lebenswelt*. Such spheres include the economic market system, medical science, technological research and bureaucratic organization. This is not just to state the very obvious fact that every society is a mixture of cultural, economic and political influences, each generated by its own system of people, institutions and ideas. Rather it is to point to the existence of highly specific spheres which specialize in pursuing precisely determined goals in an efficient and effective manner. This they do according to strictly formal rules and procedures. As they operate with a high degree of relative autonomy, it would be simplistic to assume that moral principles from the *Lebenswelt* can be applied in precisely the same way both to it and to the functional spheres.

Once this differentiation is acknowledged, several issues become evident. I will argue that, due to the relational nature of the human person and of society, the differentiation is not absolute. However, this differentiation and *relative* autonomy may appear to preclude any normative claims made by Christianity or any other ethical tradition. If it does not, then what level of moral autonomy can a functional sphere rightly claim? How should moral accountability be demonstrated and to whom? What are the criteria which legitimate a moral claim by the *Lebenswelt*?

---

7. At the time Weber was writing society, while not homogeneous, was much less pluralistic and multicultural than our own. Nevertheless, I think it legitimate to point to dominant cultural and moral spheres, aware that these will often have contested aspects to them.

If some level of autonomy is accepted, then business ethics (within which financial ethics has to be located) cannot simply be conceived of as applied ethics, as Velasquez does.[8] It cannot be assumed that there are universally valid moral principles which simply have to be applied to a business context. If one wishes to use some general norm, it will need to be argued for, rather than assumed. It is not obvious, for example, how general moral principles alone can tell business what kinds of anti-competitive practices are morally permissible or what business itself should do about unemployment. Neither is it obvious how business managers are to choose between the concerns of the shareholders, the workers and environmentalists when these concerns are in conflict.

This possibility of non-applicability of universal norms arises, as Rahner concluded,[9] from an 'inexpressibly individual' element in the concrete instance, bringing with it individual obligations. Individuals, whether persons or collectives, are confronted by historical tasks which do not allow us always to be guided by general norms. Today, even when recognizing the usefulness and binding nature of universal norms, we often find ourselves at a loss when confronted by questions of politics, economics, pollution and so on. No moral theory can provide simple solutions to such practical questions. Therefore business ethicists who propose simple, straightforward 'decision models' should be viewed with caution.[10] In questions such as these, individuals require the maturity to take responsibility for decisions which cannot be legitimated by universal norms or standard decision models alone. It is for this reason that the Roman Catholic tradition, for example, repeatedly points out that in the economic sphere it may offer guidelines towards solutions, but not the concrete solutions themselves.[11]

This is because each sphere is characterized by a set of socially recognized goals or purposes which do not remain static through time; the conquest of empire or its administration was an acceptable activity for companies like the East India Company, but is rejected today. These socially recognized goals then count as justificatory values for their respective spheres, and ethical standards of a particular sphere are justified in relation to these values (as well as others).[12] So, for example, locking up someone against his will is justifiable within the criminal justice sphere, given its socially approved role of restraining convicted criminals.

---

8. Manuel G. Valasquez, *Business Ethics: Concepts and Cases*, 5th edn, 2002.

9. Karl Rahner, 'Reflections on the Adult Christian', *Theology Digest* 31 (1984), pp. 123–26.

10. For example, Elaine Sternberg, *Just Business: Business Ethics in Action*, 1994 and Elizabeth Vallance, *Business Ethics at Work*, 1995.

11. For example, John Paul II, *Centesimus Annus*, 1991, n. 43.

12. Thus it would be incorrect to presume that social approval of the goals and their attendant values alone can be the criterion for moral correctness.

It would not be a justifiable activity in the business sphere. Again, it would be inappropriate to judge disciplinary and grievance procedures within a firm by the standards required of a criminal court of law. It follows that *a significant criterion for ethically evaluating a particular sphere is in relation to its reasonable values, constrained by how it impacts on other spheres.* I am not just saying that the circumstances must always be taken into account. Rather I am stressing that it is the *socially ascribed role* which provides the context for the particular circumstance.

While there is not complete continuity between the spheres, neither is it correct to assume that there is complete discontinuity. In large measure these spheres are defined by those roles which are socially assigned and approved as having a contribution towards the provision of some good for society. Thus, although there is an economic sphere, society as a whole has not sanctioned the formation of business firms to manufacture and distribute cocaine or 'snuff' films, even though there is a market and substantial profits are to be made. There is a running debate between society and the technological/economic sphere on the question of 'should we do what we are capable of doing?' Examples of this debate are cloning and genetically modified organisms.

The very basis of business ethics refers to how business fits into the whole of society. It must address how, if at all, moral claims on business behaviour can be made by the *Lebenswelt* which both respect the relative autonomy and functional competence of business and at the same time prevent the disintegration of society into unrelated, mutually exclusive fragments. Talcott Parsons,[13] whose work underpins much of modern social-systems theory, developed the concept of 'zones of interpenetration' between social sub-systems. In his analysis, it is through such zones of interpenetration that different spheres communicate and maintain the integrity of the overall system. Each system is independent, but influences the others directly and indirectly through the process of continuing interaction. Others have developed his work, but have maintained his concept of 'boundaries' which enable the observer to know where one sphere stops and another begins.[14]

Parsons' view is that the spheres interpenetrate externally – the image that comes to mind is a series of Lego® bricks. Social science, and much of philosophy, is still based on Newtonian images of the universe. We manage by separating things into parts. We believe that influence occurs

13. Talcott Parsons, *Structure and Process in Modern Society*, 1960 and *The System of Modern Societies*, 1971.
14. For example, Lee E. Preston and James E. Post, *Private Management and Public Policy: The Principles of Public Responsibility*, 1975 and Michael Novak, *The Spirit of Democratic Capitalism*, 1982. Another variant is that of 'interactive' systems; cf. James E. Post, *et al.*, *Business and Society: Corporate Strategy, Public Policy, Ethics*, 9th edn, 1999.

as a direct result of force exerted by one person, or one 'system' on another, and we engage in complex planning for a world we keep expecting to be predictable. 'The whole corpus of classical physics and the technology that rests on it is about the separateness of things, about constituent parts and how they influence one another across their separateness.'[15]

In this world of things there are well-defined edges; it is possible to tell where one stops and the other begins. Yet our reality is that social spheres, and society as a whole, are in a constant state of flux. It may be comforting to imagine we inhabit a world of stable systems, but we do not. I take the view that a more accurate term than Parsons' 'interpenetration' would be 'integration'. This term highlights that there is an internal type of relation, where spheres may fuse and mix. This respects the dynamic plurality of roles carried by any individual, as well as the 'colonization' of other spheres by the economic. This colonization will be discussed more fully in Chapters 2 and 3. The term also enables the identification of a central paradox: that of functional differentiation within inter-connectedness, a state of high diversification without clear boundaries. This paradox will be an underlying theme throughout the whole book, but will particularly inform the discussion of the next section.

This social framework enables the identification of a number of issues which I will explore more fully in subsequent chapters. First, the possibility that economics' presumption of deterministic individualism prevents an adequate conceptualization of social complexity and integration, and therefore the legitimacy of moral claims from the *Lebenswelt*. Secondly, the possibility that the move to justify business behaviour apart from its inter-relatedness with other social spheres (a move discussed later in this chapter) necessarily fails to preserve the social legitimacy conferred by the wider community which business needs if it is to carry out its function. Thirdly, that the reductionism inherent in the standard explanations of business behaviour and motivation (as I will discuss in Chapter 3) will exacerbate social fragmentation and personal alienation.

The 'Positioning' of Business within Society

My choice of framework permits discussion of the positioning of business within society. This will be particularly important in looking at the finance sector. The relationship of the sector to the rest of the economy is a complex one, with finance assuming an ever greater centrality. The sector also shares with the rest of business a relationship to society as a whole.

15. Danah Zohar, *The Quantum Self: Human Nature and Consciousness Defined by the New Physics*, 1990, p. 51.

How business is positioned within society will be particularly important when considering issues such as the purpose of the sector and the relative power it has.

More than twenty years ago Useem presented an impressive body of evidence to support his thesis that a politicized leading edge of senior executives and directors in a number of major corporations has had a major role in defining and promoting the shared needs of large corporations in the USA and the UK.[16] Rooted in inter-corporate networks through shared ownership and directorships of large companies, this phenomenon is an unforeseen consequence of the decline first of family capitalism, then managerial capitalism which is being replaced by institutional capitalism.

> In the era of institutional capitalism, it is not family or individual corporate interests that serve to define how business political activity is organised and expressed but rather concerns much more classwide – the shared interests and needs of all large corporations taken together. Increasingly a consciousness of a generalised corporate outlook shapes the content of corporate political action.[17]

He takes issue with, and refutes, those theories of business–government relations which see business as either too little organized to act politically at all, or so fully organized that it acts as a single, politically unified bloc. Instead he presents evidence of a still highly imperfect fashioning of the main elements of public policies suited to serve the aggregate welfare of the corporate community by what he terms an 'inner circle' which transcends company, regional, sectoral and other politically divisive fault lines within the corporate community. More than a decade later, Hood – although he seems unaware of Useem's work and does not use the same terminology – provides examples which are fully in line with Useem's argument.[18] Boswell and Peters' examination of the ideas of British business leaders on political, economic and social issues since 1960 brings the research up to the 1990s.[19] Their work reveals the distinctive contributions made to both public policy and thinking about capitalism by elite business opinion.

Yet business ethics has failed to address this phenomenon. Corporate decision-making is viewed exclusively as a product of the internal logic of the firm. This perspective is accurate for many, indeed most, decisions of large companies. However, when decisions are made on the nature and

16. Michael Useem, *The Inner Circle: Large Corporations and the Rise of Business Political Activity in the US and UK*, 1984.

17. Useem, pp. 4–5.

18. John M. Hood, *The Heroic Enterprise: Business and the Common Good*, 1996.

19. Jonathan Boswell and James Peters, *Capitalism in Contention: Business Leaders and Political Economy in Modern Britain*, 1997.

direction of its philanthropic activities, the allocation of company funding
to lobbying, consultation with the highest levels of national and multi-
national government, public defence of the free-enterprise system and so
on, there is an external logic as well. Useem argues persuasively that the
logic of classwide benefits obtains here, involving considerations that lead
to company decisions beneficial to all large companies, even if, at least in
the short term, there is no direct gain for the individual firm. This reality
should be prompting business ethicists to revisit their conceptions of the
firm, of corporate decision making, of the relationship of business to the
wider socio-political environment and of agency theory. Yet there is little
evidence that this has happened, resulting in central issues of business
roles, power and resources being bypassed. Given the enormous influence
of the finance sector on, for example, the International Monetary Fund
(as I will be discussing in Chapter 9), the ways in which it has successfully
ensured government action which benefits the sector over the last 60 years
and its centrality within the economy, this oversight is not trivial. Mainstream business ethics has remained resolutely micro-focused, with good
conduct within existing structures being seen as its remit. Even in discussion on social responsibility – where it might be thought that almost by
definition a wider horizon would have to come into view – the issues have
been conceived in micro- and unilateralist forms. By selecting a wider
perspective than that used in standard business ethics, I will seek to illu-
minate some of the blind spots resulting from a micro-focus.[20]

Business Values – A Chimera?

The discussion so far on justificatory values may appear to beg the
question 'Does business *in itself* have values which should be prized and
by which it can be judged?' Milton Friedman, along with many economists and business practitioners, believes that it does not. He argues that
regulation of business by the current moral rules and general values of
society is both appropriate and sufficient. Such a suggestion is disin-
genuous in the extreme. The role of business interests in making the rules
that govern their own operation, and their use of lobbying about both
general and issue-specific regulations, means that obeying the rules of
society does nothing whatsoever to resolve dilemmas between business
and society.

Friedman denies that business is a proper object for separate ethical
analysis at all, arguing, in one of the most famous articles about business,
that the only social responsibility of business is to make profits, as that is

---

20. This is not to suggest that a micro-focus has no value. Clearly it does, but business
ethics needs more than one level of analysis.

its distinctive purpose.[21] In other words, the social and ethical responsibilities of business are exhausted in terms of market-place performance. As long as business uses its resources efficiently, it has fulfilled its responsibilities; nothing more need be said. Any other view would show 'a fundamental misconception of the character and nature of a free economy' and would 'thoroughly undermine the very foundations of our free society'.[22] He views the market, and therefore business within it, as something which achieves its end precisely by the impersonal nature of its activity.[23] There is a lack of coherence in this view. By claiming that the current moral rules and values of society are appropriate and sufficient, he appears to be suggesting that there is a pre-modern unity in society. At the same time, he is proposing a completely autonomous market system, with its own normative principle: maximize private profits and reduce costs. Such a degree of separation has the corollary that, while society may try to exercise some degree of control over business through the non-moral mechanisms of legislation and market rules, there is no place for it to make moral claims. Despite its logical incoherence, Friedman's view has been immensely influential, particularly among business practitioners. Despite the growth of 'social responsibility reporting' which may appear to go against this view, much of this reporting is with an eye to reputational protection and enhancement, which indirectly feeds in to the bottom line. Indeed, much of the incentive for doing this type of reporting is explicitly appealing to the impact on profitability.[24]

Another form of separation is to suggest that the only proper subjects for ethical enquiry are individuals, rather than organizations and their structures. John Ladd argues a commonly heard theme, although perhaps not always so bluntly put. He asserts that business organizations in particular are not entities which can be treated as moral agents. 'We cannot and must not expect formal organisations or their representatives acting in their official capacity to be honest, courageous, considerate, sympathetic, or to have any kind of moral integrity. Such concepts are not in the vocabulary, so to speak, of the organisational language game.'[25] Hayek[26] suggests that it is no more sensible to discuss the morality of the market than it is to discuss the morality of the climate. He bases this on the

21. Milton Friedman, 'The Social Responsibility of Business is to Increase Its Profits', 1970; reprinted in George D. Chryssides and John H. Kaler (eds.), *An Introduction to Business Ethics*, 1999, pp. 249–54.

22. Milton Friedman, *Capitalism and Freedom*, 1962, p. 133.

23. Friedman, *Capitalism*, p. 15.

24. See, for example, 'The Good Company: A Survey of Corporate Social Responsibility', *The Economist*, 22 Jan 2005.

25. Quoted in Robert C. Solomon, *Ethics and Excellence: Cooperation and Integrity in Business*, 1992, p. 132.

26. Fredrick A. Hayek, *The Constitution of Liberty*, 1960.

assertion that market outcomes are not directly chosen or intended by the individual. Rather they are the cumulative result of a multiplicity of separate, individual decisions.

However, those who believe that they can dispose of ethics and the posing of value questions overlook the fact that economic activity places enormous moral demands on individuals. It requires a moral attitude that the economy alone cannot produce. In addition, while the economy can show individuals the relative prices and the optimal allocation of their resources for certain goals, it cannot relieve them of the choice between goals and values. Ladd's view would require that business practitioners live their lives in discrete compartments, operating as a different *type* of moral agent in different contexts.

The extensive literature on corporate culture makes clear that the working environment is not, in fact, neutral. Ladd, and this line of argument generally, ignores the well-documented fact that any organization quickly evolves some sort of corporate culture which will contain either implicit or explicit moral expectations. Schein[27] describes culture as a model of basic assumptions – invented, discovered or developed by a particular group as it learns how to confront its problems of external adaptation and internal integration – that have been influential enough to be considered valid and consequently taught to new members as the correct way of perceiving, thinking about and experiencing these problems. Study of these cultures has verified that many of the thoughts and actions of individuals in organizations are culturally influenced. Individuals can act and operate according to different standards and criteria depending on the context, and socialization processes in organizations are usually aimed at shaping individuals to fit into a normative structure.[28] The values of the organization shape the expectations of managers and staff and their views about 'right' or 'wrong' behaviour in a corporate context. The question then arises of how the members of that organization can evaluate the demands of the culture in which they find themselves. Ladd's perspective would not allow for this to happen. Neither would it have any contribution to make on the rights and wrongs of, for example, whistle-blowing. What it would entail, however, is that the role of business practitioner must take precedence over all other roles. In this view, if one's personal morality is such that it conflicts with business practice, one either has to suppress that morality or give up business.

While Friedman's position maintains a connection between society and business activity, at the very least he falls into the trap of assuming that

27. Edgar H. Schein, *Organisational Culture and Leadership*, 1985.

28. See, for example, A. Kennedy and T. Deal, *Corporate Cultures*, 1982; Linda K. Trevino, 'A Cultural Perspective on Changing and Developing Organizational Ethics', *Research in Organizational Change and Development* 4 (1990), pp. 195–230.

society has an homogenous moral framework from which those in business can draw unambiguous guidance. In addition, he makes no allowance for the complex interplay between individual and corporate ethics or for the particularities of business. His analysis, although still very influential, evolved before the impact of globalization; now a firm's business interests do not necessarily coincide with the home country's national interests. Above all, however, it masks the place of the market as ideology. As with all highly successful, established paradigms, its fundamental assumptions tend to be taken for granted, no longer to be questioned, no longer only one possible alternative among different types of economy and behaviour. It ends up assuming what it claims to be proving: in this case, that the pursuit of self-interest through market processes serves the common good.

Ladd, Hayek, and numerous followers, display an unjustified faith in the mechanical workings of the market. I will be looking at this mechanistic model in more detail. At this point, it is sufficient to say that as long as it is believed that the invisible hand of the market leads to beneficial results, the question of the morality of the market, and therefore of business operating within it, is avoided. As long as it is believed that only impersonal market forces guide the economy, no moral decisions have to be made. The invisible hand makes all decisions and choices; nobody is supposed to have market power. The striving for profit maximization is all that is required, both of firms and of individuals.

However, if there is market power, if business practitioners are making deliberate choices and decisions that influence others' lives, there must be guiding norms for such decisions. If the market is a mere social fact, as Hayek maintains, just as the climate is a natural fact, then it is beyond the control of those who work in it. However, if the market is not totally beyond our control, if we can – at least to some extent – influence the circumstances within which we act, then the question of the morality of our decisions and actions does arise. Adam Smith, to whom so many economists and business practitioners look, did not only write *The Wealth of Nations*. He had first written *The Theory of Moral Sentiments*, and the later work presupposes the earlier. Today's assessment of business must be equally broad in its perspective.

Summary and Conclusions

A bottom-up approach provides a method of ensuring that the voices of both free-market proponents and Christian theology can be heard. It might be argued that the approach of starting from an examination of business's own values risks falling into the trap, mentioned earlier, of presuming what it claims to prove. However, I believe that this approach finds a path between, on the one hand, uncritical apology and precipitate acceptance of the status quo and, on the other, presumptuous moralism and abstract imperatives.

The basis of business ethics refers to how business fits into the whole of society. I have presented a framework which respects functional differentiation within a context of inter-connectedness. I have rejected the micro-focus common in mainstream business ethics, in order to facilitate reflection on the relationships between economic activity and the wider society. However, business ethics must also respect functional differentiation. It must, if it is to be of value to those it addresses, be firmly located within the concrete context of business practice, its role and functioning within society and the actual experience of business practitioners. It will be of value because it takes seriously the *actual* goals, ideals, values, purposes and dysfunctions of the sphere in which the moral agent must operate. It will accept that sphere's assumptions and claims as being heuristically helpful, even if not correlative with ultimate reality. Beginning with an examination of 'what is' rather than a hypothetical 'what should be', it will be possible to identify those features where – within business's own value system – moral questions arise. By identifying areas of business's self-understanding where goals and values are shared, it will be possible to begin a debate which avoids sinking immediately into incommensurable moral statements and which, by virtue of being a true conversation, can provide both partners in the conversation with new insight. As finance is in many ways a paradigmatic case of business beliefs and activities, this more general discussion will establish a solid foundation for the more specific examination of the sector later on.

In the mind of the general public, business is often viewed as being amoral, if not actually immoral. In the next two chapters I will seek to show that business does have distinctive values which can provide a substantial part of its ethical justification, while at the same time providing an important element of its own critique. This critique will show how the neoclassical economic model of the market, with its pervasive influence, structures many of the assumptions about economic behaviour in a way which seems to run counter to our moral intuitions. This is so despite the claim that the market, acting as a completely autonomous social sphere, will, through the mechanism of the invisible hand, produce the optimum outcome for the whole of society. I will also argue further that, while there is indeed a degree of separation and autonomy between the social spheres, a more accurate picture will be one which acknowledges the areas of integration between them. This and Chapter 3 together provide the building blocks for the examination of the finance sector.

Chapter 2

ETHICAL CLAIMS OF THE MARKET

The finance sector is often viewed as the most complete expression of free-market principles. We can, therefore, expect that free-market characteristics will be evident in the sector: what is claimed for the free market will be mirrored in some way in how the sector operates. Therefore, how the free market justifies itself will form part of the finance sector's own justification. This chapter will be concerned with the ethical claims made for the operation of the free market as a whole. These claims have emerged out of the particularities of the business context itself and must be taken seriously in their own right if ethical reflection is to be accepted by business practitioners. My aim here and in the next chapter is not to present an exhaustive evaluation of the free market. It is a more modest one, that is, to identify both the ethical claims of the free market and the limits to those claims. The purpose of identifying the limits is that it is at those points that contributions from other perspectives may be helpful.

The capitalist free market, as any economic system, is a co-ordinating system for economic activity. It regulates what things are produced and by what means. It determines who receives them in return for which contribution. As an economic order, capitalism is usually described as being distinguished by three structural characteristics. First, the private ownership of capital and means of production. Secondly, market and price mechanisms working through supply and demand as the means of co-ordination, and finally, profit and utility maximization as the basic motivation in economic action. This last characteristic, although usually presented as a self-evident fact, is in reality a highly questionable assertion. The market is an entity and concept which is in continual and rapid change. An obvious recent example is the structural changes brought about by the process of globalization. When considering aspects of the market, we need to distinguish between the 'ideal' market (by 'ideal' is meant a model which is abstracted from the complexities of human society to see how it would work in a 'pure' form) and the concrete historical forms which correspond to a greater or lesser extent to this ideal.

The Claims of the Free Market

The ethical claims made for the market stem directly from its method of organizing productive and distributive economic activity. I shall briefly outline the claim and then examine its limits. As I want to ensure that a conversation is possible, I shall not be introducing theological arguments at this point. I am examining the limits to these claims from within the framework of economic arguments; therefore you may not find the arguments you expect to see. This does not mean that I think them unimportant; rather it is an acknowledgment that theologians sometimes move too quickly into theologizing, without sufficient clarity about where the places are at which to start the conversation. Having examined these limits, there will be an initial assessment of their internal coherence. This is not the final assessment; it will be further refined in the discussion of the finance sector.

These ethical claims are made of the ideal market, an ideal which requires those conditions leading to 'perfect competition'. These conditions can be summarized as, first, that there shall be many buyers and sellers, none of whom has a dominating share of the market. Next, that there is free, unrestricted entry to the market for all sellers and buyers. These two conditions define the situation of 'perfect competition'. The model of the ideal market assumes that all participants to any transaction are in possession of complete information about the prices, quality and quantities of goods which are available. The final condition is that all the benefits and costs of the production and use of the goods fall entirely on the parties to the transaction and on no other. In other words, there are neither positive nor negative 'externalities'. Commentators then transfer their claims from the ideal market to the real market, holding that the nearer real markets are to ideal market conditions, the more clearly will the ethical goods claimed be provided.

Justice and Efficiency

Very often when proponents of the free market are talking about equity or justice they are referring to commutative justice[1] whereas critics tend to mean distributive justice. Commutative justice is held to result from the quantity of goods available and their attached prices being in equilibrium. What this means is that prices correspond simultaneously to the value the purchaser puts on the goods acquired and to the costs borne by the seller in supplying them. It is achieved when the mutual consent of the

1. Commutative justice is justice in exchange relations and other forms of private transactions.

contracting parties is reasonable, uncoerced and fair to everyone involved. Goods fetching a greater than normal profit will cause others to enter the market and the goods in question to be produced in larger amounts until the excess profit is reduced.

A detailed examination of commutative justice under the aspect of consent to the transaction will be made in Chapter 9. It needs to be noted here, however, that commutative justice, by definition, is limited to the private sphere. The problem comes with defining what is the 'private' sphere. When privately owned corporations act in ways which significantly shape the lives of people who are not directly parties to the transaction, it seems at least arguable that they are acting in the public sphere. If that is the case, then commutative justice is not sufficient. Distributive justice is the responsibility of the state in some form or at some level. It is to do with the proper ordering of access to public goods. Once more there is the problem of defining what is to be viewed as a public good and what is a private good. Again this will be examined in Chapter 9 where the ambiguity between these two types of good will be highlighted.

Following from this is the claim that the market produces optimal efficiency, understood as the elimination of waste. Resources are invested where consumption is high and withdrawn from those areas where it is low; the preferences of the customer indicate which items are required. What people as consumers want to spend their relatively scarce resources on is what is produced. In addition – under the conditions of perfect competition – the fundamental economic problem of scarcity is eased. This is because goods are produced and resources allocated in such a way that it is not possible to improve upon the choice of productive methods or the distribution of goods resulting from their purchase. Given the appropriate conditions, the theory of general equilibrium explains how the information supplied by prices leads economic agents to achieve this outcome. Where these ideal arrangements do not occur, for example, due to monopolies, lack of information or externalities, an intervention is justified which is designed to improve the market in its own terms. So, for example, an anti-monopoly policy is an intervention to increase competition and the allocative efficiency of resources and pricing.

'Allocative efficiency' is a term which will keep recurring. Sometimes it is easier to understand a concept through an example of how it can go wrong. In March 2005 China had at least 12 trillion yuan (US$1.4 trillion) sitting unproductively in banks – unproductively because China's banks are woefully poor at lending where it is needed. The country also had thousands of entrepreneurial firms crying out for funding. If the Shanghai Stock Exchange could bring these two together it could raise the efficiency of the economy. It could not do that because Initial Public Offerings (IPOs) were banned. Instead much of that cash found its way into the property market, inflating a bubble. That was allocative inefficiency. Resources were directed to a relatively unproductive use.

Another aspect of efficiency is that of information. When trying to determine key economic decisions – what to produce, how, for whom and by whom – a major constraint is knowledge about technology, skills and desires. Any economic system, therefore, if it is to be efficient, must be capable of operating within that constraint and revealing the information required. Through its flexible pricing system – which, for example, notifies economic agents where to deploy talent and resources and which skills to train or re-train for – the market is seen as uniquely capable of over-coming the informational constraint.

Limits to the Claims

Adam Smith proposed that the 'invisible hand' of the market would ensure that the interest of the whole of society would be promoted.[2] He assumed that this would happen in the condition of perfect competition. Even within the limitation of this condition, however, the 'goods' of justice and efficiency are only present for those able to participate in the market. The needs and demands of those without the necessary economic resources (the old, the sick, children, future generations) do not, in principle, influence the market. There is, therefore, no automatic provision of the *common* good, only for the good of that larger or smaller number of people who are already part of the market.

Cumulative inequalities of income result from the market's tendency to respond to the preferences of those already participating. Relatively scarce resources are drawn to what the wealthy want and away from the necessities of the poor. Capital accumulates more to those who are already in possession of it, and the acquisition of property involves the acquisition of power. This raises questions about economic power and freedom which will be discussed when considering the relationship between free markets and democracy.

This cumulative inequality is not just within any particular society. It is also a factor in the disparity between developed and developing countries. The causes of this disparity are many; nevertheless, the in-built distortion caused by the migration of resources to those who already enjoy high levels of economic participation cannot be overlooked when assessing how far the claim of justice is vindicated. Efficiency may also suffer as great inequality of income and wealth can undermine economic perfor-mance, as it might not generate sufficient aggregate demand. Once

---

2. Adam Smith, *An Inquiry into the Causes and Nature of the Wealth of Nations*, [1776] 1976, Book IV, Chapter II.

aggregate demand is insufficient, other factors can magnify the resulting negative consequences. The best known of such factors is when, in an economic downturn, it makes sense for firms to cut back on their wage costs, either through fewer employees or wage reductions. This lowers demand, which reinforces the downturn. Inequality may, therefore, militate against economic efficiency, weakening its ethical claim.

The value contained in the concept of efficiency is that of achieving the maximum volume of goods and services which can be produced by the choice of relatively scarce resources, and the avoidance of waste in their production. However, there are many other values, and this one of economic efficiency will only have the priority 'other things being equal'. Often they are not equal. A society could maximize productivity at a cost of great inhumanity in the way in which some or all of its citizens were treated – for example, through slave labour. Economic efficiency would then no longer be a useful instrument for human purposes. It would dominate them.

It is a commonplace of economics that there is often a trade-off between efficiency and equality. Arthur Okun, one-time Chairman of the Council of Economic Advisors in the United States, wrote that this is 'our biggest socio-economic tradeoff', one which 'plagues us in dozens of dimensions of social policy'.[3] Although these two principles necessarily co-exist in a capitalist democracy, Okun maintains that the economy usually pays a price in lowered economic efficiency when it opts for greater equality, because such efforts come at the expense of the market mechanism.

This idea, however, displays a deep-seated confusion. Efficiency is not a primary objective, but a secondary one. One pursues this or that objective more, or less, efficiently. One is efficient *at* something. It is possible to value efficiency as a means, but it is always a means to something else. It might be argued that making the best use of scarce resources (a standard definition of efficiency) is a fundamental objective, especially in the light of environmental degradation. But even here there is the need for some objective by which to define what the 'best' use might be. Even if one were to accept the claim that there is a trade-off between efficiency and equality[4] the acceptance (or rejection) of that trade-off is a value judgment which needs to be defended, not assumed. I am not arguing for some form of imposed radical egalitarianism. The problems of how such egalitarianism is to be assessed and who is to be the judge are formidable. Any alternative has its own drawbacks. Rather, I am pointing out some limits to the good claimed. Whether these limits can be extended to become

3. Arthur M. Okun, *Equality and Efficiency: The Big Tradeoff*, 1975, p. 2.
4. For example: at what rate should income tax be set so that some income redistribution occurs, without it being a disincentive? Some would argue that no income redistribution should occur in this way at all.

more inclusive is a complex political/social/economic question. Many aspects lie outside the scope of a work on ethics. But ethics may point to the areas which other disciplines need to address, as well as provide a framework within which they can reflect. This aspect of inclusiveness is something I will be returning to several times.

Hence, even the ideal market can only provide partial benefits. When the technical and economic complexity of the real market is factored in, it becomes even more difficult to approach the condition of perfect competition, further reducing these partial benefits. Despite the existence of legislation in all the highly industrialized countries, there is still the creation of monopolies and oligopolies. Buyers, by virtue of that economic complexity, rarely, if ever, have all the information they need to make well-informed, and therefore free, choices. The very notion of competition requires some qualification. There is 'healthy' competition which is fair, encourages innovation, efficiency and productivity. There is also mutually destructive, negative and debilitating competition. The claim that the market promotes competition can therefore be seen as something of a two-edged sword which ethically could cut both ways.

It is a key argument of the market model that whatever the market decides must be optimal. People rationally express their true preferences in their pattern of expenditure. It then logically follows that markets accurately serve free choices and then these choices combine to form the general welfare of society. The assumption is that, by definition, people get what they want. If what they want is not currently available, some entrepreneur will work out how to provide it. This assumption is demonstrably false. For example, polls consistently show that Americans would like universal health insurance with a free choice of doctor. Other nations offer that choice, at a lower aggregate cost, than the United States' high-priced system. Yet the free market does not provide it. Another aspect of the falsity of the claim is that with the logic of mass production, nothing is produced which cannot be produced by the thousands, leading to standardized and homogenized products. Only the rich can buy variety. Although the technical apparatus of production should only pursue an instrumental function, in reality it is increasingly that apparatus itself which determines what the market aims at. It does this by supplying goods and services to meet needs which it itself has suggested to consumers through its influence on public media.[5]

This leads to a fundamental ethical question: efficient means to what end? You cannot sustain discussion of efficient or effective means to unstated ends. The model of the market as mechanistic and impersonal

---

5. See, for example, Agnes Nairn and Pierre Berthon, 'Creating the Customer: The Influence of Advertising on Consumer Market Segments – Evidence and Ethics', *Journal of Business Ethics* 42.1 (2003), pp. 83–99.

displays a highly ambiguous attitude to the question of ends. Of necessity, if the market is to be truly *instrumental*, it must accept that the ends to be pursued are those established by the wider community. Yet some of its proponents argue vigorously that intervention with market processes (however they are to be defined) is inappropriate, or even unethical. This would imply that the implicit end of the market – selling and consuming – is the only legitimate end, and all else is relative. This imperialistic claim is not acceptable to everyone, although, as we shall see, it is one which *de facto* is gaining ground.

I have described limits to the claims concerning justice and efficiency. The restriction of these benefits to those who are already market participants and the cumulative inequalities of income occur even within the restricted theoretical framework of the 'perfect' market, as well as in real markets. The presence of significant externalities and destructive competition in 'real' markets only adds to these limitations. Finally, greater clarity is needed in discussion about efficiency so that what is in fact a means does not become converted into an end, a move which is unsustainable, both logically and ethically.

Freedom

It is asserted that the market maintains the rights of individual freedom of those involved. These are not only the right to engage, or not, in the economic exchange, but also the political freedom of the individual. In contrast to command economies, the decentralization of economic power ensures that individual firms and households can make independent decisions, subject to the general conditions of the economy. Therefore, it is claimed, free markets ensure democracy. This claim of freedom is ambiguous, as its meaning differs greatly depending upon the viewpoint of the particular advocate. Friedman, for example, maintains that there is an intimate connection between economics and politics and 'that only certain combinations of political and economic arrangements are possible'. He holds that, as a component of freedom, economic freedom is an end in itself. Furthermore, 'economic freedom is also an indispensable means towards the achievement of political freedom'.[6]

The neo-Austrian school,[7] on the other hand, views democracy as no more than a technique for the selection of the administrators of public affairs.[8] As a technique, democracy cannot be considered to have the

6. Friedman, *Capitalism and Freedom*, p. 8.
7. Principally Frederick Hayek and his followers.
8. So, for example, Frederick A. Hayek, *Law, Legislation and Liberty* Vol. 3: *The Political Order of a Free People*, 1979.

character of an absolute value but, rather, 'mere convention making possible a peaceful change of the holders of power'.[9] The market is held to be a better, indeed the only true, democratic participation process because in the market no individual is prevented from realizing the exchanges he or she wishes.[10] Unlike political democracy where the minority is excluded from the exercise of power, the market has no majorities or minorities. There, no one is prevented from pursuing their own interests. It follows that as 'we cannot count on intelligence or understanding, but only on sheer self-interest to give us the institutions we need',[11] political activity ought to be drastically restricted. This restriction need not impede the development of sophisticated public policies. Michael Novak's view is that the clash of interests and perspectives within capitalist society teaches citizens tolerance and the art of compromise. This often enables them to arrive at programmes and policies which 'strike closer to the good, the true, the real than any program simply imagined by one party alone, however noble or disinterested it may think itself'.[12]

Running as a thread through the work of both the neo-Austrians and Friedman, the intellectual leader of the Chicago School, is the concept of coercion and rights. This concept has led to strong libertarian claims being made for the market. It is claimed that the market is necessarily superior to other systems of distribution in avoiding violations of rights. Frequently it is argued, from a utilitarian basis, that the market will promote efficient methods of production and exchange, leading to the maximization of satisfaction as more people will get what they want than under any other system. Libertarians such as Nozick,[13] however, reject any attempt to justify the market in such utilitarian terms, arguing that to judge institutions or actions by the ends they promote is ultimately misleading and irrelevant. Even if an institution were superior in promoting happiness or reducing pain, if it violates rights (as Nozick defines them) it would be unjustifiable. Nozick acknowledges that his position requires a very narrow interpretation of rights. In essence, rights must be restricted to 'rights against interference'. Thus, Nozick's only criterion is: are rights violated?[14]

Differing claims are being made. Rawls believes that, given the requisite background institutions, the free market is consistent with equal liberties and fair equality of opportunity.[15] Friedman maintains that it is an

9. Hayek, *Law*, p. 5.

10. Frederick A. Hayek, *Economic Freedom*, 1991, pp. 393–98.

11. Frederick A. Hayek, *Denationalisation of Money – The Argument Refined*, 3rd edn, 1990, p. 131.

12. Novak, *The Spirit of Democratic Capitalism*, p. 62.

13. Robert Nozick, *Anarchy, State and Utopia*, 1974.

14. Nozick, pp. 28–33.

15. Rawls, *Theory of Justice*, 1972, p. 272.

essential condition for political freedom. The neo-Austrians and Nozick assert that, in itself, the free market is the only true form of the democratic process, and anything which intervenes in its operation subverts the very heart of liberty, even if done by a government elected by the majority. These claims reveal varying conceptions both of democracy and of the workings of the market. They aspire towards differing visions of society and contain inherently different bases for the ethical evaluation of actions and states of affairs.

Limits to the Claim

As the meaning of freedom varies according to the viewpoint of the particular advocate, I shall treat economic freedom before political freedom. Clearly these two freedoms are not so discrete in practice.

Adam Smith presented a model of an economic order with the acquisitive attitude as its cornerstone. He justified this economic order by assuming the essential interdependence of individual economic self-interest, the free competitive market, and the common good of society. His idea of the natural harmony of individual economic interest justified individual economic liberty by asserting that a free competitive market would promote the common good through the famous invisible hand. By this he meant the prosperity of the nation, rather than that of any particular individual. He justified *individual* economic freedom from the *social* point of view; individual economic freedom is desirable because it accomplishes the *common* economic good. This surely leads to the reverse conclusion that such freedom is not desirable when its results run counter to that common good. This conclusion seems to have escaped writers who cite Smith in support of individual economic freedom.[16]

Furthermore, the justification rests on an assumption about the identity of individual and social economic goals. They both aim at an ever-increasing volume of goods for the nation and for individuals. If this identity is true it would be possible to argue away all possible conflicts of interest between society and individuals. However, if one were to admit that there can be other interests besides that of increasing the volume of goods and services – for example, the protection of the environment, or non-economic goals – then the concept of a natural harmony of interests breaks down and the possibility of moral conflict becomes apparent.

Smith himself saw that the market could not provide so-called public goods.[17] The market depends upon such goods as an educated workforce which is reasonably healthy, in a society where there is legal order. Even

16. For example, Novak, *The Spirit of Democratic Capitalism*.
17. Smith, *Wealth of Nations*, the focal point of Book V.

though such common goods are thought necessary, no private enterprise is obviously induced to pay for them. Similarly, there are public harms, such as environmental pollution. Although there is the beginning of requiring business to meet some of the costs of these externalities, for example, a few cases of 'the polluter pays', in general these costs are not taken into account by the market. This leads to items being sold at much less than their full social costs. The market fails to register the divergence between private and social accounting. Another externality not addressed is the long-term allocation of resources when that allocation calls for reduced consumption. An example is global warming. The outcomes are still held, in some quarters, to be too uncertain, the period too long, for markets to signal now that, say, the price of oil should be significantly higher than its present level if energy is to be conserved and greenhouse emissions are to be cut. This example illustrates the lack of influence of future generations on present market pricing. Whether this lack carries any ethical import depends on whether one accepts that there is any moral obligation to future generations – and not everyone does. However, even those who most rigorously deny any obligation need to account for the fact that parents act as agents for their children.

Mass consumerism is the driving force of the modern market. We are free to buy, and may come to believe that buying is an expression of our freedom. This freedom is not available to all. For those to whom it is available, the condition of mass consumerism has been broadly characterized as the *having* mode of existence, in opposition to the *being* mode; the measure of human persons is what they own rather than what they are. This increasingly affects the general orientation of society. The essential difference between being and having is between a society centred around persons and one centred around things. Most commentators would agree that the having orientation is characteristic of western industrial society.

This is one of the contributory factors which has led to the absolutization of the market model, even into areas where it is not appropriate. This has been characterized by Singer as the commercialization of our lives. Singer analyses Nozick's political theory of freedom as the non-violation of rights to show how this theory represents 'the ultimate triumph of commercialisation'.[18] Although Nozick seems to hold that it is always wrong to violate someone's rights, closer analysis reveals that what is actually held is that it is always wrong to violate someone's rights *unless* they are compensated for the violation. Thus rights themselves become commodities with a price, for what compensation can there be except money or the bartering of goods and services? And yet, for example, the person upon whose land someone has trespassed may value solitude and

18. Peter Singer, 'Rights and the Market', in Beauchamp and Bowie, pp. 72–85 (78).

quiet above all compensation. To violate that person's right to solitude with an intention to compensate may, in this instance, be an unconditional violation of rights, as no adequate compensation may be possible. It follows that to argue, as Nozick and others do, that the unrestricted market is the best protector of freedom is simplistic. By its promotion of commercialization it may, in fact, undermine the rights it claims to ensure.

This commercialization of human life can also be seen in the increasing attempts to explain all its features in market terms. Gary Becker (a Nobel Laureate in Economics) is typical of this approach. He works with the notion of the autonomous, asocial and apolitical individual who rationally calculates how to achieve his or her best advantage. Such an individual is often described as a self-interested, rational maximizer. Becker attempted to provide an analysis of the family[19] using such concepts as maximizing behaviour, equilibrium in implicit or explicit markets and command functions. Above all, he uses an 'extended utility function' to describe behaviour. This is a mathematical formulation in which all human activity is reduced to individual choice, guided by the rational pursuit of the greatest possible utility.

Becker is right to point out that there are economic factors influencing decisions within families. However, he is naïve to seek to account for such a complex social phenomenon as the family purely in economic terms, neglecting such factors as psychodynamics, culture or the difference between sex and gender. Every difference in, for example, the division of labour is described as resulting from 'biological' differences without accounting for the socially determined features of gender roles. Neither does he indicate adequately how families relate to other social structures. This is because at the heart of Becker's failure to provide a convincing account of the family is his failure to acknowledge the importance of non-economic factors and values and his dis-embedding of people from the social relations and structures within which they exist. The core of his approach is the denial of significance of any level of existence other than that of the individual. He does this by reducing people's environments to interior states or predilections. Collective norms and relationships, ethical systems and social structures are all truncated to the attributes of the individuals who happen to populate the collective. By doing so, he not only attenuates the richness of human experience and relationships; he also severely limits human freedom by disallowing the ability of non-economic factors to influence belief and action. He is implicitly assuming that intangibles can be monetized and swapped around like ordinary goods.

Becker's is an extreme statement of the assumption that individual self-interest constitutes the heart of rational-actor theory. However, the

19. Gary S. Becker, *A Treatise on the Family*, 1981.

extension of purely economic values into all areas of human life jeopardizes the non-economic values which form part of what it is to be human. Reducing the multiplicity of human relations to one of mere commercial exchange does not enhance human freedom. Although economics as a discipline is moving towards incorporating a wider range of socio-psychological motivations for behaviour in its analyses, so leaving behind the one-dimensional approach of Becker and others, the assumptions operating in the market are still generally based on this reductionist approach.

Freedom and Democracy

The logic of the claim that free markets ensure democracy runs thus: If markets thrive on well-informed consumers, then a market society requires free expression. If markets express voluntary exchange and free choice, then they are the natural server and support of liberal democracy. Although such reasoning has a surface plausibility, it can only be maintained by ignoring what has happened with real markets. A basically capitalist form of production and exchange has coexisted with Nazism, fascism, Latin American military dictatorships, East Asian autocracies and a wide range of other authoritarian regimes. Clearly, liberal-democratic values are not automatically nurtured by markets. Therefore markets are not a sufficient reason.

Nor can one claim that they are a necessary reason, due to two factors. The first is that the claim is made that only a capitalist market can produce these goods. Yet as Rawls has cogently argued[20] there is no theoretical reason why the mechanism of the free market cannot be used within socialist systems to obtain the same advantages of efficiency, liberty and justice. Since the proportion of social resources devoted to the production of public goods is distinct from the question of public ownership of the means of production, there is no necessary connection between the two. Although the system of organizing the production of commodities will differ between a socialist and a free-market economy, all regimes will normally use the market to ration out the goods actually produced.[21] Similarly, Rawls shows that the rate of saving and the direction of investment may equally be directed by collective decision or individual firms competing for funds.[22] The connection between competitive prices and the market economy is one of historical contingency, not one of

20. Rawls, *Theory of Justice*, pp. 265–74.
21. Rawls, p. 270.
22. Rawls, p. 271.

necessity. Although less fully argued, this view is also that of Knight, who saw no reason why, logically, socialism could not use the market economy.[23]

Taken at one level, the historical evidence is that free markets have been compatible with democracy. As Peter Berger points out, all democratic societies have had a capitalist economy.[24] Indeed, the underlying assumption in the West's advocacy of free markets in Eastern Europe following the collapse of communism was that this would strengthen the move towards democracy. We can now see that that assumption was flawed – without a strong infrastructure resulting from a long co-evolution of civil society, politics and economic institutions we end up with neither democracy nor a functioning free market but Mafia capitalism. Even without that example, the assumption of compatibility is becoming fragile. The argument is based in large part on the view that economic arrangements have a deep impact on the concentration or dispersion of power. As Friedman wrote, 'Political freedom means the absence of coercion of a man by his fellow men ... The preservation of freedom requires the elimination of such concentration of power [as permits this coercion] to the fullest possible extent.'[25] Because competitive capitalism, operating through free markets, separates economic power from political power, it enables one to offset the other.

However, using Friedman's own criterion of the separation of power, it is no longer clear that economic and political power do, in fact, offset each other. Just as Adam Smith in his day criticized the merchants and manufacturers for their disproportionate influence on legislation to their own advantage,[26] so many criticize business in ours, claiming that there is a disproportionate influence of business and other advantaged participants rather than a more genuine competition of diverse groups. For example, Enron, throughout its life, aggressively lobbied Congress, the Commodity Futures Trading Commission, the Securities and Exchange Commission (SEC) and the Federal Energy Regulatory Commission for less regulation and oversight. A US Senate Committee report[27] described its success at lobbying as 'impressive'. The activities of the transnational tax-services industry and of transnational corporations significantly diluted moves to

23. Frank H. Knight, 'Free Society: Its Basic Nature and Problem', in *On the History and Method of Economics: Selected Essays*, 1956, pp. 282–99.

24. Peter Berger, *The Capitalist Revolution: Fifty Propositions About Property, Equality and Liberty*, 1987. He also believes that capitalism is not a sufficient reason, p. 81.

25. Friedman, *Capitalism and Freedom*, p. 15.

26. Smith, *Wealth of Nations*, especially Book IV, Chapter VIII.

27. Senate Staff Report of Committee on Governmental Affairs, *Committee Staff Investigation of FERC's Oversight of Enron Corp.*, 2002.

reduce harmful tax competition between countries.[28] This is not, however, only a question of how much undue influence business gains through lobbying and political donations. There is also the phenomenon of classwide action discussed in Chapter 1. The question is being increasingly asked: 'To what extent do free markets, by their increasingly transnational nature, or single corporations, by their sheer economic size, escape democratic controls expressed through national governments?' This question will have particular relevance when discussing the finance sector.

This brings us to the second factor. Market theorists such as Hayek would have us believe that the free market arose as a result of inexorable historical forces which brought about a gradual and unplanned evolution. Yet, as Polanyi, in his account of the rise of the first phase of the free market in mid-nineteenth-century England reminds us, 'The road to the free market was opened and kept open by an enormous increase in continuous, centrally organised and controlled interventionism. To make Adam Smith's "simple and natural liberty" compatible with the needs of a human society was a most complicated affair.'[29] Free markets only arose as a result of state power which successfully overturned the 'embedded' social markets which had previously existed, thereby creating a market society.

This overturning came about as a result of three basic uses of state power. The first was the transformation, via enclosure, of common land into private property, especially in the period 1790–1815. This has appropriately been called 'a revolution of the rich against the poor'.[30] The state was only able to do this because the vast majority of the population was outside the political process. This transfer of property rights was to the benefit of, and under the control of, a small land-owning elite.[31] The Poor Law reforms of 1834 ensured that the level of publicly provided subsistence was both below the lowest market wage and stigmatizing. These reforms, combined with the abolition of wages councils, led to the poor being constrained to work for whatever the market set, no matter how minimal. The repeal of the Corn Laws (1846) finally removed all agricultural protection and ushered in an era of free trade which has remained the model for all subsequent neo-liberal policies.

It was the ruthless use of state power, without democratic control or justification, which established the free market and the labour conditions

---

28. Michael C. Webb, 'Defining the Boundaries of Legitimate State Practice: Norms, Transnational Actors and the OECD's Project on Harmful Tax Competition', *Review of International Political Economy* 11.4 (October 2004), pp. 787–827.

29. Karl Polanyi, *Origins of Our Times: The Great Transformation*, 1945, p. 142.

30. Polanyi, p. 42.

31. Hence Nozick's contention that one can and should ignore how property rights were originally acquired can be seen to be self-serving. His libertarian thesis requires that this be discounted if he is to maintain that they are 'natural' and morally neutral.

which it required. An analysis of the history of the second half of the nineteenth century shows that as the franchise was extended, so state intervention in the economy changed. Rather than free markets ensuring democracy, the growth of democracy ensured the cutting back of free markets. This was true not only in Britain but also in the United States. The last decades of the nineteenth century saw the rise of major capitalists (the so-called 'Robber Barons') at a time when the federal government was extremely weak. As this level of government strengthened, anti-trust legislation was passed, leading to the break-up of, for example, the Standard Oil Company. The claim that capitalism automatically serves democracy can only be held by abstracting from the realities of history.

This dependence of the growth of the free market on the use of state power was not restricted to the nineteenth century. There is a growing body of work in the discipline of International Political Economy, ably represented by Eric Helleiner,[32] which demonstrates clearly that the globalization of financial markets following the Second World War was not the result of unstoppable technological and market forces, as usually maintained. Although these factors were important, even more important were the political decisions (and non-decisions) taken by states, principally the USA and the UK, both of whom stood to gain enormously from financial globalization. The influence of financial practitioners on these decisions is clear, even within the official records. This links directly back to the first factor discussed: the question of how effective the separation between political power and economic power is in practice. Another contemporary issue is the extent to which the advance of the free market depends upon its being placed beyond democratic control through the acts of bodies such as the World Trade Organization. Once a country becomes a member, it is no longer the sovereign state which decides, for example, what is free trade and what is a restriction. It is a bureaucratic body outside the reach of any democratic legislature. This, for its supporters, is one of its strengths. However, its critics argue that instead of market forces conforming to principles of democracy, the norm becomes one which delegitimates political demands which are construed as infringing on the functioning of the market.

It would appear, then, that the relationship between the free market and democratic processes is not as straightforward as market theorists suggest. Both historically and contemporarily, a strong case can be made that the free market and democracy – rather than being compatible – can in fact conflict. Certainly the ethical contention that the free market supports and enhances democracy is weaker than claimed.

A crucial aspect of markets and freedom is the question: freedom from

32. Eric Helleiner, *States and the Reemergence of Global Finance: From Bretton Woods to the 1990s*, 1994.

what and for what? It is clear in the writings of free-market libertarians that what is principally meant by 'freedom' is freedom from government intervention. But this is scarcely an exhaustive description. Other freedoms include the freedom not to be exploited in situations of ignorance, uncertainty and unpredictability and the freedom not to be excluded by market forces from society. Libertarians deny that there is any loss of freedom in this respect, because no one is literally exercising constraint. What is ignored by those who understand freedom individualistically is that every form of human association gives rise to power structures and conflicts of interest between these power structures. Those with comparatively few economic resources, for example, those who have only their labour, are in a position of weakness and are subject to those who can exercise power in the market. To date mainstream business ethics has not addressed this issue of power in the market-place. The economic model of the perfect market defines the problems away by denying the existence of asymmetric power, and this despite work analysing the extensive effects of oligopoly.

Adam Smith, however, had no such illusions about the effect of power, because economics is about wealth and wealth is power. Furthermore, business activity, because it involves the social relationships among members of a community in their attempt to earn a living, is concerned with power. This means that a major problem of all economic activity is domination – something which standard introductions to economics seem to ignore.[33] Referring to the silence on this issue, Galbraith wrote:

> Power – the ability of some in the economic system to command or otherwise win the obedience of others and the pleasure, prestige and profit that go therewith. It is a reticence [to speak out about power on the part of the classical tradition] that persists to this day. The pursuit of power and its pecuniary and psychic rewards remains ... the great black hole of mainstream economics.[34]

In this section I have suggested that the ethical claim that free markets enhance freedom needs to be heavily qualified. Economic freedom accrues only to some market participants, with greater weight being given to the freedom to consume than to the freedom to produce. The too easy assumption of an identity between individual and social economic goals serves only to mask the possibility of moral conflict when these do in fact occur. The extension of the market into all aspects of life can, as Singer has pointed out, result in the denial of rights. It can also, as Becker's work illustrates, undermine non-economic values. The relationship between the

33. A trawl through 10 textbooks haphazardly chosen from among those published in Britain between 1994 and 2004 did not reveal any reference to power other than monopolistic power.

34. John K. Galbraith, *A History of Economics*, 1987, p. 115.

market and democratic processes is an uneasy one, whilst the reality of asymmetric power is ignored.

Summary and Conclusions

Free-market capitalism, as an economic system, has enjoyed unrivalled practical success at wealth creation. With the free market's incentive towards thrift and innovation, the modern business firm has shown itself to be one of the most efficient economic instruments in history. Since the beginning of the Industrial Revolution, it has increased per-capita incomes in Western Europe and the USA around twentyfold. It has enabled the greatest improvement in the standard of living for the average worker seen in history. This success is of enormous moral worth and is something to celebrate. The alleviation of hunger and infant mortality, the better health and greater comfort now experienced in free-market countries arise from this success. The dispersed exercise of uncoerced economic power contributes greatly to an efficient way of getting many economic decisions made in accordance with the freedom of choice expressed by participants. Many claim, therefore, that autonomy and liberty are thus served. Yet from the same point of view, problems remain. There is inequality of access (either within a country or between countries) due either to cumulative inequalities of income or to the creation of cartels, quotas, monopolies and other restrictions. The market cannot provide public goods. Neither can it deal adequately, if at all, with externalities.

These aspects seem to suggest that, at this level, the problems of business ethics are generated by the way the market works, rather than the concept of the market in itself. That is to say, these issues arise in part from the difference in operation between the textbook market and the world in which the business practitioner has to act. It lies, market theorists suggest, in the difference between perfect competition and real market processes. Yet, as the discussion on, for example, cumulative inequalities has shown, some of these aspects arise within the context of the perfect market itself. Even the conditions of perfect competition exclude those presently not participating in the market from the benefits of efficiency and justice. Neither can the perfect market adjudicate between the differing understandings of 'rights' shown by, for example, Nozick and Singer. It is, therefore, too simple to suggest, as many proponents of free markets do, that all that is required to overcome its limits is for the market to become ever more free. These issues would still not be addressed.

The ethical values claimed for the market provide a standard against which processes and outcomes may be initially assessed. In themselves, they are inadequate to address shortcomings and the moral complexity arising from clashing or competing values, for example, differing understandings of efficiency, or when efficiency itself conflicts with non-economic goals and values. They have also shown themselves to be insufficient to curb monopolistic tendencies, cartels and so on. External intervention has been required.

But issues also arise from a deeper, less tangible level, which the model of the market as an impersonal, mechanistic phenomenon only conceals. One of the most fundamental of such issues is the relationship between the values claimed for the market and more general social values. As I noted in Chapter 1, the market operates within a complex social framework. It draws upon external values such as truth, trust, honesty and obligation, as well as the values of justice, efficiency and freedom. The process is not all one-way. Business practitioners and theoreticians seek to extend the influence of the market into ever greater areas of social life.

Some of the attempts to apply these values, as understood within market processes, back into the wider society, show these values' limitations, rather than their universality. Singer reveals the fundamentally flawed nature of Nozick's theory. Becker's attempt to explain the family solely in economic terms founders on his failure to acknowledge the importance of non-economic factors and values. Yet many of these values are also essential to the market. The external values upon which it draws, and which it needs to operate, presuppose the existence of moral values within the wider society. These, however, appear to be becoming more attenuated as the plethora of books such as *The Cheating Culture*[35] seek to demonstrate and, as some would argue, Judeo-Christian influence in western society continues to wane. Business is, therefore, faced with two related questions.

First, how can these values be fostered within the business environment itself? Is it, perhaps, that the way in which ethical justification has been made for the market has, in fact, served to conceal internal values upon which business depends? Friedman's assertion about profits gives a truncated view of the purpose of business. A further example might be the great stress put upon the merits of competition. This underplays the extent to which any corporate endeavour relies on co-operation, most obviously internally to the organization, but also externally between organizations.

Secondly, to what extent is the reliance on self-interest self-defeating? It is often argued that markets are based on self-interest. If so, then the pursuit of self-interest would need to be encouraged. However, this might lead to the possibility of an increasing incompatibility between the moral character of the individual and the wider requirements of market processes. This is because the increase in self-interest could, over time, move the moral perspective of participants away from those values which support the market, so undermining the background conditions essential

---

35. David Callahan, *The Cheating Culture: Why More Americans are Doing Wrong to Get Ahead*, 2004.

to its operation. On the other hand, it is a standard utilitarian argument that it is in the self-interest of an individual to be, for example, honest because all need to be honest if the individual is not to be defrauded. However, a debate between these two points of view would ignore a more fundamental question, which is that of accepting the premise of self-interest being *the* motivating factor in market behaviour. This is one of the questions I shall be taking up in the next chapter.

The market does not operate in a hermetically sealed ethical compartment. Deeply rooted in a complex interdependency with its social context, it should not try to claim a moral self-sufficiency which it demonstrably does not have. Neither, however, is it a dog-eat-dog ethics-free zone. I take the position that markets are not *in their essence* instruments of alienation, exploitation, anarchy and centrifugal egoism. They are, or at least can be, good instruments and serve human community. Like all human things, however, they can be used inadequately, badly and for evil purposes. No less than human beings themselves, they are capable of both good and evil. They require wider criteria of ethical reflection than just those claims which they make for themselves. An acceptance of the partial validity of market claims is necessary, but it is not sufficient.

The free-market system, when compared to any obvious alternative, clearly has a range of strengths. This does not mean that it is without problems. The question is not, as in previous decades: 'Can the market system work?' but: 'Will the market system work well enough?' Keynes wrote:

> I think that capitalism, wisely managed, can probably be made more efficient for attaining economic ends than any alternative system yet in sight, but that in itself it is in many ways extremely objectionable. Our problem is to work out a social organisation which shall be as efficient as possible without offending our notions of a satisfactory way of life.[36]

A contemporary expression of this remark would need to include the question: 'Do we want a market economy or a market society?' A market society is one where all human relationships and aspirations are deemed to be economic. It is one where the logic noted by Polanyi 60 years ago is fulfilled. That is, 'no less than the running of society as an adjunct to the market. Instead of economy being embedded in social relations, social relations are embedded in the economic system.'[37] Chapter 4 will explore the view that what it is to be human is more than the reductionist version contained in the workings of a market society. Keynes' comment is as pertinent today as when he wrote it.

---

36. John M. Keynes, *The End of Laissez-Faire*, 1926, pp. 52–53.
37. Polanyi, *The Great Transformation*, p. 63.

Chapter 3

ETHICAL INSUFFICIENCY OF THE MODEL

In this chapter I will be examining two foundational assumptions of the free-market model. To the non-economist they may appear to be in the same category as the feeding habits of the starfish – only of interest to the deeply committed few. They are, in fact, highly practical in their consequences. If these assumptions are accurate, they will give us a good-enough picture of how the market works and, indeed, how it should work. If they are not, then they cannot provide an adequate basis for the market's ethical claims. This deficient base would then ultimately prevent a correct understanding of ethical business practice by distorting the true relationship of business with the good life and with society. I will be claiming that they are indeed deficient.

The insufficiency does not lie only in the differences between the perfect market and the real market. If it did, the most justifiable use of moral energy would be to work at increasing the alignment of perfect and real markets. Nor does the insufficiency lie only in an inadequately nuanced understanding of efficiency, justice and freedom. These two factors taken together severely limit the claims; but correcting them would still not address the flawed foundational assumptions. These assumptions are, firstly, the disjunction between fact and value; and, secondly, the assumption of self-interested maximization of utility (satisfaction) as *the* motivating force of behaviour.

The Value-free Market?

The economic/mechanistic model of the market operates from a point of view which sees the market as entirely value-free. It is purely a mechanism through which consumers' preferences are registered and satisfied. What they actually prefer is another matter entirely, and is not for the economist to prescribe. Economists cannot say anything about subjective human valuations of one economic good against another, or the strength of one person's satisfaction against that of another. They can only observe the weight given to these goods by what is bid for them in the market. The mechanistic model takes goals, motives and the preferences of individuals as given, and only considers means. Individual choices are based upon unquestionably accepted preferences and the force conditions of the market.

The claim that the market is value-free is too simple. The first aspect ignored is that preferences are essentially social in character. They are influenced by social status, education and training, as well as factors such as misunderstanding and manipulation, and cannot be divorced from all context. Knight himself acknowledged that economic exchange is inextricably part of the broader discussion of values. 'In large part the individual wants themselves are *created* by social intercourse, and their character is also largely dependent upon the form of organisation of the economic system upon which they are dependent for their gratification.'[1]

The second factor is that the model itself is not, in reality, value-free. Preston suggests that there are two in-built values, elegance and efficiency.[2] The issues arising from the value of efficiency being treated as an end rather than a means have already been discussed. Here I will only look at the value of elegance. Preston points out that insofar as economics is mathematical, it shares in the mathematician's criterion of elegance. The more variables which can be accommodated with the fewest number of complexities, the more elegant the theory is held to be. Yet mathematical sophistication may be far from the actual workings of the economy. The ideal market situation presupposed by the mechanistic model is not at all, as economists like to argue, an analogy of, say, 'mass' in physics, that is, a projection of predictable behaviour minus distorting factors such as friction or atmospheric gravity. As Thurow has pointed out, 'when the heavens do not conform to an astronomer's predictions, no one goes around talking about "irrationalities" or "distortions". The theory is just wrong'.[3] Yet the attempt to explain the full complexity of the market within one model continues. Now, if elegance and efficiency were all there was to the matter, I would not need to write a whole chapter. There is a great deal more to it than just that.

Fact and Value

Much of the assumption that the market is value-free comes from a dualism which has come to dominate economic theory, and, therefore, also explanations or justifications of the market. This dualism arose as economics became a distinct discipline, trying to establish itself as a science which stood apart, analysed, described and, where possible,

---

1. Frank H. Knight, *The Economic Organization*, 1969, p. 9, emphasis in original.
2. Ronald H. Preston, *Religion and the Ambiguities of Capitalism*, 1991, pp. 22–23.
3. Lester Thurow, quoted by Robert C. Solomon, *Ethics and Excellence*, p. 52.

reduced economic activity to mathematical formulae. Involvement was to be avoided. One of the very earliest professors of political economy, Nassau Senior, made the case that 'as navigation is separate from astronomy and astronomers do not offer advice on guiding a ship, so the science of political economy has no concern for practical or moral issues and economists need not or should not offer advice or criticism thereon'.[4] With the influence of Ricardo at the beginning of the nineteenth century and Walras, who made economics substantially a matter of mathematical technique at the end, ethics became largely divorced from economics.

This attitude has come to be the prevailing orthodoxy, expressed forcefully and influentially by Lionel Robbins. Rejecting the claim that economics and ethics must be associated, he writes: 'Unfortunately it does not seem logically possible to associate the two studies in any form but mere juxtaposition. Economics deals with ascertainable facts, ethics with valuations and obligations. The two fields of enquiry are not on the same plane of discourse.'[5] This in turn has affected justifications of the market and of market behaviour based on the economic theories of what markets are, and how economic agents act. By declaring economics to be a positive, not a normative, science, economists believed that they were simply dealing only with ascertainable facts. This reveals a profoundly flawed distinction between fact and value. There have been many writers of the philosophy of science who have refuted such a simplistic separation. Popper was one for whom all facts are 'theory laden',[6] and who gave great importance to our prior conjectures about the world in his account of the scientific method. Insofar as 'facts' affect beliefs which in turn have behavioural consequences, we can add, with MacIntyre: 'Every action is the bearer and expression of more or less theory-laden beliefs and concepts; every piece of theorizing and every expression of belief is a political and moral action.'[7] 'Facts' are interpreted data, and interpretation involves values. Furthermore, having established the 'facts', we then have to decide what to do with them. Do we raise interest rates to curb inflationary demand, or reduce them to stimulate exports and lower unemployment? This judgment involves issues of value.

A too easy assumption that 'facts are just facts' obscures which values are actually operative. It allows quite crude presuppositions to remain unexamined – even within what appear to be sophisticated economic calculations. In fact there is a complex and often non-explicit interplay between efficiency assessments and moral judgments. An example of this

4. Quoted in Galbraith, *A History of Economics*, p. 125.

5. Lionel Robbins, *An Essay of the Nature and Significance of Economic Science*, 3rd edn, 1984, p. 148.

6. Karl R. Popper, *Objective Knowledge: An Evolutionary Approach*, 1972.

7. MacIntyre, *After Virtue*, p. 61.

is 'Pareto optimality', a valued condition in some branches of economics. Stated simply, a social state is described as Pareto optimal if and only if no one's utility can be raised without reducing the utility of someone else. However, Pareto optimality can come 'hot from hell'. This is because a state of affairs can be Pareto optimal with some people in extreme luxury and others in misery, as long as the miserable cannot be made better off without cutting into the luxury and extravagance of the wealthy.[8]

Furthermore, there is no necessary connection between well-being and Pareto optimality. It could be that State A can produce more biological weapons than State B without reducing production of other goods. This does not, however, establish the superiority of State A if biological weapons are of no benefit. This is just one example of how efficiency and well-being can be divorced in economic analysis. With this divorce goes a further problem when one asks what sort of society is envisaged by Pareto optimality. Under this principle, practical judgments about how society should be organized are based on how social states maximize the aggregate of utility. But society is not just an apparatus for maximizing overall utility. Pareto optimality is incompatible with giving proper respect to individuals who are not merely contributors to ends that are not their own, including the end of maximizing overall utility.

Pareto optimality, on one reading, is not straightforwardly utilitarian, as it does not seek the greatest good of the *greatest* number. Those in luxury may be only a small minority. Although it is neutral about distribution, it is, however, utilitarian in that it seeks to maximize the greatest *aggregate* value of utility. The utilitarianism shown in the Pareto principle provides one of the norms for the development of economic science, and with it, the justification of the market. The widespread acceptance of utilitarianism by economists is explained by Sen (himself a Nobel Laureate in Economics) as resulting from the lack of interest economists have shown in any kind of complex ethical theory.[9] Keynes remarked that practical men who claim to be dealing only in facts are usually the slaves to some defunct economist.[10] Similarly, it might be argued that an economist who claims to be dealing only in facts is a slave to an unexamined ethics.

---

8. Amartya K. Sen, *On Ethics and Economics*, 1987, p. 32.
9. Sen, p. 50.
10. John M. Keynes, *General Theory of Employment, Interest and Money*, 1936, pp. 383–84.

Values: Ends and Means

There is a lack of coherence within economic theory concerning ends and means. Economics, as a discipline, has insisted that it has nothing to say about ends. Ends are to be decided in some other forum, be it the individual or the wider society. It is a decision which is external to economic activity, which is then seen as having an instrumental role to that decision. Yet Pareto optimality presupposes within itself an end for society – that of overall maximized utility. In addition, economists such as Becker insist that *all* human activity can be described and analysed by economic criteria. If everything is to be explained by economic criteria, then nothing is outside economics. If so, where is the sphere for deciding ends? By default, the ends become whatever the economic system is capable of producing. But an economy is capable of producing a wide variety of outputs. On what basis can there be a choice between, or a ranking of, desired or achievable ends?

This question is directly concerned with values and the relative value of things. The specification of an end is value-laden, but so is the choice of means to achieve that end. There needs to be coherence between the values of the end and the chosen means if the end is not to be subverted. If, as economists have maintained, economics is concerned with means, on what basis is the most appropriate means chosen so that the primacy of the end is assured? The preoccupation with means which is typical of neoclassical economics tends, through the process of goal displacement, to lead to the primacy of means over ends. Indeed, the means can become the end so that, for example, business activity is seen as sufficient in itself, in isolation from its social context and consequences. Coupled with what Becker has acknowledged to be a form of intellectual imperialism in the economic process,[11] this produces a system which is ethically unstable. It both seeks to be the over-arching social framework, and yet avoids any real engagement with the ethical values needed if the economy is to fulfil its function within society of contributing to the good life. This results in an abdication of responsibility for actual outcomes, and strengthens a form of technological determinism which insists that there is no choice but to follow wherever the market leads.

The ethical claims of the market cannot, therefore, be reduced simply to economics. Economics itself, and the models it uses to describe the market, contains presuppositions about values which often go unchallenged because they are unrecognized for what they are. This masks the moral complexity within which business practitioners must act. It also leads the moral problem to be reduced to an economic one through the acceptance

---

11. Gary S. Becker, *The Economic Approach to Human Behaviour*, 1976, pp. 5–14.

of given, constant goals. Ethics is replaced by economics.[12] Technique has displaced, rather than supplemented, ethical reasoning in management.

Yet it would be a mistake to suppose that this displacement has been total. The effective working of the market depends upon values such as truth, trust, honesty and obligation. Without them the countless relationships that make up the market would collapse, as it would be impossible to regulate every transaction by a legal contract. These values are an essential resource for market behaviour and provide some restraint to its tendency to imbalance. However, their existence does reveal a source of tension between, on the one hand, these background requirements of the market, and, on the other, the motivational assumption of the market model. That assumption is that *the* motivation of behaviour is rational self-interested maximization which is affected by others' well-being only indirectly.

The Motive of Self-interest

In the last quarter of the nineteenth century, economists began asking: 'Given an economy with a certain population, having certain tastes, and certain resources and techniques, how can resources be allocated through a market system, so as to maximize the satisfaction of consumers?' With this micro-analysis, economics had to consider individual behaviour, and, drawing on its utilitarian heritage (many of the early utilitarians were economists) and its more recent mathematization, it adopted a definition of rational behaviour as one which maximized satisfaction, or utility.

Edgeworth asserted that 'the first principle of Economics is that every agent is actuated only by self interest'.[13] This statement is a classic formulation of what has become a basic premise of economic theories and of explanations of market behaviour. It enables economists to make some useful, but nevertheless only approximate, predictions about the behaviour of large groups of people. Economic models require human motivations to be 'pure, simple and hard-headed, and not messed up by such things as good will or moral sentiments'.[14] One of the most quoted texts to support this position of pre-eminence for self-interest is Adam Smith's 'It is not from the benevolence of the butcher, the brewer, or the baker, that we expect our dinner, but from their regard to their own interest. We

---

12. Frank H. Knight, *The Ethics of Competition and Other Essays*, 1935, pp. 34–35.

13. F.Y. Edgeworth, quoted in Amartya K. Sen, 'Rational Fools: A Critique of the Behavioural Foundations of Economic Theory', 1977; reprinted in Amartya K. Sen, *Choice, Welfare and Measurement*, 1982, pp. 84–106 (84).

14. Sen, *On Ethics and Economics*, p. 1.

address ourselves, not to their humanity, but to their self-love, and never talk to them of our own necessities but of their advantages.'[15]

It is hard to overestimate Smith's influence, even today. But is it true to his position to cast him as the founding father of unalloyed self-interest? And does it *necessarily* follow that self-interest is 'selfish' in the sense that an individual's own best interests do not embrace the well-being of other people?

Smith and Self-interest

Smith was debating a problem which had been explored for more than a century before him: the relationship between self-interest and the public welfare. Most writers had been keen to refute Hobbes' position[16] that self-interest was destructive of society, and in so doing, they helped shape the values of classical economics.[17] Smith's work is a logical extension of these earlier positions. He sought to prove the identity of self-interest with social interest, and did this by using the principle of the division of labour. Each individual capitalizes on their own differences in order to pursue that kind of work most suited to their personal skills. This leads to higher productivity which is rewarded by greater income. Society also benefits from the higher collective productivity which generates a greater social wealth. Thus, self-interest could have clearly beneficial results, such as thriving economies and a more comfortable level of living for all. It is from this argument that the utilitarian claim is derived that if business is single-minded in its pursuit of profit, then society will be better off.

One of the principal messages of the *Wealth of Nations* is that if a nation is to develop economically, it must promote the principle of the division of labour. Trade is carried on by engaging other people's self-interest. It is based on each party to the transaction believing that it is to his or her advantage to do for the other what the other requires. Consequently, the division of labour arises from the desire to serve one's self-interest, but in such a way as to engage the self-interest of others. Having established the fundamental importance of the division of labour, Smith analysed those economic conditions and policies which promote it. He believed that the free market was the environment in which division of labour could thrive.

With this message in mind, it might be thought that Smith was in favour of unfettered self-interest. However, he was doing no more than specifying why and how normal market transactions are carried out, and why and

---

15. Smith, *Wealth of Nations*, pp. 26–27.

16. Thomas Hobbes, *Leviathan*, [1651] 1981.

17. Milton L. Myers, *The Soul of Modern Economic Man: Ideas of Self-Interest: Thomas Hobbes to Adam Smith*, 1983.

how division of labour works. He defended the idea that self-interest is not, in itself, either antisocial or destructive. Nevertheless, although Smith saw that self-interest played a part in many actions, he specified limits to it. In the *Theory of Moral Sentiments* Smith commended self-interest as a necessary virtue among others.[18] However, he stressed that along with other 'affections' it is useful when it is confined to a certain degree of moderation and disadvantageous when it exceeds the proper bounds.[19] Indeed, he went so far as to call Mandeville's system of morality, based on self-interest, 'wholly pernicious'.[20] A view often heard is that *Wealth of Nations* represents a rejection of his earlier position. Not so; Smith published a revised edition of *Theory of Moral Sentiments* in 1790, fourteen years after he published *Wealth of Nations*.

Smith was no Hobbesian individualist, but emphasized the importance of social relationships. Putting *Theory of Moral Sentiments* and *Wealth of Nations* together, we see that Smith understood self-interest to be 'proper regard for self' – 'that degree of self love which elicits the approval of the impartial spectator because it does no harm to others'.[21] He argued that a person should not regard himself as 'separated and detached, but as a citizen of the world, a member of the vast commonwealth of nature'. It follows that 'to the interest of this great community, he ought at all times to be willing that his own little interest should be sacrificed'.[22] This limiting of individual freedom by the requirements of the common good has already been referred to in Chapter 2. It is a limitation not much adverted to by the more vigorous proponents of the free market. Although modern economic theories see self-interest as the necessary and sufficient motivation underpinning all social interaction,[23] Smith proposed it in specific contexts, and did not see it as adequate for a good society. Nor did he even see it as an automatic consequence in the economic sphere. Smith's actual wording when referring to the mechanism of the invisible hand is: 'By pursuing his own interest he *frequently* promotes that of society';[24] not always, only frequently. He was discussing a particular question about investment and adds 'as in many other cases'; not all cases, only many cases. Those who see Smith as *the* proponent of untrammelled self-interest are reading modern attitudes and assumptions back into his work.

18. Adam Smith, *The Theory of Moral Sentiments*, [1759] 1976, pp. 302–6.

19. Smith, *Moral Sentiments*, p. 306.

20. Smith, *Moral Sentiments*, p. 308.

21. Jeffrey T. Young, *Economics as a Moral Science: The Political Economy of Adam Smith*, 1997, p. 24.

22. Smith, *Moral Sentiments*, p. 140.

23. For example Becker, 'I am saying that the economic approach [which assumes maximizing behaviour] provides a valuable unified framework for understanding *all* human behaviour', *The Economic Approach to Human Behaviour*, p. 14, emphasis in original.

24. Smith, *Wealth of Nations*, p. 475, emphasis added.

Self-interest and Rationality

Coupled with self-interest as the explanation of all market behaviour is the assumption of rationality, with rationality tightly defined. Becker confidently asserts that 'everyone more or less agrees that rational behaviour simply implies consistent maximization of a well-ordered function, such as a utility or profit function'.[25] It is assumed that all human beings behave in this rational manner. Given this assumption, characterizing rational behaviour is not ultimately different from describing actual behaviour. Sen gives a critique of the identity of rational and self-interest in economic behaviour. He argues that because of the development of a 'scientific' methodology, economics neglects the influence of ethical considerations in actual human behaviour. He disputes whether people can so comprehensively shun the question: 'How should I live?' as the economic model requires.[26] He also doubts that it makes sense to assume that people actually behave in the rational way characterized.

Sen is not alone in challenging the accuracy of this assumption. Simon suggests that 'we stop debating whether a theory of substantive rationality and the assumptions of utility maximization provide a sufficient base for explaining and predicting economic behaviour. The evidence is overwhelming that they do not.'[27] Here both Sen and Simon are, perhaps, underestimating the impact that any model, consistently articulated, will have on behaviour. Several studies have shown that behaviour can be modified by the rationality assumptions of economics and that, to some extent at least, how agents function is how they are assumed to behave.[28] Given the pervasiveness of the model of the 'good life' as self-interested consumption presented through advertising and television programmes, it is not difficult to see how extensive is its scope for influencing and limiting the type of life towards which people aspire. The model of self-interested maximization provides the context of most people's lives in western societies,[29] and context, environment and circumstances of life are highly influential in what an individual can conceive and know. It is very difficult to aspire to something which one has not seen modelled and for which there is a strong countervailing influence. This point is of particular relevance for business ethics, as one of the criticisms of business culture is

25. Becket, *The Economic Approach to Human Behaviour*, p. 153.

26. Sen, *On Ethics and Economics*.

27. H.A. Simon, 'Rationality in Psychology and Economics', *Journal of Business* 50.4.2 (October 1986), pp. 209–24 (223).

28. For example, Jai Ghorbade, 'Ethics in MBA Programs: The Rhetoric, the Reality, and a Plan of Action', *Journal of Business Ethics* 10 (1991), pp. 891–905.

29. MacIntyre isolates three 'central features of the economic order', that is, 'individualism ... acquisitiveness and its elevation of the values of the market to a *central social place*'. *After Virtue*, p. 254, emphasis added.

that it socializes people to prefer and be content with an inferior concept of the good life than they might otherwise have had.

The predictive ability of the standard economic assumption of rationality is highly prized by economists, as is the assumption that what flows from individual rational (as economically defined) decisions will, through the 'invisible hand', work to the common good. Certainly the market is superb at solving what is known as the 'co-ordination problem' – how do you ensure that the goods people want are in the right place (more or less) and in the right quantities (more or less). The example of failed co-ordination in centrally planned economies should be persuasive on this point. However, that is not necessarily the same thing as the common good, and to assume that rational decisions taken at the micro-level will automatically extend to the macro-level is unjustified. A series of rational actions does not automatically produce a rational cumulative result. Cumulative irrationality can be seen in the example of the choice of cars for personal transport because they are quicker and more convenient than public transport. An ever greater number of car journeys results in traffic jams – so the journeys are no longer quicker. As travellers have 'revealed' a preference for cars, this leads to resources being diverted away from public transport in order to widen the roads, so leading to even less public transport and yet greater numbers, therefore, turning to cars. This type of action/consequence is often called the 'cumulative fallacy'.

It follows that it cannot automatically be assumed that the results of aggregated maximization will produce the desired or maximally achievable common good. The actions of the tobacco industry illustrate that we cannot assume that unconstrained self-interest will automatically translate into actions which serve the welfare of society. Neither can the assertion be sustained by trying to build up from the level of individual decision. The financial model assumes that the agent has 'perfect knowledge' of all the factors relevant to the decision. However, real agents, operating in real time, have to make their decisions under conditions of uncertainty or ignorance.[30] Keynes perceptively wrote, 'Nor is it true to say that self-interest is generally enlightened; more often individuals acting separately to promote their own ends are too ignorant or too weak to achieve even these.'[31]

One conclusion to draw from the actual conditions of ignorance is the ethical import of information. The ethical nature of information – who

---

30. This point goes further than Simon's concept of 'bounded rationality'. Rationality is bounded in the sense that there is simply too much information of too great a complexity for any individual agent to process. While that is true in itself, what is being argued here is also the further point that economic decisions are made in real time in which the future, which will itself be partly created by the act of deciding, is unknowable.

31. John M. Keynes, *Essays in Persuasion*, 1931, p. 312.

has it, how much, when and under what conditions – will form a significant part of the discussion of the finance sector in Chapter 9. A second conclusion is that if, in practice, one cannot rely on individuals to act in their true best interests, to argue that the 'invisible hand' will produce the 'right' answer in the end, one which serves the self-interest of all, stretches credulity. Yet through a libertarian understanding of the form and structure of market demand, financial economics holds that freely expressed market demands must be both self-interested and produce morally acceptable aggregate results. The discussion of Pareto optimality has put a question mark over the second assertion. It is now time to look at the first: that freely expressed market demands must be self-interested.

Revealed-preference Theory

The way in which neoclassical economics has succeeded in characterizing any and all behaviour as 'self-interested' is through the theory of revealed preference. Choices are observed and preferences are then presumed from these observations. If, in choosing x, you reject y, it is declared that you have 'revealed' a preference of x over y. Only by inconsistency (sometimes choosing x, sometimes y) is it possible, under this definition, to avoid maximizing your own utility (satisfaction) by every isolated act of choice. So, for example, if I choose a Big Mac over an organic salad, I have revealed a preference for Big Macs.

However, it is a jump in logic to say that internal consistency is rational. It is possible to choose consistently actions which go directly against the achievement of one's stated objective, that is, to choose irrationally. There must, presumably, be some coherence between the objective sought and the actions taken to realize it. Satisfying preferences arising from error, for example, the belief that Big Macs are a balanced meal, could lead to results contrary to the person's best interests: I could end up obese and lacking essential vitamins and minerals. Or it could be that my choice does not, in fact, indicate what I prefer: I would like an organic salad, but I am broke and Big Macs are cheaper. Yet preference theory equates the satisfaction of preferences or desires with human well-being – a theory which is clearly inadequate.

It is also a jump in logic, despite the apparent straitjacket of the definition, to say that internal consistency shows self-interest. 'If you are consistent, then no matter whether you are a single-minded egoist or a raving altruist or a class-conscious militant, you will appear to be maximizing your own utility in this enchanted world of definitions.'[32] A consistent chooser might have any degree of egoism that one cared to

32. Sen, 'Rational Fools', p. 89.

specify. Except in the purely definitional sense required by the theory, the question of self-interest is left unresolved. Therefore, to the extent that revealed-preference theory aims to shed light on motivation, it is a conceptual failure, in that it does not reveal meaningful distinctions.

Revealed-preference theory underestimates the fact that an individual economic actor is also a social being, with choices that are not rigidly bound to his or her own preferences. Preferences are influenced by things such as social class, sub-culture and so on, as well as being subject to the distorting effects on 'rational' choice caused by advertising and media depictions of 'the good life'. In addition, as Sen argues,[33] allegiance to groupings or class interests can quickly call into question the emphasis on individualized self-interest. There are many intermediate groups between an individual and all others which provide the focus of many actions and choices. Because many of the choices made are profoundly shaped by social institutions and groupings, it is misleading not to take account of the inextricably linked nature of interests. It is also misleading not to recognize common interests with others.

Even if there is internal consistency and a correspondence between what one tries to achieve and how one goes about it, that does not justify linking rationality indissolubly with self-interest. The inevitable corollary is that non-self-interested action is irrational, a conclusion which on the face of it appears absurd. It is not at all clear why rationality should not involve the intelligent pursuit of all one's goals and values, rather than just one class of goals, that is, self-interested ones. The assumptions about individuals and self-interest are flawed; but what of organizations? This is the issue we look at next.

Self-interest and Business Activity

Economic thought shapes economic practice. This is not just the practical models of business behaviour developed by consultants, journalists and various other commentators to which business feels it has to respond. The economy is also increasingly forced to change itself in order to match the descriptions of abstracted models that are produced by academic economists.[34] What those models are therefore becomes of vital importance. The economic model of business takes the values and goals of the agent as given, and focuses its attention on individualistic materialism. This assumption presumes that the end towards which all agents strive is that of utility-as-wealth maximization. The further presumption of

33. Sen, 'Rational Fools'.
34. See, for example, the studies in James G. Carrier and Daniel Miller (eds.), *Virtualism: A New Political Economy*, 1998.

opportunism is built into the model in order to deal with the expected diligence with which agents will pursue personal wealth. The firm is seen as essentially a place for mitigating the effects of opportunism so as to achieve economic efficiency; as a legal fiction which serves as a nexus for a set of contracting relations among individuals.[35] It takes rationality as a given, seeing it as an inevitable law of nature. Jensen and Meckling, for example, in their seminal article on the theory of the firm, dismissively call any consideration of alternative possible behavioural motivations a 'Nirvana' form of analysis.[36]

Any argument which wishes to counter this assumption of opportunism faces a problem. To co-operate with others, that is, to trust others, in the face of a majority of opportunists, is potentially to place oneself in a precarious position. What is required is an account of rationality with which to oppose that of the economic tradition which sees rationality as nothing more than consistent maximization of a utility or profit function.

The economic theory of self-interest holds that each individual is a rational self-interested maximizer. Given that 'self-interested' is usually defined as acting in one's own interest at the expense of others, in the event of a conflict of interest the individual will always put his or her self first. This view can expect no loyalty, only opportunism. However, the business environment is also routinely described as one which, given the size and complexity of today's economic organizations, requires an extensive reliance on agents (employees) who act on behalf of principals (owners). Agents are required to set aside their own interests to act in the interests of principals. This requirement contains expectations of loyalty, fidelity, trust and concern for others. This, however, is not self-interested behaviour. Hence the paradox that a system which is predicated as resting on self-interested behaviour relies on a significant proportion of participants giving up their self-interest. The view that all behaviour is motivated by self-interest carries within itself the seeds of the destruction of its own environment. If only self-interested action is rational, then to be loyal at a cost to oneself is irrational. Yet experience reveals that in business there is loyal behaviour. Here is another instance of the model's failure to predict and account for actual behaviour.

Co-operation is a necessary component for achieving social good. The traditional view of business has tended to over-emphasize competition and correspondingly under-emphasize co-operation. It assumes that the relations between the participants in the market are impersonal, and that each proceeds independently of the other in an anonymous market with each out to maximize what she can gain. Yet one of the most distinctive

35. M.C. Jensen and W. Meckling, 'Theory of the Firm: Managerial Behaviour, Ownership Costs and Ownership Structure', *Journal of Financial Economics* 3 (1976), pp. 305–60.
36. Jensen and Meckling, p. 310.

features of the market system, and modern society in general, is that of many individuals joining together in creative enterprise. This shows itself in, for example, the joint-stock company, the corporation, pension funds, unions, political parties and many other forms of social organization. This does not seem to mirror the atomistic world of economic theory. Although the theory is highly individualistic, life in modern societies in practice demonstrates complex organized forms of life. Nowhere is this more clear than in business. Most business activities are associative, not individualistic. Few business enterprises can be conducted by just one individual alone and none can succeed in isolation. Business activities are inherently relational.

There is a balance to be struck between the individual moral agent and the supportive culture and structures in which that agent acts. With its focus so firmly on the individual, the neoclassical model is unable to create that balance. Corporate decisions and actions are usually the consequences of an accumulation of individual decisions and actions within the firm, no one of which may strike the individual as ethically particularly serious. Policies are frequently formulated over a long time and as a result of many different internal and external considerations. No one person will feel responsible for the results of such a long drawn-out process. More likely the individual will go along with what Galbraith calls 'institutional truth', that is, what serves the needs and purposes of the organization.

An adequate business ethics must include an acknowledgment that structures have a pervasive influence which can escape the notice even of those who operate them. Structures are not deterministic, but they do acquire almost an existence of their own, making them, as management reports so frequently point out, difficult to remove or even alter. The business corporation, as an entity, is inadequately dealt with in economic theory and the reductionist view it takes fails to account for the variety of motivation for action within the organization. As was pointed out in Chapter 1, corporate culture, which is the body of shared values, expectations, beliefs and norms of behaviour, provides the immediate context of most business activity. In consequence, that culture is crucial to ethical behaviour because it is the vehicle through which the moral values and principles of the organization are transmitted and maintained. In the long run, corporate business cannot be viable, socially as well as economically, if it does not pay attention to its own institutional character.

Profit as an End

The final aspect of business that I shall look at in the context of reductionist assumptions is that of profit. This is not only an aspect of the assumption about motivation; it is also an ethical claim. It differs

somewhat in type from those discussed earlier. Justice, efficiency and
freedom can be viewed as ethical goods provided for society as a whole by
the market. This claim is more than *how* the market provides these goods
is ethically justified. It is the claim of the moral integrity of making a
profit.

There is genuine debate about what actions are morally legitimate in
creating a profit. This includes issues of employment conditions, environmental impact and other externalities not included in the cost of production. The true costs of production are far higher than those shown in
company accounts. There is also a wide range of issues in the shareholder/
stakeholder debate. There is, therefore, considerable latitude for questioning what counts as true profit, and what constraints upon its creation
can legitimately be imposed. Such issues, while extremely important, are
not directly relevant here. Rather, my focus is on the presumption of
profit-maximization within the context of business's position within
society, as discussed in Chapter 1.

There I argued that the question of social reality, and therefore of the
distinctive *purpose* of the business firm lies at the heart of business ethics.
The particular type of social reality of the business firm as an economic
organization means that profits are vital for production and a primary
economic requirement in a free-market system. They stimulate and reward
innovation, risk bearing and the adjustments of the allocation of
resources. The abuse of a good thing – profits – should not blind us to the
value of that thing in itself. Since the social justification for the business
sphere is held by many to be its economizing role[37] profitability is a primary value for business.

However, to say that because something is a primary value it is therefore *the* primary value is a logical mistake. It does not follow that because
a primary value of for-profit organizations is to make profits, the only
purpose of business is to make profits. This distinction is important
because what is conceived of as the purpose of something will determine
when that something is acting or being used appropriately. If the only
purpose of business is to make a profit, then to maximize that profit can
be the only legitimate criterion by which business can be judged. Others
would make the distinction between profit-maximization and maximizing
shareholder wealth, with the latter having priority.[38] However, both of

37. 'Economizing' means prudent, careful, rational actions which produce greater outputs
or benefits from a given amount of resource inputs. The difference between input and output
is 'profit'. A firm which fails the economizing test records a 'loss', meaning that its actions
diminished, rather than multiplied, the potential output from a given amount.

38. For a standard financial management approach, see Arthur J. Keown *et al.*, *Financial
Management: Principles and Applications*, 9th edn, 2004.

these approaches are structurally the same, having as their aim the accumulation of wealth as the sole criterion.

This approach has become the dominant orthodoxy, and like any belief which is repeated often enough, it assumes for many the status of a fact about which nothing can be done. When writers such as Bowie and Duska suggest that the primary function of business is the provision of goods and services,[39] the standard riposte is that if goods or services are not profitable, they will not be provided. This answer demonstrates confusion between motives (or subjective reasons) and purposes (which justify). The two have become conflated. The motive for business may well often be the desire to make a profit, but that is not its purpose. As noted in Chapter 1, profits can be made from selling cocaine or 'snuff' films, but that fact is not considered as justifying the activity. Profits are a means for achieving the purpose of business and as such should not usurp the end. As an executive remarked, 'Profit is like health. You need it, and the more the better. But it's not why you exist.'[40]

In addition, there are many in business who do not see their goals reflected in that of an exclusive concern with profit-maximization. If one is looking at what motivates economic behaviour, profit-maximization is not a sufficient explanation. Kenneth Arrow summarizes very succinctly the arguments, exposing the fallacy that it will *necessarily* provide the basic motivational power.[41] The motives of the firm frequently include its self-preservation, its growth, its ability to innovate, rather than profit-maximization. His opinion is shared by, among other, Galbraith, who also stresses that the balance between these various motives will differ, depending upon the size of the firm.[42]

Many owners of business are proud of the particular goods and services they offer. Their primary source of satisfaction is with the delivery of a quality product which genuinely benefits customers. The neglect of such owners by mainstream business ethics is not surprising, however, as owners in general, of whatever persuasion, rarely feature. Most writing in the field is directed at managerial behaviour. If profit-maximization were to become an absolute, as many writers suggest, then there would be no possibility of evaluating this or any other goal of business in the light of a broader human good. However, even within a managerial focus, the actual motivation of many seems to have been miscast. Handy, for example, writing of his time as a manager in an oil company, says:

---

39. Norman E. Bowie and Ronald F. Duska, *Business Ethics*, 2nd edn, 1990.

40. Quoted in Thomas J. Peters and Robert H. Waterman, *In Search of Excellence: Lessons from America's Best-Run Companies*, 1982, p. 103.

41. Kenneth J. Arrow, 'Why Profits are Challenged', in *New Challenges to the Role of Profits*, 1978, pp. 49–61.

42. John K. Galbraith, *Economics and the Public Purpose*, 1974.

It was not the shareholders but my own self-respect which drove me. Sitting in that far-off country, the idea of maximum earnings per share was very remote, very intellectual, very unreal. I had ... a much more serious social function ... I was there to help produce things which were badly needed, in good condition, at a fair price, on time, without mucking up the local scenery or upsetting the local councillors or villagers among whom we lived and worked.[43]

People such as Handy, and he quotes many instances besides himself, do not fit into the profit-maximization straitjacket.

There needs to be much more clarity at the level of *purpose* in business ethics. Even the purpose suggested by Bowie and Duska stops short of a full analysis. When considering the purpose of business it is not sufficient to assert what the essential goal of business is – whether that goal is profit-maximization or the provision of goods and services. There is what might be termed a 'for-the-sake-of' relationship. It is, therefore, also necessary to ask further: 'What are the goods, and the ultimate good, for the sake of which the purposes of business might be pursued?' In the end one is asking: 'What is the ultimate good of human life?' Conducting an ethical investigation in some domain of human activity requires a reflection on the goals of that activity in the light of the ultimate goods of human life and community. This will be taken up in Chapter 5.

Summary and Conclusions

The neoclassical model of the free market is utilitarian, rationalist and individualistic. Being based on the actions of individuals taken in isolation, analysis of economic behaviour has been dominated by methodological individualism. Drawing on Smith's 'invisible hand' and the analysis of the division of labour, the presumption has been that the ultimate reason for action would be the agent's perceived best interests.

The characterization of economic agents as self-interested maximizers – while useful for making limited economic predictions – does not allow a dynamic analysis of choice and has led to a serious distortion in the understanding of economic behaviour. Stemming from this is an inevitable distortion of what can be viewed as ethical economic behaviour. Ideas have behavioural consequences. They influence the way issues are defined and therefore the potential ways in which they may be resolved. They provide points of view and present and legitimate particular goals. What we think about ourselves and our possibilities determines what we aspire to become. Assuming that individuals in all possible roles are motivated by self-interest may well make analysis more tractable and

43. Charles Handy, *The Age of Paradox*, 1994, pp. 158–59.

simple, but will not do much to raise issues of ethics and social responsibility in society. Instead this assumption serves the purpose of legit-
imizing thinking and behavioural patterns which themselves are essential
components of the problems faced.

The theory of rational self-interest is not, as most economists seem to
assume, morally neutral. In fact, it is here that the pernicious effects of the
theory become clear. The theory tells us that to behave morally is to invite
others to take advantage of us. It encourages us to expect the worst of
others and in doing so becomes self-fulfilling, bringing out the worst in
ourselves. It provides the foundation for a structural antagonism between
economic behaviour and ethical norms which, in this perspective, are
viewed merely as constraints upon action. Neoclassical theory tells agents
that they act in one way. Ethical norms may well suggest that they act in
another. Two views of reality are presented, from which the individual
must choose. Indeed, through the tyranny of formalized, deterministic
maximization rules, any ethical space for individual decision or action is
abolished. There is no place for the exercise of moral judgment.

Economics assumes a society of perfectly rational and omniscient
maximizers. However, it is not, in general, a good idea to assume that
something is the case that in fact never is. Why should anyone, including
ethicists, concern themselves with the actions of totally rational, self-
interested maximizers, with perfect information and consistency of
desires, when few, if any, such people exist? Despite the claims of the free
market model, many business practitioners do not act in the way predicted. The opportunism expected by, for example, the standard debt-
market model, is not always shown. Indeed, some research demonstrates
clearly that some honest behaviour is *necessary* to the function of the debt
markets.[44] Phelps[45] has cogently argued that altruistic phenomena are also
crucial; people do not always behave in the maximizing way that is
implied by the model of the perfect market. Producers may advertise their
products truthfully when they need not; many firms pay fairly, keep their
word, refrain from undetectable pollution and so on.

It is true that self-interest is a feature of many moral actions. There is a
proper place for self-interest in human motivation – basic physical survival requires it. However, I am arguing for a more multiform reading of
moral motivation, and denying the dominant (if not exclusive) role given
to it in economic analysis. It is misleading to try and separate out into
neat, mutually exclusive categories, those choices which are self-interested
and those which are other-directed. There is an 'I-aspect' for all healthy

44. John Dobson and Ken Reiner, 'The Rationality of Honesty in Debt Markets', in Uric
Dufrene (ed.), *Finance and the Ethics Debate*, 1996, pp. 11–19.
45. Edmund S. Phelps, *Altruism, Morality and Economic Theory*, 1975.

individuals, but also a 'we-aspect' as suggested by Etzioni.[46] Many choices and decisions are shaped by the social context, including families, the market itself, friendships and social class. To understand and follow our own interests requires that we recognize that our choices are inextricably linked with others'. It is here that terminology may be particularly unhelpful. Within religious circles the debate is most frequently couched in terms of self-interest turning, in its excesses, into greed. I do not underestimate the motivational power of greed (and fear). However, it may be more useful to re-examine the issue of self-interest from the perspective of the obligation, both personal and communal, to take care of one's responsibilities. From this stance it may be possible to envisage the creation of wealth as being an activity which has as its first purpose the common good, and its second as enabling the individual to attend to personal and communal responsibilities. It is within such a perspective that a healthy understanding of profit might be located.

Individual pursuit of self-interest still remains largely unchallenged; instant individual gratification, individual self-help and individual success are the most commonly promoted framework for choices and actions. To question this framework is to open oneself to the accusation that one is against these things and therefore in favour of some sort of imposed collective choice. Individualism or collectivism, that is the dilemma. Except this polarization is a false dilemma. It is not the case that the only alternative to atomistic individualism is face-grinding, life-denying tyranny. There are many possibilities between these extremes. For the properly constituted self there is no place for a false antagonism between 'selfishness' and 'altruism'. A more reasonable conception of the self is one which acknowledges the intimate relations between the individual and the other, and the reality of mutually interested actions which place the individual within a community. There is no incompatibility in positing as a final good one's own happiness and positing as a primary constituent of that final good acting towards others out of genuine altruistic regard. There is no reason *prima facie* why the good of others cannot matter to me independently of my own interest, just because it is introduced as something required by my final good.

The neoclassical economic model fails to predict and account for this actual behaviour. The reason does not only lie in its unrealistic assumptions about motivation. It also lies in its cultural myopia and in its social philosophy of business. Taking first the cultural assumptions; the model fails to advert to the fact that it is deeply rooted in Enlightenment philosophy with its particular form of individualism. While some cultural differences in markets may be noted (for example, the structural differences between western conglomerates, Korean *chaebol* and Japanese

46. Amitai Etzioni, *The Moral Dimension: Toward a New Economics*, 1998.

keiretsu), this fundamental feature is passed by. There are profound questions to be asked about the nature of capitalism in cultures which have arisen from a different philosophical and religious matrix, have a different mix of public and private sectors and a social framework which is less individualistic. The model's social philosophy of business sees the economic system as a separate social sphere, operating mechanistically and autonomously. It fails to take account of the degree of integration of the social spheres. It is correct in seeing that the economic sphere requires a specific functional social role from its participants. However, it is inadequate in that it does not allow for the degree to which participants have a dynamic plurality of roles.

The separation model, coupled with the motivational assumption of self-interest, legislates away the possibility of many moral conflicts. There can be no conflict between individual self-interest and the interests of society as a whole, not only because of the presumed workings of the invisible hand, but also because there is no 'place' for moral claims from the *Lebenswelt* legitimately to impact on a functional sphere. With the procedural rationality assumption, as long as business achieves the best cost–output ratio, no more can be asked of it. The model assumes that each component entity of the system is isolated from every other one (as in Friedman's image of a series of Robinson Crusoes), and interactions take place *only* by means of transactions, that is, through the mechanism of market exchange. Thus, the model has to predicate self-interest as the sole motivation; it has no other string to its bow to explain how social interaction occurs.

It cannot draw on such factors as cohesiveness or a broad commonality of interest – and hence bases for co-operation rather than conflict – among social entities. However, if one were to draw upon a model of social spheres which acknowledges a degree of interaction along with *relative* autonomy – so that no one sphere completely controls or is controlled by another – not only would one have a model which more accurately reflects social reality, one would also begin to have a conceptual tool for considering potential differences, conflicts and compatibilities among the social spheres and the overall social environment, the *Lebenswelt*. Such a model could accommodate both the separateness of, and possible conflict between, business and societal goals as well as their mutual goal adjustment.

The limits of the ethical claims made by the neoclassical economic model of the market discussed in the previous chapter, together with the foundational defects discussed in this chapter, combine to leave a profound dissatisfaction with the picture painted of business life. The dialectical nature of the relationship between the model and the actual market has had a deeply harmful effect on how agents view their choices and actions in the economic sphere. Given the restricted concept of the good life which this model presents, it is not surprising that the sector of the market which is viewed as most approximately the model's realization, the finance sector, is one which is often perceived as being the most ethic resistant.

Chapter 4

THE HUMAN PERSON

The last two chapters have identified a number of ethical issues which are
inherent both in the theoretical bases and in the practical workings of the
free market. The free market also fails to address the issues raised in
Chapter 1 concerning the proper relationship between the economic
sphere and other social spheres – indeed it makes the problem worse with
its tendency to extend itself from a market economy into a market society.
These problems do not appear to be resolvable from within the neoclassical model itself. As Einstein is often quoted as saying: 'No problem
can be solved from within the consciousness which created it. We must
learn to see the world anew.' We need to step outside that consciousness
and view the problems from a different perspective while still talking in
mutually understandable terms. I am, therefore, now leaving the economic model to present an alternative. I shall be doing this in two stages.
The first stage, in this chapter, will be to look at the human person as one
pole in the relationship between the individual and society. The second, in
the next chapter, will be to examine the relationship of the individual and
the economic sphere with other social spheres and society as a whole,
through the mechanism of the common good.

I have argued that economics is mistaken in seeing itself as operating
and reflecting in a value-free way. Here I have to own up to the fact that of
course my analysis has not been value-free either. Despite my best
endeavours to remain entirely within an economic framework, what I
have argued will inevitably be shaped by the values I hold, by my world-
view. What anyone considers to be the meaning of life will influence the
priority given to values and influence behaviour. The questions I have
chosen to ask, the things which I have identified as problematic, the
aspects I view as weaknesses, will inescapably be informed by my religious
convictions. It is time, therefore, for those convictions to become more
explicit so that they too can be a part of the conversation.[1]

Non-economists will by now, I hope, see why economics is important in

---

1. Elements of this chapter appeared in 'A Christian Reflection on Work, Culture and
Society', in Anthony O'Mahony, Wulstan Peterburs and Mohammad Ali Shomali (eds.),
Catholics and Shi'a in Dialogue, 2004, pp. 378–91.

order to understand business activity, and therefore the finance sector. I now have to show non-theologians why theology is also important in that endeavour. Theology has as its subject God and God's relation to the world. Its purpose is not simply to uncover and present 'knowledge' but to serve a way of life. Its task is not merely to describe a plausible intellectual vision, but, far more importantly, to give a compelling account of a way of life. Theological ethics is an important bridge between more speculative theological reflection and living that way of life. It is not the case (contra Hauerwas) that Christian ethical insight based on theology cannot be shared except with those who also share in the faith from which it comes. This means that Christian ethics should be seen as evoking and enriching ethical insights which are capable of being intelligible to others. Christian ethics have their source in a vision of human existence, our common human life. Its contribution will be in terms of the increased possibilities for human flourishing which it can enable. This it must do through the means of conversation with those who hold different points of view and within the context of the different spheres in which that way of life must be lived. Ethics has to be persuasive as well as declaratory.

But to many, the idea that there can be a real conversation between such divergent viewpoints as economics, business and religion is not much more than nonsense. The cultural shift from modern to postmodern means that the very possibility of shared discourse about meaning, values, purposes is being challenged. Postmodern theorists assert that we can no longer seriously pursue questions of purpose and objective meaning. Others may not go quite so far, but it is difficult to deny that fewer and fewer convictions are held in common, and public discourse suffers increasing fragmentation, and subjectivism and relativism increase. In a pluralistic context Christian faith is seen as just one option among many. Life and faith no longer simply overlap. Life is seen as a multi-interpretable concept, and beliefs about the world must be explained in terms of their social, political or psychological usefulness to human beings. 'God' only 'explains' anything for 'those who believe in God'.

Christians today are also postmodern people. We participate in a culture in which God's role has been obscured and in which profoundly human or religious experiences no longer refer us directly and automatically to the God of Jesus. Instead it is often argued that appeals to God only reveal the psychological needs of those who continue to believe in God. Religion has been described as 'less a public affirmation of faith than a private consolation, along with philosophy, literature and cricket, against the cruel indifference of the world, personal failure and inevitable death'.[2] In such circumstances, it can seem foolhardy to suggest that there

---

2. D.J. Goldberg, '"An Intelligent Person's Guide to Religion" by John Haldane', *The Independent*, 26 April 2003, p. 24.

can be sufficient unity between faith and daily activity to permit the sort of conversation I want to have.

Furthermore, postmodern theorists would argue that the aim of a life in which faith is integrated must fail. The self, they argue, is inescapably multiple and fragmented. This is due, among other things, to the diversity of roles which people inhabit, the complex, numerous relations we have, the multiple forms of discourse in which we take part, and the social construction of gender. Therefore to attempt to discuss, let alone live, an integrated life would be either illusory or oppressive; illusory because such an attempt would need to deny the multiplicity of the self, or oppressive because it would have to impose a false unity.

Yet such unity of life is integral to the Christian vision. The Christian tradition, with its strong emphasis on the active presence of God in the world, insists that the whole of life is to be lived in conformity to God's will. Therefore all aspects of our existence should be ordered to serve the end of virtuous and pious living; this includes economic activity. Christianity does not hold that an escape from the economic realities of life is the ideal for a religious person. Rather, the religious relationship with God comes in the midst of the living of daily life, and economic dimensions of that life are as religiously significant as any other. The connection between faith and life means that theological ethics must respond in a Christian manner to the basic moral question of how we should live. It is this question which is at the heart of moral reflection. It is not a question about the immediate. Neither is it a question about what I should do now or next. Rather it is about a manner of life.

The rise of modern thought – and particularly modern science and economics with their abstraction from questions of purpose – have, as I have argued with relation to economics, sundered fact from value and left us with the challenge of finding a ground for ethics that cannot be reduced to individual preference or social convention. Earlier I referred to the need to find points of entry into the conversation. One such point is the economic model's reductive view of the human person.

The Human Person

Every ethics is based on an image of the human, on an *anthropology*. How the person is conceptualized will, in a dialectical manner, be related to the type of moral theory that evolves. For example, the utilitarian concept of a person is based essentially on a person's desires. From this viewpoint, desires form a person's real self, both as a moral and as a non-moral concept. As a result, utilitarianism attempts to show that the source of one's actions, whether moral or non-moral, is the set of one's present desires.

Since moral theories direct their explanation of the institution of morality to a certain kind of person, 'person' is not a theoretically neutral concept. It includes an implicit normative aspect in the sense that it states what is morally important and relevant, and what can be left to one side. It seeks to show how acting as *this* type of person is to act morally. Thus 'person' as a moral concept is pivotal. Rudman's study *Concepts of Person & Christian Ethics*[3] demonstrates how contentious 'person' is in moral debate. His analysis of the positions held by Tooley, Singer and Parfit reveals how their different conceptions of 'person' lead to profoundly different notions of personal identity, moral responsibility, moral relevancy and the possibility of possessing rights. As Schweiker rightly points out, systems of commodification that reduce value to only one system of measurement, for example, money, pose a pervasive threat of the loss of 'persons'. 'The inability to articulate a robust sense of the worth of persons is a fact in most commercial cultures.'[4] However, a robust sense is precisely what we need.

The account of the human person which I shall be presenting arose from the work done initially by Louis Janssens, but then by many others, to explore what the description 'the human person integrally and adequately considered' might mean. The work done so far has tended to concentrate on biomedical and sexual ethics. This is not surprising given that questions in these fields are closely related to the debate about what is a 'person' and what is 'natural'. However, this account is equally useful for social ethics. It is disappointing that much of the vast literature on social justice seems to have been written with little reference to personalism beyond that of human dignity. Human dignity is a vital component of ethical evaluation. The problem is that it is being made to do all the work, when perhaps a more nuanced approach would give a range of evaluative tools. Used on its own it can drift into the sort of narrow individualistic view of the human person which plagues economic and business analysis.

The moral anthropology I am presenting is not a static *de facto*, but a proposal of what is humanly desirable, a project, a vocation to be realized. We are, you might say, called into an ever-expanding 'becoming'. This non-static moral anthropology is one which is open to the multi-dimensional reality of the person, and sees the moral relevance of acts as flowing from the fact that they are the acts of the human person.[5] Although these

---

3. Stanley Rudman, *Concepts of Person & Christian Ethics*, 1997.

4. William Schweiker, 'Responsibility in the World of Mammon: Theology, Justice and Transnational Corporations', in Max L. Strackhouse with Peter J. Paris (eds.), *God and Globalization* Vol. 1: *Religion and the Powers of the Common Life*, 2000, pp. 105–39 (108).

5. Kevin Kelly, *New Directions in Moral Theology: The Challenge of Being Human*, 1992, p. 30.

dimensions can be outlined and analysed individually, they cannot be separated from each other. 'These aspects or dimensions belong to one and the same human person: they are interwoven and form a synthesis because each is proper to the integrity of every person.'[6]

Selling suggests that 'we think of "person" as a focal point, where all these dimensions converge ... These dimensions are "continuous" because they are always present, whether we are conscious of them or not ... the person is a unity, not simply exhibiting but actually constituted by these dimensions.'[7] Another way of thinking of this unity is to say that there is no separate 'I' which *has* these dimensions. I *am* these dimensions. There is no priority of dimensions, only the unity of the person.

Janssens proposes eight fundamental dimensions of the human person. The human person is (1) a subject called to be conscious, to act according to conscience, freely and responsibly. As a subject, no one may be reduced to an object or used as a mere means. (2) An embodied spirit – our body forms a part of the integrated subject that we are. There is a psychosomatic unity of the person. (3) Part of the material world – bound up in an intrinsic and essential relationship with the rest of creation. (4) Essentially inter-relational with other persons. We become an 'I' only in relation to a 'Thou'. (5) An interdependent social being, not only because we are open to each other in the 'I–Thou' relationship, but also because of the need to live in social groups with appropriate structures and institutions. (6) Called to know and worship God – open to the experience of transcendence. (7) Historical – thus a personalist ethic must necessarily be a dynamic one. (8) Equal but unique. Created in the image and likeness of God (*imago Dei*); each and every human person, sharing the same human nature and condition, enjoys dignity and is worthy of respect. Fundamental equality explains why some moral obligations apply to all. But each is also non-substitutable; each is a unique individual.[8]

When these essential dimensions are taken together, they constitute what is meant by 'the human person integrally and adequately considered'. Thus the personalist criterion for ethically evaluating an action is: An action is morally right if it is beneficial to the person adequately considered in himself or herself (that is, as a unique, embodied subject) and in his or her relations (that is, openness to others, to social structures, to the material world and to God).[9] In our actions, we must account for the whole person – our being-a-subject and in our essential openness. To

6. Louis Janssens, 'Artificial Insemination: Ethical Considerations', *Louvain Studies* (1980), pp. 3–29 (4).

7. Joseph Selling, 'The Human Person', in Bernard Hoose (ed.), *Christian Ethics: An Introduction*, 1998, pp. 95–109 (98).

8. Janssens, pp. 5–13.

9. Janssens, p. 13.

ignore one or more dimension of the person is to neglect a source of moral responsibility. Another way of looking at this is to say that authentic human flourishing requires that attention be paid to all dimensions of the human person.

One objection that needs to be faced immediately is the view that, with our greater awareness of diversity in all its forms, such a characterization, which claims to be applicable to all persons, is unsustainable. However, Janssens' proposal is not culturally specific. For example, our relationality and embodiment point to the need to have some reasonably stable structure for the nurturing of children. It does not prescribe what the form of that structure should be. It could be extended family, nuclear family, clan, patriarchal, matriarchal, and so on. What such a framework does require is a lot of hard work to ensure that what is cultural is not unwittingly proposed as normative for everyone. Furthermore, the insistence that we are historical beings means that we have only a gradual discovery of ourselves: many aspects of our psychology, physiology and inter-connectedness with the environment were unknown even 30 years ago. It follows that further information about ourselves can call into question previously accepted conclusions in ethics. Just as our beliefs about physics or medicines are revisable in the light of increased knowledge, so too are our ethical beliefs.[10] There is, therefore, a need for a certain humility in any attempt to make claims about all human beings, whether the claim is religious, economic or within business ethics. This anthropology seeks to hold together the universal and the particular, recognizing that great care needs to be taken in how the relationship between them is maintained. Norbert Rigali summarized this well.

> Formally, [universal human nature] is a principle, in every human being, of embodied spiritual self-transcendence in culture; and in this respect it is universal and unchanging. Materially, however, it is a principle, in every human being, of a particular historical model of embodied spiritual self-transcendence, possible within the limits of a particular culture; and in this respect human nature is particular, historical and variable.[11]

The Contribution of Personalist Ethics

I will not be discussing every possible contribution of personalist ethics, as my ultimate focus is the finance sector. So, for example, much that could be said about ecological concerns stemming from our intrinsic and

---

10. Gerard J. Hughes, 'Natural Law', in *Introduction to Christian Ethics*, 1998, pp. 47–56.
11. Norbert Rigali, 'Christian Morality and Universal Morality: The One and the Many', *Louvain Studies* 19 (1994), pp. 18–33 (29).

essential relationship with the rest of creation (dimension 3) will be passed over – although not entirely. From a business point of view (and hence, indirectly, the finance sector) it has enormous implications for how we are ethically to assess pollution, exploitation of natural resources, sustainability, genetically modified organisms and so on. In addition to the general aspects discussed here, more specific contributions will be brought out in later chapters.

Relationality

Mainstream business ethics, in line with most modern ethical theories, typically supposes that the basis of human life, the most fundamental level of the human situation, is an individualistic one.[12] Such theories can only rest on what I have argued is a counter-factual foundation. Its unsupported premise is that we are non-socially organized individuals. It must approach our living together in society, therefore, as something which is inherently *not* in our nature. The rational-individualist model of the economic actor omits relationship with others, so excluding a significant and distinctive feature of personhood. Economic rationality provides too thin an understanding of what it is to be human and prevents reflection on the ways in which self-interest and other-interest interact and modify our choices and decisions.

Personalism, with its retrieval of the importance of relationality, corrects this counter-factual bias towards rational individualism. (I use 'retrieval' as relationality is clearly visible in biblical texts and Patristic writers.) The individualism of the free-market model and business ethics can then be critically assessed in the light of the fact that we live in a social, cultural context. Selling comments:

> The irony of an individualist attitude is its ignorance of the dependence of the individual upon the tools of social commerce to assert the very individuality that is being claimed. 'Different from' implies something from which to differ. The 'individual' springs into awareness only within the experience of contrast that is possible in a social context. Autonomy is the result of separation, which in turn is completely dependent upon identification with a group.[13]

Feminist writers have repeatedly drawn attention to the fact that abstract, atomistic individualism is a patriarchal construct.[14] This has yet

12. For example, Hobbes' war of all against all is the explicit background to Thomas Donaldson and Thomas W. Dunfree, 'Towards a Unified Conception of Business Ethics: Integrative Social Contracts Theory', *Academy of Management Review* 19 (1994), pp. 252–84.

13. Selling, 'The Human Person', p. 102.

14. See, for example, Iris Marion Young, *Justice and the Politics of Difference*, 1990.

to be adequately accounted for in both economic analysis and business ethics. What is also overlooked in business ethics is how culturally specific the individualistic assumption is. The socio-cultural context of the birth of business ethics, along with management schools and academic management journals, is the post-Second World War United States, a time which coincided with US economic dominance. This was the context for the elaboration of a theoretical view of business, its purpose and its management which, with the emergence of transnational corporations and prestigious MBAs, has become the dominant model. Boyacigiller and Adler's meticulous survey of the relevant literature[15] shows how pervasive US cultural assumptions are in terms of business research. One of their primary conclusions is that due to this parochialism, theories have been developed which are insufficiently aware of non-US contexts, models, research and values. 'Most American theories ... have been developed and presented as if they were acultural ... [but selected examples] demonstrate how US values regarding free will, individualism and a low-context orientation profoundly affect how the field conceptualises organizational behaviour.'[16] 'Low-context' is particularly worth elaborating with regard to personalist ethics. Hall explains the concept:

> A high-context communication or message is one in which most of the information is either in the physical context or internalised in the person, while very little is in the coded, explicitly transmitted part of the message ... A low-context communication is just the opposite; i.e. the mass of information is vested in the explicit code ... Although no culture exists exclusively at one end of the scale, some are high, while others are low.[17]

The low-context orientation of the United States may well explain the generally minimal emphasis that business ethics and organizational theory have placed on such contextual features as history (dimension 7) and social setting (dimension 5) which together create culture. Failure to take account of cultural factors affects, for example, reflection on trust and business agreements. The low-context orientation of the United States is evident in the emphasis on written legal agreements, whereas many other cultures put more faith in face-to-face agreement where it is the relationship, not the legal document, which binds the agreement. Another aspect is accountability and responsibility. US culture includes the beliefs that individuals can affect their immediate circumstances, are responsible for their actions and can influence future events. In contrast, many other cultures are more deterministic and so generally define accountability and

15. Nakiye Avdan Boyacigiller and Nancy J. Adler, 'The Parochial Dinosaur: Organisational Science in a Global Context', *Academy of Management Review* 16 (1991), pp. 262–90.
16. Boyacigiller and Adler, p. 272.
17. Edward T. Hall, *Beyond Culture*, 1981, p. 91.

responsibility more diffusely than cultures which rely on free will. In more deterministic cultures (such as the Chinese, or many Moslem countries) people cannot assume responsibility for many events because such events are perceived as being outside of their control.

Other examples of such cultural differences include differences in motivation and commitment to the organization (which would directly affect how agency theory is conceived), time, authority, the meaning of work and other features which impact on business conduct. Clearly, therefore, an insistence on the importance of the social setting and culture is not an added luxury, but a necessary part of an ethics which seeks to safeguard all the dimensions of the human person. Culture, which embraces the value systems of a society, contributes, in important ways, to the complexity of ethical decision making. How, for example, is corporate governance to be envisaged in the context of irreducible diversity? (It is here, to anticipate the next chapter, that solidarity and subsidiarity will have a role.) The emphasis on the relational, social and cultural aspects of the human person is a necessary and valuable corrective to the atomistic, supposedly acultural, economic actor found in much business ethics. The absence of this richer characterization prevents any realistic assessment of many motivational considerations of actual behaviour. Its presence allows us to assess critically how business assumptions may undermine the social cohesion required by the market.

Transcendence and Identity

The first dimension listed was that the human person is a subject, called to act according to conscience, freely and responsibly. Implicit in that description is the claim that my ability to form moral judgments is linked to my deepest identity. It implies a high estimation of the capacity to lead the sort of integrated life which I referred to earlier. However, I have already referred to an increasingly common feature of contemporary culture which is that many experience their self as fragmented, dispersed through a multiplicity of roles, purposes and values. We move quickly among so many different experiences, contexts and value schemes that the question: 'Who am I?' becomes hard to answer. Advertising, however, assures me that by submitting to the embrace of the market I will find myself, whole and entire. It is through consumption that the individual receives identity. It is conferred through the market. Ultimately what is bought is unimportant. It is the purchasing process itself which becomes central and which clothes itself in religious features: the wide airy spaces of shopping malls are our new cathedrals, temples to consumerism and places of pilgrimage.

Religion itself becomes functionalized by the market. As Taylor has noted, the modern world is a disenchanted place.[18] With postmodernity, however, there is a re-enchantment – although this time an enchantment which the market has moved in on.[19] De-traditionalized and stripped of its classic integrative dimension by the continued assertion of the primacy of choice, religion becomes a commodity on the market, to be chosen (arbitrarily) by the consumer. People are still free to believe what they like; in fact, the need for some sort of spiritual life is increasingly recognized. The market is quite capable of meeting the needs generated by such a spiritual life. Demand can be met through a welter of artefacts, rituals and experiences under both generic and brand names. Thus the 'religious' person is presented with all the necessary items to compose their religious identity according to their own choice of 'pick-and-mix' components. The illusion is fostered that individuals are capable of giving themselves an identity, whereas the reality is that it is the market which has given it.

It is not surprising, therefore, that should a business practitioner proffer religiously based moral reasoning, colleagues will find this somewhat bizarre. This is not only because of the arguments I discussed in Chapter 1 which suggest that if one's personal morality conflicts with business practice, the person either has to suppress that morality or give up business. It is also because of the way in which religion is increasingly viewed. Religious identity is increasingly seen as a life-style choice which speaks of our personal development and personal fulfilment: religion as personal hobby. In the public world, religious identity is not considered either primary or necessary. It is, therefore, not a valid basis for coming to decisions in a public context. To suggest otherwise might well be viewed as intolerant of other people's valid choice of lifestyle.

This subverts one of the most basic moral questions of human life – the question of what identity-conferring commitment(s) ought to characterize and guide our lives. It is not the commitments which I have (some given, some chosen), commitments which carry values through time, which ground and guide my choices. Now it is my consumer choices, whimsical, arbitrary, fleeting, which bestow my identity, an identity which, apparently, can be taken up and discarded at will. We can reinvent ourselves continuously. To quote an advert for a watch: 'Who will you be for the next 24 hours?' Choices are only a matter of what works, and what serves my self-interest (narrowly construed). They therefore have no existential or ethical meaning. Increasingly, expediency becomes the only viable option for moral decisions, as principle cannot operate in the world of the arbitrary. This reveals one of the major challenges people face: how can my personal identity be grounded so as to enable me to come to moral identity?

18. Charles Taylor, *Sources of the Self: The Making of Modern Identity*, 1989.
19. This re-enchantment is not limited to a market phenomenon, but goes much wider. See, for example, John D. Caputo, *The Prayers and Tears of Jacques Derrida*, 1997.

The arbitrary nature of a market-conferred identity, if it does not lead to expediency, will increase relativism. People act in diverse social roles in numerous social practices which seem to have their own local moral rationality. No values are superior to other values, because, it is held, there is no such thing as truth. In the public sphere the space left by the absence of a comprehensive notion of truth will be filled by power and vested interests. The interests of dominant groups will come to dictate the events of daily life and instead of independent criteria for truth, group biases will be considered sufficient. This renders opposing perspectives impotent. This is particularly marked in the sphere of work. Economic groups and interests exert considerable political and social power, not least by the way in which economic, instrumental rationality has contributed to the privatization of other modes of truth. In addition, the work environment will be affected by those attitudes and aspects of corporate culture which I discussed in Chapter 1. When questions of morality are relevant only for individuals, not for institutions, these institutions tend to become ends in themselves, and cannot accurately be described as morally neutral.[20] But, as I have already argued, because we can – at least to some extent – influence the circumstances within which we act, the question of the morality of our decisions and actions remains.

I said earlier that the heart of ethics is about a manner of life. I have also suggested that it is identity-conferring commitments capable of carrying values through time which should ground and guide moral choices. It follows, then, that ethics addresses the question of the project to which we ought to commit our lives. For theological ethics this is the question of the moral meaning of Christian faith. This moral meaning cannot be restricted to the purely personal (if there is such a thing). There is a false dichotomy between public and private morality – they are both on the same continuum. Conscience cannot be privatized. As Tracy puts it, no Christian 'alert to the radical theocentrism at the heart of theology can rest content with the fatal social view that religious convictions are purely "personal preferences" or "private opinions" '.[21] All very well, but if it were as simple as that, we would not have the problems we do.

Part of our problem arises from the schematic way that morality is often handled, at least at the pastoral level. When treating the practical outworkings of morality, this is often done by examining the Ten Commandments, which are frequently divided into two blocks corresponding to the two great commandments of Christ (Mark 12:29–30). The first

20. Kathryn E. Kuhn, 'Social Values and Bureaucratic Reality', in Gerard Magill and Marie D. Hoff (eds.), *Values and Public Life: An Interdisciplinary Study*, 1995, pp. 139–66 (158).
21. David Tracy, 'Defending the Public Character of Theology', *Christian Century*, 1 April 1981, pp. 350–56 (351).

block, consisting of commandments one to three, is discussed under the heading: 'You shall love the Lord your God with all your heart, and with all your soul, and with all your mind'. These deal with what are often described as 'our duties to God'. The second block, consisting of commandments four to ten, is discussed under the heading: 'You shall love your neighbour as yourself', and deals with our relations to one another.

In general, moral reflection flows from this second block. It is where most Christian moral teachings are located (think of how many books, articles and sermons are based on issues of sex and death). It also forms the basis of most ethical discussion with those of other beliefs or none. It is not hard to see why it is much easier to confine ethical discussion in the public forum to this second block, which is much more likely to be accepted as being relevant to daily life. There exist some areas of commonality across a wide spectrum of groups and beliefs. It is possible to find at least some common ground on which to build, such as: 'does this action or type of action lead to human flourishing?' It is an approach which is, however, quite inadequate to address the challenge identified here. Because the tendency is to look at discrete acts or types of act, it can quickly reduce the moral life to quandary ethics: specific actions viewed from the minimalist perspective of being right or wrong. Vision, moral imagination, virtue, goals and many other aspects of the moral life do not easily find a home in such an approach. Such aspects become subordinated to an understanding of morality based primarily on a legal model. It reduces Christianity to moral precepts.

In the face of such a situation there is no one solution which will solve all the issues, no magic bullet. But there is one ingredient which, I believe, could make a significant contribution. It draws on the combination of two dimensions described earlier: dimension 6 (called to know God – open to the experience of transcendence) and dimension 8 (created in the image and likeness of God, equal but unique). It is a proposal which sounds deceptively simple. I say 'deceptively' because it is, I suggest, rather like Wendell Holmes's 'simplicity on the far side of complexity'. It is not based on the morality of acts, but rather in the universal call to holiness which reveals the exalted vocation of all the faithful in Christ. The suggestion is that the question of the 'project' to which we commit our lives, a commitment which both grounds our identity, and is capable of carrying values through time, and removes the false dichotomy between public and private, is the project contained in the first commandment: 'I am the Lord your God ... you shall have no other gods before me'.

My core identity can be summed up in the statement: 'I am the person I am because God is *this* God'.[22] If I am created in the image and likeness of

22. I am pointing here to a Trinitarian understanding of the creating God. See, for example, Ilia Delio, 'Does God "Act" in Creation? A Bonaventurian Response', *Heythrop Journal* 44.3 (July 2003), pp. 328–44.

God, and if God creates *ex nihilo*, then I am constantly held in being by God; I continually emerge from out of the creative impulse of God. My identity *as me* is being continuously confirmed, rooted and strengthened. It is embodying an aspect of the infinite, inexhaustible God. As such I hold equal dignity with all other persons, but the inexhaustibility of God also ensures that my uniqueness is not merely based on the particular combination of character traits, experiences and gifts I have; it is inherent. (This safeguards the theological justification of the value of diversity – a value often proclaimed without being given a theological grounding.) Nothing can remove this identity; no matter what I do I cannot discard it. It is not arbitrary, not re-inventable. It is given. This choice, because it is God's choice, has both existential and ethical meaning.

It might be objected that this notion is still a privatized one, a variation on 'me and Jesus'. It lacks a social dimension. This can be answered in several ways. It is true that there is an intensely 'private' dimension, if by that is meant intimacy. This God is, as Augustine put it, 'nearer to me than I am to myself'. Faith, seen as participation in God, means that one identifies with God because that is where one's focus is fixed. Life then becomes a continual interaction with God, fed by God. Aquinas, in his theory of charity, which is both theological and ethical, conceives the union between the human being and God as one of friendship,[23] a conception which indicates the threadbare nature of considering the first commandment solely under the heading of 'duty'. However, alongside this is Aquinas' treatment of the inner unity between the love of God, self and neighbour[24] which he develops from the New Testament presentation of *agape*. There it has the constant meaning of the creative love of God for human beings, the responsive love of human beings for God, and included in that love, the love of human beings for one another. Many today would wish to add here that it includes the love of human beings for the whole of God's creation. The moral life is seen in terms of the person's multiple relationships with God, self, neighbour and the world.

Here we can see the beginnings of how this notion can provide a basis for our social morality. It provides motivating reasons, as well as justificatory ones. The source and ground of moral values is not social convention, human creativity or personal preference. The source and ground of value is God. '"My God" is not a name that provides for a good night's sleep, but a passion that disturbs our rest and keeps us on the alert.'[25] Morally and religiously serious people are interested in transforming the world, making it better. And this faith in God can be united with daily life, as moral injunctions may be unified as distinguishing

---

23. Thomas Aquinas, *Summa Theologica*, II–II, q. 23 ff.
24. Aquinas, II–II, q. 25–26.
25. Caputo, *The Prayers and Tears of Jacques Derrida*, p. 334.

characteristics of a single way of life, the life of living the first commandment. The demands of discipleship are based on the uniqueness of God before whom everything else disappears. Everything is an application of the first commandment.

A second answer, which highlights the indivisibility of the personal and the social, lies precisely in the identity of the 'we' of the Church. If I, as an individual Christian, have my identity because of who this God is, then so do we, who are the People of God. It liberates us from the modern myth that we are really solitary beings, each pursuing his or her own private good in fierce competition. The deepest truth of our human nature is that we are not, as the market insists, selfish and greedy, but rather that we hunger and thirst for God and in God we find each other, for we meet others at the depth at which we allow ourselves to be met by God. Human life finds its unity in adoration of the one God. The commandment to worship the Lord integrates us and saves us from endless disintegration.

Another objection is that, due to its particularity, this approach will be divisive. To take the first commandment as a main foundation for social ethics will inevitably block the possibility of the conversation I say is so important. Yet we cannot ignore the boundaries separating moral communities. Sometimes they are irreducible. Acknowledging these boundaries, however, does not mean that discourse between different communities is impossible. What it does require is that we avoid trying to find and impose an illusory semblance of commonality. I am not seeking to dismiss the value of the search for commonality, indeed I hold it to be vital, but to suggest that we must allow for moral differences. If Christians do not, why should others? Pluralism is real and cannot be airbrushed out of the picture by attempting to present differences as largely superficial, merely different ways of expressing a common experience. Commonality and consensus are not to be so easily found. Moral particularity is not something to be afraid of; rather it is the place where we must begin our moral and ethical reasoning.

I take Walzer's warning that problems can arise when a person is dominated by a single source of identity. The 'singular self', where one particular membership totally defines identity, is apt to be an ideological or religious fanatic.[26] Such a self is unable to engage in dialogue with others; ideologically driven or god-possessed, he or she is unable to listen to other voices, neither those of other people, nor the internal voice of self-criticism. However, what I am proposing here is not an exclusionary source of identity, but a more complex one which both underpins and integrates other partial sources of identity. Dialogue with other traditions, whether religious or secular, can only begin from the basis that no one

26. Michael Walzer, *Thick and Thin: Moral Arguments at Home and Abroad*, 1994, pp. 96–100.

human tradition has the monopoly of wisdom; the Holy spirit works in all traditions. By the same token, therefore, Christians have their own contribution to make. We do a service to no one by denying particularity. The Christian churches either subordinate their witness to an externally defined agenda or they identify from within their own tradition their own authentic social mission and the grounds of their own identity.

It might still seem that this notion only intensifies the problems I began with. I do not think so, and I believe that there is no alternative. We communicate the integrity or fragmentation of our lives in the manner of our responding to the questions which life poses us. One of the myths of modernity is that the good is a matter of choice and that such choice is an exercise of objective, uninvolved reason. In the Christian tradition, however, the moral self is characterized by the radical willingness to be open to God implied by the first commandment, leading to involvement. Engagement, not retreat, is the real possibility and demand of faith. We must live the expectation; the hope; 'the hope against hope' in a transforming future. Without that hope we are reduced to the present, the immediate and to mechanistic rationality.

A Free and Responsible Subject

The concept of participation flows from seeing persons as created in God's image who are meant to be subjects, that is, responsible agents, of the institutions to which they belong. If they are not allowed to share in the important decisions that affect their lives, they are reduced to mere objects. This participation has implications for corporate strategy and organizational ethics, as work is not to be seen as a special kind of merchandise, nor as a force (the 'work force') needed for production. It calls into question personnel practices such as viewing workers as 'human resources', a practice which points to the tendency to treat workers as depersonalized factors of production, perfectly interchangeable.

By placing business activity within the context of a participating subject, open to transcendence (including self-transcendence) and with an orientation to the future implicit in being historical, one sees that the 'ends' of business activity go well beyond that of the 'end' of the market: buying and selling. Both the formulation of profit/shareholder value-maximization and of the production of goods and services are thereby shown to be inadequate in that neither includes within its focus an explicit reference to the human person who undertakes that activity and for whom it holds a deeper, richer level of meaning than just earning enough to live, however comfortably.

Such an understanding challenges that view of business and ethics which emphasizes ethics as something which is introduced 'from the outside'. The nature of the human person, and an appreciation of the ways in which work is (or can be) a vehicle for responding to God's calling of us into deeper discipleship, provides a framework for seeing ethics as something which is already part of the very nature of business activity itself, and human existence more generally. This understanding of the worker is far from universal. Hammer and Champy's influential book on business re-engineering[27] characterizes employees as, at best, morally marginal, without personal lives or histories and easily malleable. The understanding I am proposing leads to a rejection of any assumption that ethics is alien to most people's experiences and dispositions. An examination of the 'case-study' literature in business ethics reveals the extraordinary concentration on examples of misdeeds, reinforcing negative stereotypes. The implication seems to be that the only way of learning about what is ethical is to study every variant of non-ethical behaviour that the author can drum up. As a contribution to the formation of good judgment it is inadequate. At the very least, authors need to ask if there is a balancing need for good role models. A changed understanding would, perhaps, reduce the emphasis in so much business ethics on prevention through enforcement mechanisms like regulations and ever stiffer penalties.

Most emphatically this is not to underestimate the reality of sin, of our often distorted priorities and perceptions, of the ways in which we can be blind to the injustices in which we are caught up. Nor am I ignoring the often negative effects of corporate culture. The context within which behaviour takes place has a powerful effect on behaviour, limiting and shaping opinion. Rather, I am arguing that there are moral values *in* the organization and its culture, the people who work there and the interaction between these two. Some of those values will be highly questionable. Others, however, are of great worth, and if these are ignored then what tends to happen is that people live down to the low expectations held of them – as educationalists know only too well.

Summary and Conclusions

The task of ethics is not limited to establishing the criteria for right actions or to defining the context of obligation. A personalist ethics insists that ethics must examine questions which deal with the problem of what makes a life meaningful and explore what it is to be a human agent, a person, a self. The ways in which we understand ourselves as persons has a direct link with how we organize ourselves in social groups. An integral understanding of the human person will, therefore, contribute to a society

27. Michael Hammer and James Champy, *Reengineering the Corporation: A Manifesto for Business Revolution*, 1993.

in which, however imperfectly, each dimension of a person is valued and fostered. Conversely, a reductionist anthropology will contribute to a society in which one or more dimension is undervalued and perhaps even oppressed. It is, therefore, an essential criticism of liberal capitalism, and those strands of business ethics associated with it, that it allows human *functions*, for example consumption, to take the place of human *persons*.

By placing the business practitioner within the totality of life, both individual and social, the anthropology of personalist ethics enables moral reflection to begin from a positive stance. The atmosphere of much business-ethics writing is negative, with its primary focus on errors, or on what should not be done. I have argued that personalist ethics can provide an important corrective. Although it may arrive at outlining attitudes and actions which should be avoided, it begins by focusing on what the moral agent is and can become. By locating identity within the theology of *imago dei*, it points towards a positive end (*telos*) of our becoming. The negatives are then understood in the light of the positives. Just as a student, if she wishes to obtain a first-class degree, will avoid a frenetic social life in the run-up to her exams, so individuals, in choosing the project to which they commit themselves, and thereby choosing what sort of person they will become, will avoid certain types of conduct. In addition, the anthropology of personalist ethics, while including the rational and analytic, appeals also to another side of human knowing – what may be termed the intuitive side, the side which draws on wisdom, imagination, creativity and so on. This opens up the possibility of drawing on the full richness of moral imagination.

That moral imagination will be fed by the vision of our lives as rooted in God, sustained by God and destined for God. It is the fundamental truth from which all our actions should be seen to flow. In the context of postmodernism, truth cannot be claimed merely on the basis of the authority of institutions or institutional leaders. This will be resisted as an imposition. Not only must we live the hope, we must also live the truth, do the truth. Truth is not a claim, it is witnessed to by how we live. Our relationship with truth is personal, not abstract. When that truth is God, we do not possess it but love it. As Rahner said, the Christian of the future will be a mystic or will be nothing at all.[28] A Christian, like other people, tends to see the world initially with herself at the centre. We ask: 'What place does God have in my life?' We need constantly to re-learn that the question is: 'What place do I have in God's life?' This leads to seeing, evaluating and judging all things in relation to God, to unifying all our actions into the one project to which we can commit ourselves – God's project for us as individuals and for the world. We lose our very selves if we concentrate our ethical reflection solely on actions.

28. Karl Rahner, *Theological Investigations*, Vol. 7, 1971, p. 15.

Chapter 5

THE COMMON GOOD

Having examined one pole in the relationship between the individual and society, it is now time to look at the other pole, particularly a basic moral dilemma: 'How is the tension between the individual and society to be maintained in a healthy, productive way?' We should not seek to resolve that tension by dissolving one end or the other. Both are required. Therefore, neither the neoclassical understanding of the free market, which comes down firmly on the side of the individual alone, nor communism, and all those models which elevate the society at the expense of the individual, will be adequate. The ideal is to keep both ends in fruitful tension. One way of doing this is through the concept of the common good. Although this concept is rightfully recognized as a core value in the Roman Catholic tradition, it also holds an important place in Protestant reflection.[1]

How useful, or otherwise, the concept of the common good is, hinges on questions such as: 'What conditions are required for human fulfilment?' 'What makes a good society?' 'What is the relationship between the individual and society?' Society is full of competing claims. How do we adjudicate between them so that society does not dissolve into just a collection of special interest groups, each fighting for its particular concern? Many people believe that the invisible hand operates as an adequate mechanism for ensuring the common good. This claim is based on the belief that the market allows freedom to choose according to self-interest, yet promotes efficiency and prosperity from which all benefit. On the contrary, the invisible hand, as a mechanism, is severely limited. Furthermore, revealed-preference theory fails to recognize and value common interests and interdependence, so putting a false antagonism between self-interest and other-interest, with no space for mutually interested actions which place the individual within a community. It incorrectly assumes that rationality requires action which is self-interested, narrowly conceived as excluding consideration of the interests of others except

1. See, for example, studies in Dennis P. McCann and Patrick D. Miller (eds.), *In Search of the Common Good*, 2005; Eric Mount Jr., *Covenant, Community and the Common Good: An Interpretation of Christian Ethics*, 1999.

indirectly. It therefore has little to say about competing claims except, perhaps, to assume that the claim made by the strongest group will win out over the others.

Writers such as Becker illustrate the tendency described by Giddens[2] of adopting the methodological tactic of beginning the analysis assuming that agents are ignorant of the 'real' stimuli to their activity. Agents' own reasons can then be discounted. That stance has strongly defined and potentially offensive political overtones. If people have no worthwhile understanding of the reasons for their actions, then their views can be disregarded in any practical programmes of social organization. That approach is opposed by a personalist ethics with its view of the person as a responsible, participating subject, inherently social and with personal goals and aspirations which should be respected. As one of the first tasks of ethical reflection is to ensure that all voices in the debate are heard, the voice of moral agents who claim motivations other than economic rationality cannot be discounted *a priori*. Using the concept of the common good provides the structural space for differing voices and motivations to be heard.

Defining the Common Good

The concept of the common good is based upon the capacity of human reason to discern the good, even if only partially. Reason also recognizes that some human goods are shared in common, and that these form part of the good human life. Reason reflects on experience, and therefore its understanding of the common good will necessarily be dynamic. Pope John XXIII defined the common good as the sum total of those conditions of social living whereby people are enabled more fully and readily to achieve their own perfection.[3] He noted that the common good progresses and that the general norms by which it is defined are in accord with the nature of things and the changing conditions of social life.[4] It is, therefore, impossible to define the common good in a final way, irrespective of changing social conditions. In its practical daily manifestations and requirements, it will appear very different in, for example, a basically agricultural society to its appearance in a hi-tech western society.

The definition was extended some years later so that 'the common good embraces the sum total of all those conditions of social life which enable

---

2. Anthony Giddens, *Central Problems in Social Theory: Action, Structure and Contradiction in Social Analysis*, 1979, pp. 71ff.
3. John XXIII, *Mater et Magistra*, 1961, 65.
4. John XXIII, 220.

individuals, families and organisations to achieve complete and efficacious fulfilment'.[5] As the origin, subject and ultimate purpose of society and all institutions is the human person, the common good is grounded in a vision of what it is to be human and cannot be determined without having regard to the human person. Although we speak of 'the common good' (singular), this, I think, is potentially misleading. It could give the impression that it is some sort of unified, general condition. If that were the case then, in conditions of irreducible diversity with a plurality of conceptions of the 'good', such a notion would be a non-starter. However, the conditions spoken of refer primarily to the social systems, institutions and environments on which we all depend. The common good will be served when these work in a manner which benefits all people. Examples of the common good are a just legal and political system, an effective system of public safety and security, an unpolluted natural environment, a flourishing economic system and international peace. It would be a mistake, however, to limit the concept of the common good to such 'common goods' as these which are produced by forms of co-operation. The concept also includes the *kind of community* brought into being and sustained by those forms of co-operation and interaction. As Mount says, the concept affirms the centrality of community and resists 'the extremes and neglects of Western individualism with its suspicion of any effort to advance a common good because of plural versions of the good and its tendency to make all associations voluntary and contractual'.[6]

Building up an overlapping consensus in support of such common goods as those I've just listed among people who otherwise hold differing values and convictions requires a certain commonality of interest and activity. On what basis might we build? One theologian who has explicated the foundation of the common good in human fulfilment is Grisez. He identifies a number of 'basic human goods' which fulfil persons. These are: (1) self-integration, which is harmony among all the parts of a person which can be engaged in freely chosen action. (2) Practical reasonableness or authenticity, by which is meant harmony among moral reflection, free choices and their execution. (3) Justice and friendship, which are aspects of the interpersonal communion of good persons freely choosing to act in harmony with one another. (4) Religion or holiness, which is harmony with God. (Grisez later broadened this to: peace with God or the gods, or some non-theistic but more-than-human source of meaning and value.) (5) Life itself, including health, physical integrity and safety and the handing on of life to new persons. (6) Knowledge of various forms of truth and appreciation of various forms of beauty or excellence. (7) Activities of

---

5. Second Vatican Council, *Gaudium et Spes*, 1965, 74.
6. Mount, *Covenant, Community and the Common Good*, p. 1.

skilful work and of play, which in their very performance enrich those who do them.[7]

We do not have to accept Grisez's list of goods as final and definitive – indeed, given our knowledge of past errors of judgment about what it is to be human, and the evidence of previous development in thinking, it would be foolish to do so. Nevertheless, such an understanding represents a reasonable approximation in our time of what contributes to human flourishing. Neither are we obliged to accept the contention of Grisez and his collaborators that each of these goods is absolute and, from its own point of view, the most important. Instead, we can take the same position here as with the dimensions of personalist ethics. That is to say, though these goods can be delineated and analysed individually, they cannot be separated from each other. They are interwoven and form a synthesis because each is proper to the integrity of every person.

One of the paths for working towards the common good would be to analyse social structures to assess their impact on the possibilities for realizing these basic goods. Do they facilitate or frustrate them? Are these structures enabling or oppressive? Such an analysis might cause us to seek to transform the structures, and in doing so, we could well find that we clarify further our recognition of the basic goods and what is required for their realization. How they are realized will, in large part, depend on a host of factors (not least culture), factors which themselves will change over time. No analysis can, therefore, be a once-off. Nor, despite the universal nature of the basic goods (and therefore of the values they embody) will such an analysis ever be other than particular. It is precisely 'the inculturation of these universal values in the shared meanings, values, and institutions of a particular culture [that] constitutes the universality-in-particularity of morality'.[8]

When, therefore, we speak of conditions which enable complete and efficacious fulfilment, it is these basic human goods to which we point, that is, goods which are aspects of the person, not extrinsic things such as property. These extrinsic things can be valuable by being useful to persons, they are human goods, but they are not directly and in themselves fulfilments of persons; they are instrumental. Neither are these goods relativistic, despite the fact that the conditions which enable them will vary due to differing social conditions. This is because the concept of the common good is grounded in an anthropology found across cultures. It points to features of our shared humanity and provides a starting point for the commonality I referred to. For example, Nussbaum uses myths and stories from widely differing times and places as illustrations of what

7. Germain Grisez, *The Way of the Lord Jesus* Vol. 1: *Christian Moral Principles*, 1983, p. 124.

8. Norbert Rigali, 'Christian Morality and Universal Morality', p. 32.

we think it is to be human.[9] The resulting 'non-relative values' are strongly reminiscent of Grisez's basic human goods, although she is working outside of a Christian framework.

The concept of the common good thus provides a more global philosophical perspective than does the individualistic, western model of self-interested rationality. It shares common ground with a wide range of religious perspectives as well as secular communitarianism and is more amenable both to Islamic and Oriental cultures. For example, the Japanese term *kyosei* was popularized by the Chairman of Canon Inc., Ryuzaburo Kaku. The term, which Kaku translates as 'living and working for the common good', is what he saw as describing the purpose of Canon. What Kaku means by 'common good' may differ in some respects from the understanding I am presenting. Nevertheless, it indicates a reaching towards something similar. It seems, then, that the common good could function as a concept which facilitates cross-cultural dialogue on what constitutes the good life and the good society.

The common good today, therefore, can be characterized as a dynamic concept, concerned to ensure that the social systems, institutions and environments on which we all depend work in a manner which benefits all people, so underpinning a robust understanding of social justice. It points to more than these systems, institutions and environments, however, in that the kind of society created by working for the common good is itself a good to be sought. Being rooted in a particular vision of what it is to be human, its anthropology ensures that, while it is flexible with regard to the form it might take in a particular context, it is not totally relativistic. In an increasingly globalized context, it has the potential to function as a cross-cultural platform for debate.

With its linking together of individuals, families and social groups the tradition does not presume a *necessary* incompatibility between the good of individuals and social groups, but sees the good of the former as inextricably linked to the latter, without either subsuming the other. Because the good of society is also the good of each member of society, if it is not the good of some sector, class or group, then it is not the *common* good. The common good is common both to the whole and to the persons who comprise that whole. The common good avoids the extreme of collectivism because it demands that the good be distributed to the persons who make up society. It also avoids the extreme of individualism by giving importance and meaning to society and the community. It is also the 'common' good because the basic human goods must often be pursued with others in a social context. For human beings, life in a community

---

9. See, for example, Martha Nussbaum, 'Aristotelian Social Democracy', in *Necessary Goods: Our Responsibilities to Meet Others' Needs*, 1998, pp. 135–56.

which nurtures such goods is a precondition – necessary, but not sufficient – for personal happiness.

However, it is here that the common good can become imprecise, prescriptive rather than analytic. Phrases like: 'the state must provide for . . .' or 'society has an obligation to . . .' do not add much to the stock of human knowledge. What is often lacking is a straightforward, explanatory, functional analysis of how various institutions condition and are conditioned by the common good of the individuals and groups which comprise them. What is also needed is an analysis of how both institutions and their constituent members function in concert to establish the common good of the wider community. Using the anthropology and personalist ethics which I have described does, however, enable us to at least approach an understanding of how the good of the individual, the intermediate groups and the whole of society might come together into the common good. Using these tools allows us to identify what sort of individual and communal life truly and fully benefits human beings. It also reminds us that to be a person is to be related, to have loyalties and allegiances, responsibilities and associations.

I have already suggested that many of the basic human goods must be pursued in common if any individual is to enjoy them. The relationship between the individual and society is reciprocal and even somewhat paradoxical. The human person seeks good, but cannot achieve it except in society. For that reason, seeking the good of society is one way of securing our own personal good. But at the same time, the common good is oriented towards the person, who does not exist for the sake of society. The human person has a goal of his or her own, a transcendent goal (dimension 6) which is higher than society. Thus the common good has to respect the human person, not merely use him or her as a means to an end (totalitarianism).

But it would be a great mistake to think that the goods that an individual might seek are, therefore, individual goods. This is the fundamental error of contractarianism (for example, that of Rawls). In this perspective society comes into being as a result of a contract between equals who, in order to ensure the collective peace needed to pursue their personal aims, surrender some part of their personal freedom to the state. Community is an optional association, a mere means to private ends. Society is no more than an amalgam of individuals who have no choice but to co-operate in order to survive. Such a society cannot contribute to their development as persons. All it can do is to facilitate maximum co-operation in the pursuit of individual interests and guard against arbitrary violence. It follows that, as there are only individual goods, there can be no common good, no common purpose. The most that one could speak of would be a common interest. However, that is a false assessment of how we achieve many of the goods we seek. The things that individuals might value (authentic self-expression, certain works of art, outcomes based on frankness and equality, or whatever) presuppose a certain culture, a certain society which gives these goods meaning. As Taylor argues:

> If these things are goods, then other things being equal so is the culture that makes them possible. If I want to maximize these goods, then I must want to preserve and strengthen this culture. But the culture as a good, or more cautiously as the locus of some goods (for there might be much that is reprehensible as well), is not an individual good.[10]

Neither is it an instrumental good. It makes no sense to think of the goods which culture makes possible as somehow capable of existing on their own and culture only acting as their mere instrument. It is a good in itself, a common good, something which Taylor designates as an irreducibly social good. Culture is not the only non-individual good which enables individuals to achieve goods. Institutions can also perform this function, a possibility which I shall return to shortly.

Subsidiarity and Solidarity

It is often thought that the Catholic tradition of the common good, because it has a strong emphasis on the demands of justice and charity, and because it advocates solidarity, would give self-interest pretty short shrift. In fact this is not the case. *Rerum Novarum* (a document which is usually held to have inaugurated the modern period of Catholic social teaching) argues that self-interest is not condemned under Christian charity.[11] There is no demand that all self-interest be uprooted and replaced with self-sacrifice. Rather, self-interest is to be tempered with generosity. The commitment implied by the common good requires personal sacrifices only when these have some prospect of being both useful and indispensable.

Even to speak of 'personal sacrifice for the common good' raises problems. Appeals to the common good in such situations may well be interpreted as merely a cloak for the interest of some particular group. 'Suspicions about the common good begin with who defines it and whose voices are not heard in the process of definition.'[12] All too often those being summoned to self-sacrifice are the already poor and marginalized, and those doing the summoning are the articulate and powerful. Christians too have been guilty of advocating forms of self-sacrifice which have

---

10. Charles Taylor, 'Irreducibly Social Goods', in *Philosophical Arguments*, 1995, pp. 127–45 (137).

11. Leo XIII, *Rerum Novarum*, 1891, 20–21.

12. Mount, *Covenant, Community and the Common Good*, p. 31.

been both gender-biased and supportive of repressive forms of piety, rather than being concerned with individual welfare. How the *content* of the common good is arrived at is, therefore, of vital concern. The history of the twentieth century shows that there is always the danger that a distorted notion of the common good could collapse into totalitarianism. Merely asserting that the common good must promote and protect human dignity is not enough. Nor can one rely on tradition to provide the rules for social life, insofar as tradition can be oppressive in itself and/or subject to interpretation by an elite. Additional safeguards are required to ensure that the content of the common good is truly *common*.

A protection against totalitarianism is the concept of subsidiarity. By insisting that it is 'an injustice and at the same time a grave evil and a disturbance of right order to assign to a greater and higher association what lesser and subordinate organisations can do',[13] limits are placed on political society. This is seen as only one community among others and therefore should be limited so that it will not displace or absorb others. By extension one can argue that the economy is limited by the concept of subsidiarity so that it too does not displace or absorb other social spheres. Subsidiarity is most frequently used in relation to the state; it is a key principle, for example, in the workings of the European Union. However, it also lends itself to business activity through its obvious connection with freedom and participation. It also has implications for management systems, particularly in a global context of irreducible diversity.

Inherent in the concept of subsidiarity are two essential features. The first is decentralized decision making; the second is an institutional framework enabling the construction of a strong but flexible network of participating subjects. This structural arrangement carries two criteria: co-determination and decisional complementarity. This leads to an evolutionary mechanism (rather than a pre-determined one) so that rules and decisions emerge from the process of interaction. Because decisions are decentralized, the necessary reciprocal recognition among the participants becomes possible. This, however, does require that the highest institutional levels create the conditions to enable the weaker parties to participate effectively in the collective endeavour. Subsidiarity therefore implies that the content of the common good cannot be imposed 'top-down'. There is a tendency for the common good to be presented as something which is objectively knowable by observation of social conditions. However, in a pluralistic, secular society, the content can only emerge as a result of a genuinely public dialogue, not as the precondition for one. It will take place within the context of creatureliness, that is to say, by people who are limited, have only partial insight (even if not actually perverse), and who are influenced by history, sectional interests

13. Pius XI, *Quadragesimo Anno*, 1931, 79.

and self-serving preferences. As these conditions apply to all human beings, no elite need step forward to do our thinking and deciding for us. Only after real dialogue will a proposal emerge as the object of true consensus – or fail to do so.

A second safeguard against a totalitarian version of the common good is the concept of solidarity. The common good, by definition, has to be inclusive or it is nothing. The 'we' of the common good has to include a great many individuals and categories of persons who will not be immediately (or perhaps ever) congenial to us. It is a moral stance or attitude which is rooted in the fact of our shared humanity. No one is outside the moral community, so everyone is to be treated in accordance with the common human dignity shared by all people. It cannot, therefore, rely on a cosy, sentimental foundation of 'togetherness'. When called on to collaborate with others, the *virtue* of solidarity, because it is not simply a matter of feelings,[14] requires us to take account of the means and ends to ensure that they avoid the danger of selfish particularism and oppressive totalitarianism.

Solidarity is the antithesis of the individualist attitudes of distrust and selfishness. Solidarity (seen as commitment to community) is directly opposed to some understandings of freedom which see freedom as purely absence of the constraint which is entailed by communal responsibility. Atomistic individualism assumes conflict between individuals whose interests are incompatible with one another. This assumption in fact contributes to our both interpreting and constructing social interaction in terms of conflict. The expectation of conflict is a self-fulfilling prophecy leading to a diminishment of social cohesion. This is illustrated with great clarity by Patrick Riordan in his examination of different attitudes of those working within the penal system.[15] Social solidarities do not, however, come about as automatic consequences of individual initiatives. They have to be worked for as a goal of any form of social organization.

This highlights one of the ways in which the common good differs from communitarian ethics, with its emphasis on the ideal of 'found' community. By this is meant the 'family or community or nation or people, as bearers of this history, as sons and daughters of that revolution, as citizens of this republic'.[16] The problem with this is that it may give traditional communities and relationships such normative weight that unjust social

---

14. 'Not a feeling of vague compassion or shallow distress ... [but] ... a firm and persevering determination to commit oneself to the common good.' John Paul II, *Sollicitudo Rei Socialis*, 1987, 38.

15. Patrick Riordan, *A Politics of the Common Good*, 1996, pp. 6–27.

16. Sandel, *Liberalism and the Limits of Justice*, 1982, p. 179.

patterns are perpetuated.[17] We can concede the influence of these communities without having to endorse it; as I have already suggested, an essential part of working towards the common good is the need to challenge destructive social structures. Another danger is that communitarian ideals may be essentially exclusionary. Privileging unity over difference excludes those who are different and suppresses the differences of those who are considered the same.[18] By holding equality and originality together, personalist ethics informs our understanding of the common good so that equality is not limited to an imposed or preconceived uniformity, allowing social differentiation without exclusion. As communitarian ethics lacks the concept of solidarity, it cannot explore rightful obligations and expectations *across* community lines, and is therefore potentially highly partisan. Given our increasingly globalized context, its basis in the 'found' community results only in a disconnected series of special pleadings, rather than genuine dialogue between differing communities.

A third safeguard against totalitarianism within a Christian understanding of the common good lies precisely in what a secular observer might assume to be its most problematic feature: that is to say, in its religious grounding. Insofar as Christians are fallible, limited human beings, then the fear may not be misplaced; any human activity can potentially be misused, distorted into becoming its opposite. This does not, however, take away its basic validity. What safeguards the common good is the conviction that the final good of every person – that is, God – transcends any good that can be achieved politically, economically or culturally. I will need to build up this argument in stages.

The commandment to love one's neighbour as oneself demands commitment to the common good. Love of neighbour, descriptions such as 'people of God', the 'body of Christ' and the social nature of the human person, all point to the fact that individual persons only attain their destiny together in community. This does not imply that the individual gets lost in some amorphous mass; our destiny is always personal, but 'personal' is not the same as 'private'. The common good of this world is not of absolute value; only God is absolute. Therefore all realizations of the common good (political, economic, cultural) are partial and limited. Each of these goods is valuable, but may not be absolutized or allowed to become dominant. This requires that, in working for the common good, we should respect the transcendent dignity of the person because human

17. Marilyn Friedman, 'Feminism and Modern Friendship: Dislocating the Community', in Eve Browning Cole and Susan Coultrap-McQuin (eds.), *Explorations in Feminist Ethics: Theory and Practice*, 1992, pp. 89–97.

18. Young, *Justice and the Politics of Difference*, pp. 226–56.

beings are destined for a good (that is, God) which is beyond civil society and the state.

The next step comes from considering one of the implications of being created in the image and likeness of God. The Christian understanding of God is as a Trinitarian communion, a person-in-relation-to-other-persons. We too are social beings, relational beings. As beings created in the image and likeness of God, the implication is that the full common good exists only in the communion of all persons with God and with each other in God. Colin Gunton, in his reflection on the Trinity[19] argues that the only way to understand the meaning of human society is in the light of Trinitarian theology. Modernity's championing of particularity has led to a loss of any sense of relationship between particulars. For Gunton a true sense of particularity will be through particular existence lived in relationship with both God and others, with God understood as truly relational. Thus the common good demands support for the main forms of relationship in which personhood is realized. These will include friendships, families, civil society, politics, voluntary associations and relationship with God. Therefore, any theory which makes the good of society the highest good, or which grants absolute sovereignty to the state must be rejected. In other words, the common good, fully understood, is thoroughly anti-totalitarian.[20]

Comparison of the common good with other approaches highlights a number of its strengths. Firstly, it gives *appropriate* weight to society, that is to say, it avoids the opposing errors of collectivism and individualism. Unlike utilitarianism, it is concerned with the good of all, not just the aggregate good which may conceal great inequalities. It is, therefore, able to address the shortcomings identified in Chapter 2 concerning the limits to the claims for justice and freedom. Furthermore, it provides a richer framework for discussing the ends for which efficiency is a means. Rooted in a thick understanding of human fulfilment, it identifies and provides for the nurturing of many cross-cultural values. Subsidiarity and solidarity guard against particularism, exclusion and totalitarianism. Subsidiarity also ensures that the content of the common good is arrived at by means of the public forum, safeguarding participation and freedom. Finally, it allows for an analysis of the influence that structures and corporate decision making have in a complex society.

There are weaknesses, however. Talk of the common good can too easily assume the possibility of harmony. There is frequently insufficient acknowledgment of social conflict and pluralism, with sometimes deeply

19. Colin Gunton, *The One, the Three and the Many: God, Creation and the Culture of Modernity*, 1993.

20. For an extended examination of the implications of a Christian understanding of the common good, see David Hollenbach, *The Common Good and Christian Ethics*, 2002.

diverging views on fundamental social values. Even where there is general agreement on public goods, for example education and public health, reasonable people may still differ in how they wish to allocate limited resources between these goods. Here the witness of the Churches is more important than is sometimes realized. How the Churches model for others diversity, conflict resolution and subsidiarity in their internal life and external relations will either persuade others that working for the common good is a viable path to take, or it will convince them of the opposite. I suggest that much more needs to be done here, especially in their internal life.

Another tendency, at times quite marked in some theologians (for example, Grisez), is to view the contemporary understanding of the human person, human goods and the implications to be derived from them, as the 'definitive' understanding. This then forecloses on developing moral understanding, and with it the common good, in a dynamic way. The final weakness is that, by concentrating its analysis on the relationship between society as a whole and the individual, some presentations of the common good (for example, in Catholic social teaching) have neglected the role of intermediate systems and institutions. In later chapters, I shall be taking up and applying the concept precisely in those neglected areas. Here, however, I want to situate economic activity within the concept of the common good.

The Relativization of the Economy

Those engaged in business will often perceive Christian ethics as being of only marginal relevance. The very frames of reference seem to be coming from different planets. Those discussing business will be taking as some of their basic assumptions such features as utility theory, portfolio theory, market efficiency, maximization of shareholder value and the capital asset pricing model. Christian ethics will be referring to such assumptions as human flourishing, the nature of the human person, the demands of community, solidarity and the rest. So how can we go about evaluation if we are using such different models? How do we know what to do with the guidelines offered by Christian ethics? The first thing to state is that Christian ethics cannot go beyond its competence (for example, by providing over-detailed economic plans). We need to remember Aristotle's salutary warning that we must not expect more precision from ethics than it can provide. Ethics may offer guidelines towards solutions, but it cannot offer the concrete solutions themselves.

What it can do is ask different sorts of questions so as to arrive at guidelines. The first question concerns purpose. If we want to know whether a pen is a good pen, we have to know what pens are for, what the purpose of a pen is. We need to know that pens are for writing with, not for eating soup. So too with the economy. If we want to know if this is a good economy, we have to know what the purpose of the economy is. It is with such fundamental questions that we have to begin. If we cannot agree on the underlying purpose of the economy, we will not come to agreement on other issues such as the role of the business firm, or its relationship to the wider society.

When considering the purpose of the economy as a whole, I have already suggested that it is not sufficient to assert what the essential goal of business is. The goal will be important but it should neither dominate the discussion of the whole economy (for the economy is more than just the business sector), nor should it be assumed that this goal can stand in isolation. I have referred to the 'for-the-sake-of' relationship. It is necessary to ask what is/are the good(s), and the ultimate good, for the sake of which the purposes of business might be pursued? How does it contribute to the purpose of the economy? What is the relationship between economic activity and the wider society? The moral justification of the market can only lie in the nature of its object, that is, the purpose of the economy. In the end one is asking: 'How does this activity contribute to the ultimate good of human life?' A succinct summary of that purpose would go something like this:

> To provide all the goods which the resources of nature and industry can procure for all members of society. These goods ought to be plentiful enough to satisfy all those needs which are requirements for people to be able to realize their full and equal personhood, and raise society's members to a reasonable level of comfort.

It is worth noting here that reasonable people may reasonably disagree over what constitutes 'reasonable'. By definition it will be contingent; some expressions of needs will be legitimately socially determined. But also by definition it places in question whether some people in some places have more than is reasonable – particularly in the light of environmental degradation and depletion of natural resources.

What we have here is a clear assertion that the economy has a purely *instrumental* function, it is a means to an end. It is not an end in itself. This can be seen clearly in *Gaudium et Spes*.

> The ultimate and basic purpose of economic production does not consist in the increase of goods produced, nor in profit nor in prestige; it is directed to the service of man, that is of man in his totality, taking into account his material needs and the requirements of his intellectual, moral, spiritual and religious life. Economic activity is to be carried out according to its own methods and laws, within the limits of the moral order, so that God's design for mankind may be fulfilled.[21]

21. *Gaudium et Spes*, 64.

An important relativizing move has been made here – a relativizing of economic activity so that we can understand how the economic sphere interacts with other dimensions of human existence. This relativizing contrasts sharply with the commercialization of our lives discussed earlier and with the assumptions of economic rationality. There is a defence of the right of social spheres to their own appropriate autonomy. However, precisely because of this, the importance of spheres other than the economy is also defended. As I have already said, the common good does not subscribe to a reductionist anthropology which sees the human person as no more than *homo economicus*, or to a view of society which, by absolutizing the market, diminishes society to an adjunct of it. The market, as only one aspect and one dimension of human activity, is not to be absolutized. Nor should the consumption of goods be society's only value. What follows from this is that efficiency is inadequate as an end in itself. I am not denying the need for economic efficiency. It is rather that when efficiency becomes the dominant factor, it distorts any understanding of society and the individual. Like the economy itself, efficiency is relativized by its social context and the demands of the common good. It then becomes possible to avoid the criticism of attempting to sustain discussion of efficient means to unstated ends.

This relativizing of efficiency means that the economic determinism which claims that whatever the invisible hand produces must be the best – and only possible – outcome of economic activity is to be rejected. What that implies is a more modest role for business, one which is truly instrumental. That is not a trivial change of perspective – at least not in some circles. If this more instrumental role is to be a reality, the issues I raised concerning the negative impact of the free market on democratic processes would need to be addressed. What Christian ethics could contribute to business ethics at this point is the provision of a theoretical justification for denying validity to the claim that business should be allowed to act unhindered by political and social constraints. We can now move to looking more specifically at business within the common good.

Business and the Common Good

Given that earlier I stressed the transcendent ground of the common good, it may seem a bit odd to suggest that something as prosaic as business has a distinct contribution to make. However, because life in all its particularity is within the creating, sustaining and saving work of God, there is no inherent contradiction. An example of why it is often overlooked is evident in Grisez' list of basic goods. His work omits reference to an important element in the definition given in *Gaudium et Spes*, which not only refers to the complete and efficacious fulfilment of individuals and families; but also the complete and efficacious fulfilment of *organizations*. Each social group, institution, or society, because it has its own goals and structure, has its own common good, the content of which will differ from that of other groups. The common good of a family will have more intimate components than that of a residents' association. It is important, therefore, to identify the common good of the community of persons under discussion and the particular goods proper to it. It would be foolish to try and construct any form of standardized common good, applicable to all organizations. The particular goals of individuals within differing organizations will also vary considerably. The common good is concerned with creating the conditions needed to enable those involved to achieve their particular goals.

Business activity in itself can be a way in which personal goods are realized. This is through the cultivation of such things as professional excellence; virtues such as diligence, reliability, and fidelity; and skills such as teamwork and creativity. These personal goods are most often realized within some institutional structure, whether the size of a transnational corporation or a local garage. The business institution itself (unless a particular institution has become highly dysfunctional) can provide the possibility of the realization of these goods. This is one form of the common good – a localized one, it is true, but real nevertheless. 'The common good of people cooperating in practices ... includes the institutional means which sustain the practices.'[22]

To the extent that corporations are now one of the most dominant institutions of contemporary life, affecting every aspect of people's existence, they can no longer be considered a matter of purely private interest. Corporate leaders are being confronted with two basic questions: 'By what right do you, who manage these huge corporations, exercise your power?' and 'What means do we have to ensure that corporate power will be exercised in accord with some generally accepted notion of the public interest?' There is a broad issue of public accountability here which the concept of the common good can go some way towards addressing. Much of what I have said in the more general sections can be applied here. Business activity is one of the social structures to be assessed against its impact on the basic human goods. There are also questions such as: 'Does its use of political power promote or impede the forms of public dialogue required by subsidiarity?' Within a corporation, do the decision-making processes take sufficient account of these forms of dialogue? Are the management structures and corporate culture based on assumptions of conflict?

Such an analysis will not, in the abstract, provide any universal norm. A case-by-case evaluation will be required if the precise circumstances and

---

22. Riordan, *The Politics of the Common Good*, p. 63.

relationships are to be identified. Such a requirement is itself coherent with the principle of subsidiarity. In each case there will be a different type of 'society' formed by different participants, and therefore a different common good. This procedure will include the company recognizing that in some relations it will be the participant with a particular good who in fact is found to be part of some larger common good. That larger common good may be up to and including all humankind, including future generations, as well as the non-human world.

This links with one of the ways in which business is increasingly being asked to view its relationship with the wider community, that is, through taking fuller account of its various stakeholders. I do not propose to give a detailed discussion of stakeholder theory here. There is already a vast literature on it, some of it drawing on the concept of the common good.[23] I would only say that in contrast with the usual 'interest' foundation offered for stakeholder theory, the concept of the common good removes the somewhat arbitrary nature of the formulation of a company's rights and duties. Rather, what is proposed here is a position of mutuality and interdependence. It is one of mutual obligations which recognizes that business is woven into the very fabric of society and cannot be viewed as a discrete activity. It also, through the concept of 'goods', gives due prominence to right behaviour rather than to merely avoiding wrongdoing. It provides a multi-level approach which situates the company 'downwards' towards its more immediate stakeholders and 'upwards' towards the wider community. The requirements of subsidiarity acknowledge the reality of asymmetrical power which is ignored both in the neoclassical economic paradigm and in utilitarianism, where each individual counts as one and only one. Because the concept of the common good as I have outlined it here is not prescriptive, it is flexible enough to be applied to a very wide range of circumstances and groups, while at the same time, enabling intergroup dialogue to proceed on the basis of a shared vocabulary.

Another reason for not dealing with the theory in detail here is that it is not applicable in a straightforward way to financial institutions. Most of this literature looks at the internal relationships of the firm (shareholders, employees of every grade) and its external relationships (suppliers, customers and the communities in which the firm is located). As I shall be showing in Chapter 7, the terms 'customers' and 'suppliers' have a different meaning, as well as different structural relationships, in the finance sector. Nor do financial institutions always have a localized presence in quite the same way as firms who produce goods and other services. Later chapters will be examining in more detail how the sector's activities impact, for good or ill, on the common good.

23. For an excellent collection of interdisciplinary studies see S.A. Cortright and Michael J. Naughton (eds.), *Rethinking the Purpose of Business*, 2002.

Summary and Conclusions

In sharp contrast to the neoclassical model of the free market, which lacks coherence concerning ends and means, Christian ethics insists upon the relativization of economic activity. At the same time it also acknowledges the importance and moral worth of that activity, and therefore proposes an answer to the question raised in Chapter 1 concerning how business fits into the whole of society. Issues of how moral claims from the *Lebenswelt* might be legitimated, the 'social legitimacy' of business itself and its 'positioning' within society, and a way of understanding business behaviour and motivation which does not exacerbate social fragmentation and personal alienation, can all be addressed within the framework of personalist ethics and the common good understood with the elements of solidarity and subsidiarity.

It is often argued that in a global context there is no alternative to big organizations taking the dominant role in decision making. Citations of the famous quotation which I used to define subsidiarity usually begin where I did myself: 'It is an injustice . . .'. However, in its original context it begins: 'It is indeed true, as history clearly proves, that owing to the change in social conditions, much that was formerly done by small bodies can nowadays be accomplished only by large corporations.' In other words, it was precisely in view of the growth of such large organizations that the concept of subsidiarity was first articulated. The free market exists to meet the needs of a complex modern society and yet, as I suggested in Chapter 1, it is a sphere which all too easily colonizes the *Lebenswelt*, destroying the space for the sort of dialogue I have been arguing for. Instead of reaching a consensus, decisions become based on money and power alone. It is here that subsidiarity, by its insistence on the primacy of the *Lebenswelt*, draws its primary importance and strength. By defending such a primacy, what is being safeguarded is the sphere where the moral and spiritual life of human beings are lived. It reminds us of what is essential in life and seeks to ensure that social institutions and systems serve that, rather than the other way round. It is, in effect, a stance which asserts the importance of relativizing the economy.

By relativizing economic activity, a personalist understanding of economic activity acknowledges that its intermediate end is providing for human material need and satisfying human wants. However, it also includes the recognition that the final end reflects the fact that while humans are material *beings*, they are not reducible to material *objects*. They are, each and every one, fundamentally precious human persons, with a worth far beyond their value as economic instrumentalities. This understanding clearly parts company with a broad swathe of business ethics. An example is Barry's definition of the purpose and end of business. 'Since commerce is an activity that responds to people's desires, it seems the ideal candidate for favourable evaluation by a moral doctrine [utilitarianism] that exclusively understands good and bad in terms of want-satisfaction.'[24] I have argued that Christian ethics sees commerce as an activity which responds to people's desires *plus* a great deal more. Utilitarian business ethics, by concentrating more on the objective dimension of work, in fact has a much less rich, less extensive view of business activity.

I have also pointed to the neglect of the cultural aspect of the human person. Every people with a culture of its own has an idea of the kind of society it calls 'good'. Ignoring this cultural vision will not guarantee economic success. Consulting a people's cultural vision of a good society will mean their active participation, both in the decision-making and implementation phases of work. Failure to do so will result in the continuing destruction of cultures and values. It is to deny to other cultures the very thing which the free market claims to be so good at – the freedom to choose, in this case, the freedom to choose how to incorporate change and on what terms. Involving people in defining goals and in participative action towards their attainment is to treat them as people of dignity. There is a need, however, within Christian circles to extend further our understanding of cultural factors. This is required to provide a counterweight to a one-sided stress on structural change which has given little attention to cultural values and attitudes which underpin social structures and govern their working.

Much of the commentary on social policy today reflects the tension between the philosophy of self-interest and the philosophy of the common good. Much business ethics, in line with modern ethical theory, treats our social interaction in terms of the pursuit of self-interest. Here and in Chapter 3 I have argued that this way of thinking leads us to act in ways which undermine social cohesion. Yet our experience of social life reveals possibilities for acting within a wider horizon which includes both self- and other-interest. There is, therefore, a need for a language and an explanatory model which is adequate for this experience. Despite its present ambiguities and lacunae, the concept of the common good does articulate something of that experience more adequately than other approaches.

Drawing all these points, and those made in earlier chapters, together clarifies the purpose of business. This can be characterized as an instrumental activity with a threefold requirement. First, rightly ordered, business provides the material goods and services without which society cannot flourish. This is consistent with both the biblical affirmation of the goodness of the material world and of our mandate to manage its resources for human well-being. Secondly, through the production of

24. Norman Barry, *Business Ethics*, 1998, pp. 18–19.

these goods and services, the company increases economic value; that is to say, it creates wealth for all those participating in the company. If it does not do so, it cannot be justified in economic terms. Even if the nature of its business is irreproachable, a company which does not generate sufficient income to give satisfactory remuneration for the work done and the capital used cannot be justified. The marginal efficiency of capital needs to be respected.

The third requirement is for business to contribute to the common good. This common good is understood as the all-round realization of the human person as envisaged by personalist ethics, and the social conditions which enable that realization. The contribution that business can make needs to be carefully articulated, with a clear understanding that it is not boundless. It is also necessary to respect the nature of a for-profit organization in a competitive market. Business organizations cannot be expected to solve all social problems – expecting them to do so is to undermine the relativization of the economy for which I have been arguing. However, notwithstanding this caveat, there will be companies or practices which, despite creating wealth, cannot be morally justified because the type of activity in which they are involved causes material or spiritual harm to the people who form society.

The common good has, potentially, a major contribution to make to a globalized market. The present globalization and regionalization of the market economy has led to economic activity becoming increasingly borderless. Economic power is moving from the state to the market. There is, therefore, an increasingly urgent need for a new articulation of the common good which recognizes the changed political reality and sets the concept within a global perspective. This global common good would not exclude the national, just as the common good in general does not deny the individual. It must complement the national. Among nations, wide economic regions and world economic organizations, the principle of solidarity will have to prevail if the good sought is to be truly the common good.

Both voices in the conversation have now been introduced. The context which both shapes and is shaped by the finance sector has been presented, with an analysis of factors which in many cases will be heightened by the sector, its assumptions and its operations. It is time to look at finance specifically.

Chapter 6

A PHILOSOPHY OF MONEY

It is a commonplace to suggest that economic factors are pivotal in driving globalization forward. A globalized economy is far more advanced than a globalized politics. However, if we are to understand what is happening, we need to refine that observation. I will be doing this in two stages. Finance is central to the working of the free market because finance itself drives the economic factors of globalization. But finance is itself driven. The first stage, therefore, is to examine the most pervasive and influential underlying phenomenon which itself drives finance; that is to say, money. The second stage, which will be the next chapter, is to show the centrality of finance to the workings of the free market.

I am going to examine money through a neglected route, that of a philosophy of money.[1] I will show how the very nature of money as *a symbolic reality* needs to be understood if ethics in the finance sector is going to have a strong foundation. A philosophical understanding of money was once the framework for financial ethics within the Christian tradition, as can be seen by the mediaeval teaching on usury. That teaching developed from what was then understood about money, and it was that understanding which underpinned all the misgivings about the taking of interest. Money was seen then as inflexible and dissociated from the fluctuations of life. It appeared to be, and actually was, more solid and substantial,[2] more starkly contrasted with other things, than in modern times. Today it appears and operates in a much more dynamic, variable and pliable way.

The teaching was based on what was thought to be the Aristotelian notion that it was unnatural for money to engender money.[3] That money

1. Some elements of this chapter appeared in 'Money, Morality and Finance in a Global Economy', *New Blackfriars* 86 (March 2005), pp. 216–27.

2. In the mediaeval period money was not only made of metal. One of its forms was leather. There was also the wooden *sh'tar*, or tally stick.

3. Sen argues persuasively that the main focus of Aristotle's attack on usury has been thoroughly misunderstood. This misunderstanding arose by taking a particular passage from the *Politics* and ignoring the more substantive argument in it and proximate passages. The serious claim made was that it is unnatural to get a reward for *lending* money, for money is not in itself a creative activity, even though creative things can be done with resources bought

was not regarded as a productive power can be seen in such features as the condemnation of interest as theft, because the capital repaid equals the borrowed capital; the argument that money does not wear out by use and that it was not profitable, as were the objects of a lease, to the creditor; and finally, the doctrine of Aquinas that in the case of money, whose sole end is to be spent, use and spending were identical, and that therefore the use of money, unlike the use of a house, could not be sold separately. It is important to note that money at this period was essentially seen as a *substance*. As the understanding of the nature of money, and the relationship between money and time changed, the teaching was first adapted and then finally dropped.[4] Although reflection on economic matters continued, it did so without developing a new understanding of money to replace the one left behind.

This is important because in money finance possesses a distinguishing characteristic which in part explains the fascination and power which it exercises. The most fundamental distinction between the finance sector and business in general arises from what the finance sector trades in, that is to say, money. Failure to acknowledge this, and to explore its consequences, lies behind the unsatisfactory nature of much of the work that has been done in financial ethics.

Despite a widespread obsession with money, it is one of the most nebulous concepts in economic activity. Most of what counts for money has no physical existence – it is merely electronic traces in computer memories. That last sentence contains one of the basic problems: not the statement about its non-physicality, but the phrase 'what counts for money'. Because 'what counts' is in a constant state of flux.

At the individual level we think we know what money is. Yet money, like time for St Augustine, tends to become more elusive the closer it is examined. There is a vigorous and, so far, inconclusive debate about how it is to be measured, rendered almost insoluble by the impossibility of defining what we want to measure. Hence the proliferation of definitions: M0, M3, M4 and so on. Yet these definitions are forever mutating – a problem which has come to be known as 'Goodhart's law'. As soon as a particular instrument or asset is publicly defined as money in order to be controlled, that asset ceases to be used as money because substitutes will

---

with money. It is clear that Aristotle is also discussing the equally substantive issue that in some types of financial or business activity, there may be little social gain – in fact considerable loss – even though the activity yields large private profits. Instead the simpler theme that 'usury is unnatural breeding of money from money' was taken and repeated constantly. Amartya K. Sen, *Money and Value: On the Ethics and Economics of Finance*, 1991, pp. 32–38.

4. For a detailed analysis see: John T. Noonan, *The Scholastic Analysis of Usury*, 1957.

be produced for purposes of evasion.[5] This leads to difficulties in monetary policy and regulation. 'Failure to define money satisfactorily renders its measure and control mostly a matter of educated guesswork and psychological gerrymandering, a craft rather than a science.'[6]

Despite that, money is taken for granted by economics in the sense that it is abstracted from its social and cultural context, and treated in isolation from its deep symbolic functions. It is not possible, therefore, for economics to debate many of the ethical issues attached to money, simply because there is no suitable framework for such a discussion. Neither does the standard approach of business ethics towards the finance sector help, as it treats money, by ignoring it, as if it were simply a commodity like any other commodity. It is not. Nor is it even a commodity with significantly different characteristics to other commodities produced and consumed. The obscuring of its essential differences from other commodities has prevented a clear analysis of the very nature of the ethical implications of money, particularly for the finance sector operating, as it does, within a mature money economy.

Therefore an analysis of the finance sector must include an analysis of money itself, for that is what determines the nature of the sector, its activities, and the relationships within it and the rest of the economy. Most contemporary discussion of money and monetary problems has been highly mechanical, focusing on the technical details. Both classical and neoclassical economics suggest that money is simply a neutral, transparent token which mediates the exchange of goods and services. It is, however, much more than this. We need to focus on the *social relationships* that monetary transaction involves, not the objects which mediate those relationships. Because of its cultural and symbolic associations, money has also had a profound influence on the features of the free market which I have already discussed: freedom, individualism, power and the very nature of the market.

Less Helpful Approaches

A new understanding of money which is able to reflect on the social and cultural features which it exhibits has not happened from within the Catholic tradition, despite the example of its own history. In this, as in so many other ways, *The Modern Development of Financial Activities in the Light of the Ethical Demands of Christianity*, the only document in recent

5. Charles A. E. Goodhart, *Money, Information and Uncertainty*, 2nd edn, 1989, p. 100, n. 1.
6. Nigel Dodd, *The Sociology of Money: Economics, Reason and Contemporary Society*, 1994, p. xii.

years from the Vatican which deals exclusively with the finance sector, is deeply disappointing.[7] The document makes only the most cursory reference to money *per se*, and that in its Preface.[8] Its analysis of the reason for the condemnation of interest on loans must surely be one of the simplest – and most terse – on record. The writers simply assert that it is explained by 'the context of the early Middle Ages (abuse by the usurers, absence of precaution savings)'.[9] It is not only Catholic social teaching which has neglected to reflect on the nature of money within a mature money economy. So has business ethics in general, even in works devoted exclusively to financial ethics.[10] Such a framework is needed in order to evolve an ethical forum which satisfies both practitioners and the wider community because it is able to focus on the institutional dimension of the sector. I cannot hope to fill such a large gap. Instead by reflecting on some aspects of money I hope to begin the endeavour and shed some light on a number of issues.

There has, of course, been much reflection both on the economy in general and on money from a Christian perspective. Most of it, however, is directed to the individual or the Churches themselves, or takes what De George caricatures as the 'agapaistic' approach which often gives the impression that the writer thinks the problems of international poverty will dissolve before love and charity.[11] An example of the too individualistic theological approach to money is one which is more concerned with consumerism than with confronting systemic problems. Equally typical and unhelpful in this regard is taking biblical passages and using them as little more than proof texts. Although some of the conclusions arrived at may, in themselves, be worth considering, the methodology will be unconvincing to anyone who is not already committed. As an approach it does not provide an avenue for dialogue with others. Unfortunately many works fall into these two broad models. An honourable exception is Craig Gay's *Cash Values: The Value of Money, The Nature of Worth*,[12] which, although it does not examine the systemic implications, does begin to look at how money shapes our understanding of the world and of values.

7. Antoine De Salins and François Villeroy de Galhau, *The Modern Development of Financial Activities in the Light of the Ethical Demands of Christianity*, 1994.

8. De Salins and de Galhau, p. 7.

9. De Salins and de Galhau, p. 15, n. 1.

10. For example, Andrew McCosh, *Financial Ethics*, 1999; John Dobson, *Finance Ethics: The Rationality of Virtue*, 1997; Uric Dufrene (ed.), *Finance and the Ethics Debate*, 1996; Andreas R. Prindl and Bimal Prodhan (eds.), *The ACT Guide to Ethical Conflicts in Finance*, 1994; Antonio Argandoña (ed.), *The Ethical Dimension of Financial Institutions and Markets*, 1995 and John R. Boatright, *Ethics in Finance*, 1999.

11. Richard T. De George, 'Theological Ethics and Business Ethics', *Journal of Business Ethics* 5 (1986), pp. 421–32.

12. Craig M. Gay, *Cash Values: The Value of Money, The Nature of Worth*, 2003.

The more substantial work of Ellul,[13] who perhaps has had more influence on continental-European debate than on Anglo-Saxon, contains many valuable insights but is still highly problematic. It illustrates a widespread problem with much Christian reflection on the economy, in that his approach is one of 'total critique' – that is, a rejection of the entire monetary system and its functioning within the economy. Important ideas are presented without being adequately developed. So, he rightly points to the fact that money has become abstract in that it is no longer valuable in itself. What is possessed is purchasing power.[14] But he does not tell us how this has come about or explore its consequences in any comprehensive way. Similarly he points to money's impersonality because its use, rather than signifying personal control, seems instead to be a mere echo of distant and complex interactions.[15] Again he does not tell us how this arose, and so leaves it as an unsubstantiated claim. He then proceeds to the next claim that as society accepts the abstraction and impersonality of money, 'there is only one question left to ask: How will this money be distributed?'[16] Anyone who has read much Christian discussion about the economy will know that distribution is usually the major and sometimes the only focus. But although his conclusions might be valid, we are unable to test them. They are presented in a 'take-it-or-leave-it' manner which precludes dialogue.

On the basis of his conclusions, he argues that 'if money is an economic reality tightly linked to the social complex ... the individual act can hardly be taken seriously'.[17] This leads to an attitude whereby moral and individual problems are subordinated to the collective problem, to the total economic system. He identifies the displacement of all responsibility for the problem of money (which he sees as greed, envy, theft, covetousness, injustice) onto what is presumed to be the objective interplay of economic operations.[18] This, together with the abstraction of money, leads to the tendency for ethics to 'disappear', apart from questions of distribution, due to the assumption that, whatever the problem might be, I, the individual, can do nothing until the system is changed. 'All I have to do is to campaign for socialism or conservatism, and as soon as society's problems are solved, I shall be just and virtuous – effortlessly. My money problem will take care of itself.'[19]

For Ellul, to seek systemic change is hypocrisy and cowardice. It is to evade my individual responsibility for my attitudes towards money and its

13. Synthesized most clearly in Jacques Ellul, *Money and Power*, 1986.
14. Ellul, p. 10.
15. Ellul, p. 10.
16. Ellul, p. 11.
17. Ellul, p. 11.
18. Ellul, pp. 15–27.
19. Ellul, p. 15.

power over me. I evade responsibility, but am left passionately engaged with money. However, his desire to counter this displacement of responsibility leads to an over-vigorous denial of the value of systemic action in favour of personally responsible action. This results in the divorce of theology from any dialogue with the system. Those who work within the system are denied any ethical reflection on vital aspects of their lives and are instead left with little more than a pious personalistic faith. Ellul attempts a total critique of the system which aims to go deeper than any partial critique. This renders his account hard to recognize as a basis for ethics. What, constructively, and in our daily lives, are we meant to do with it? A similar problem occurs with the work of Milbank[20] and Long.[21] If ethics is to be lived, it must relate directly and yet critically to our ordinary discourse.

Simmel's Philosophy of Money[22]

In economics, money is commonly identified as having three standard properties: a medium of exchange, a store of value and a unit of account. Money, however, is a much more central institutional phenomenon, situated within human action in general. By locating money within a basic framework of human action (or 'purposive action'), it is possible to give a deeper and more wide-ranging account than the economic one, and to identify further properties of money. It also enables a focus on the consequences which the objectification of modern culture has on the inner life of individuals. This enables us to understand more fully what shapes the attitudes, perceptions and dispositions which inform how individuals actually handle money. The following analysis draws extensively from Georg Simmel's masterly exploration of the nature of money. I shall first give a descriptive synthesis and then draw out some of the implications.

The Instrumentality of Money

At the base of these further properties is the instrumentality of money. Human action is characterized primarily by its goal-oriented rather than its impulse-propelled nature. Action to realize any end or goal requires effort and the use of means if that goal is to be realized. This gives rise to the formation of purposes and, more broadly, to purposefulness. Purposive action engages us in a teleological series of actions, where the

20. John Milbank, *Theology and Social Theory: Beyond Secular Reason*, 1990.
21. D. Stephen Long, *Divine Economy: Theology and the Market*, 2000.
22. Georg Simmel, *The Philosophy of Money*, 1978.

attainment of the end is only achieved by the attainment of intermediary ends. This requires the use of means. These teleological series are chains of means which are co-ordinated to produce a certain goal.

Central to this purposive action is the concept of a tool. A tool can be seen as a mere object which is mechanically efficient, but it is also an object that we not merely operate *upon* but operate *with*. It is not itself an end. Social institutions, for example, can be tools which we use to achieve ends for which our personal abilities would never be sufficient. Legal forms of contract, testament, adoption, etc., are collectively established tools which multiply an individual's powers, extend their effectiveness and secure their ends. Structures which embody the principle of tools are organized in such a way as to release the flow of certain goods. It is at this point that money finds its place in the interweaving of purposes.

Money is the purest form of the tool, one which has no inherent relation to the specific purpose which it helps to attain. It is a pure instrument, an absolute means, which has no value except in its use. On the one hand it has no intrinsic value that is determined univocally by any other specific series of valued object. On the other, it has no purpose of its own and functions impartially as an intermediary in the series of purposes. What money in its totality mediates is not the possession of an object, but the exchange of objects. It is the scope of this exchangeability with other objects which is money's most prominent feature, and enables goods to be valued relative to one another. It also empowers the individual by virtue of its purchasing power and the freedom of choice which it provides.

Particularly in a mature money economy which has developed a system of banknotes and bills of exchange, the instrumental quality of money is heightened by its 'transportability' and its 'concealability'. These instrumental aspects of money can uniquely assist those who are strangers to a given society or who occupy a marginal position in it, to accumulate economic power. This is because with money the relational nature of the transaction has changed from one which required close and continuing links within a specific community to one of impersonality, independence and differentiation.

The move from 'substance' to 'function' is completed with the identification of two further properties of money. The first is its dynamic character which expresses itself in money's tendency to circulate relentlessly, to focus its power on an ever-changing variety of uses. The meaning of money is that it will be given away for an object or to achieve a state of affairs (for example, security in some form). If it stands still it is no longer money according to its specific value and significance. The second property is the functional character of money. Properly understood, money, whatever it represents, does not so much *have* a function, but *is* a function. Of all possible objects of ownership it is only money that merges completely with the function we assign to it.

Based on this attribution of instrumentality and purposes, we can examine the institutional environment which money requires if it is to exist and function effectively.

The Fiduciary Character of Money

Money has a fiduciary dimension lacking in neoclassical economic analysis. It requires an atmosphere of generalized trust which goes beyond the trust generated by the mutual familiarity of the members of a narrow community. It is a 'claim upon society' that money can serve us as a pure instrument of exchange. To function properly, money requires that everyone be willing to accept it from everybody, that is, it entails a claim to the performance of others. This is because, in contrast to barter, the pivotal point in the interaction is not in the direct line of contact between the parties to the transaction. Instead, it moves to the relationship each of them has with the economic community which accepts the money, and which demonstrates this fact by having money minted by its highest representative.

Yet money is merely a symbolic reality. Willingness to accept it presumes an attitude of trust, a shared awareness of money's virtues and effects, together with a disposition to act so as to confirm and make use of them. Since each bit of money at bottom constitutes a promise, money can only be routinely accepted if the risk of disappointment is taken to be minimal. Credit only makes this dependency on trust more obvious. This is not just the trust that this particular person will pay back whatever it is I have lent – after all, that sort of credit does not require money. What credit requires is an additional element of willing, a 'supra-theoretical' belief which Simmel compares to faith in God. It is worth quoting this more fully.

> To 'believe in someone', without adding or even conceiving what it is that one believes about him, is to employ a very subtle and profound idiom. It expresses the feeling that there exists between our idea of a being and the being itself a definite connection and unity, a certain consistency in our conception of it, an assurance and lack of resistance in the surrender of the Ego to this conception of it, which may rest upon particular reasons, but is not explained by them. Economic credit does contain an element of this supra-theoretical belief, and so does the confidence that the community will assure the validity of the tokens for which we have exchanged the products of our labour in an exchange against material goods.[23]

23. Simmel, p. 179.

There are two institutional elements of the diffuse mental and moral atmosphere required for a functioning money economy. The first is the political arrangement of a given society. This is external to the economic sphere and the phenomenon of money itself. In order for there to be operational assumptions concerning the conduct of third parties so that money can be a public reality, public institutions – especially the state – must both back it and sanction it. The state does this by monopolizing the creation of ordinary money (some exceptions to its monopoly will be referred to later) and by exercising its jurisdictional powers. The value of money rests upon its security, and it was only as central political power came progressively to be its guarantor that the immediate significance of metal could be replaced. Only a stable and closely organized society will be able to provide sufficient safeguards to enable such an easily destroyed material as paper to become the representative of the highest money value. Earlier forms of money, especially those made of scarce and esteemed substances, ensured that there was an intrinsic value to a piece of money. Paper demonstrates the loss of that necessity in a particularly clear way. Without the backing of, for example, a gold standard, it is no longer even a promise to pay. It is merely a promise on its future re-exchangeability.

The second condition to be satisfied if money is to preserve its moral standing and to function correctly is internal to the monetary realm itself. Money must be stable, must preserve its value over time. As we know, trust in money can break down during, for example, hyperinflation. This is a serious deficiency, for such breakdowns are integral to the operation of money, highly consequential features of the cultural conditions which make the existence and circulation of money possible.[24] As Keynes was only too aware, the greatest evil of a change in the value of money came from its social consequences because its incidence is unequal and because:

> When the value of money changes, it does *not* change equally for all persons or for all purposes ... a change in prices and rewards, as measured in money, generally affects different classes unequally, transfers wealth from one to another, bestows affluence here and embarrassment there, and redistributes Fortune's favours, so as to frustrate design and disappoint expectation.[25]

---

24. Dodd, *Sociology of Money*.
25. John M. Keynes, 'The Consequences to Society of Changes in the Value of Money', (1922) reprinted in *Collected Writings of John Maynard Keynes* Vol. IV: *A Tract on Monetary Reform*, 1971, pp. 1–36 (1), original emphasis.

Teleological Series and Quantitive Assessments

Tools extend our intention and decision far beyond the present moment. Money, as a supremely flexible tool, has an enormous number of unpredictable uses. It becomes the ultimate way to construct and co-ordinate series of means to given ends in purposive action. Under modern conditions money allows the construction of longer and longer means–ends chains, in which more and more of the apparent goals have no ultimate significance but matter purely as means, as way stations to further goals. This leads to fewer and fewer points of satisfaction for purposive action. Satisfaction – in any ultimate sense – is endlessly deferred as money enables these teleological chains to extend themselves on and on.

Not only that. Because the extension of the length of teleological means–ends chains implies a greater distance between the person and the object of his endeavour, it increases the probability that ends become obscured and that means become ends, or for ends to be confused with means. This is because money becomes conceived as *purpose* and, in consequence, things that are really ends in themselves are thereby degraded to mere means. But since money itself is an omnipresent means, the various elements of our existence are caught up in an all embracing teleological nexus in which no element is the first or the last. We lose our ability to distinguish between means and ends.

But the way that money constructs these longer means–ends sequences has advantages. These sequences can be more complex, and therefore longer. It can do this because it side-steps potential disputes about intended ends or goals. A worker does not have to agree particularly with the ultimate ends of the productive process she is engaged in because she is paid in money. This allows her to pursue independently her own ends. This is not as unproblematic as it might sound. Through money, exchange relations become increasingly complicated and mediated, with the result that the economy necessarily establishes more and more relationships and obligations *that are not directly reciprocal*. The structure of our relationships obliges distance within them, thereby eroding the 'humanness' of our interactions.

A primary aspect of the mental and moral temper of modernity is the intellectualization of existence, which is associated with money. Within the context of action, evaluations, feelings and emotions tend to focus on ends. However, means primarily require a cool, cognitive orientation. This latter orientation becomes prevalent in modern society because of the central significance of that tool *par excellence*, money itself. This, together with the decreased ability to distinguish between means and ends, leads to a further feature resulting from the dominance of money: the premium placed on the quantitive orientation to reality. This replaces the subjective appreciation of objects, goods and services with an objective evaluation of them in terms of their monetary value, and in the process it often debases them. To quote Oscar Wilde's famous epigram, people know 'the price of everything and the value of nothing'. The more things become available for money, the more money becomes the central and absolute value; then the more objects are valued only to the extent that they cost money. The quantity of value with which we perceive them appears only as a function of their monetary price. The significance of money replaces the significance of things.

In this way money quantifies the qualitative; it expresses the modern prevalence of the interest in 'how much' over the interest in 'what and how'. That orientation towards the quantitive brings about a disposition to calculate, together with an emphasis on precision. It imbues a mathematical character to the elements of life, a way of determining parity and disparity, a certain unambiguousness in understandings and arrangements. This feeds back into the quantitive orientation, in that we seek to measure, and then only value what we can measure. Aspects of our lives which are ambiguous, or not susceptible to measurement in any real sense, are then experienced by many as being of less worth. Without a price tag on something, how do I know that others value what I value? This may well be a contributory factor in compensation claims where the claimant often asserts that 'it's not about money; it's about recognition of what I have suffered'. What this seems to suggest is that only money confers that recognition.

Freedom

It is now possible to establish a number of ways in which money shapes the modern understanding of freedom. By defining money as pure instrument, it is possible to see more clearly the types of freedom of choice which its possession confers. Money obviously empowers its holder by virtue of its purchasing power. It also gives freedom of choice. It adjusts with equal ease to every form and every purpose that the will wishes to imprint it with. Yet it has not led to greater human creativity. Rather, it has diminished it, limited it. We can contrast freedom *from* something with the freedom *to do* something. What money gives in a mature money economy is something closer to the first possibility, that is, freedom *from*. It is a freedom empty of any content, having only the negative connotation of the removal of constraint. It opens up freedom of *choice*, but does not enhance our freedom *in choosing*. In itself freedom is an empty form which becomes effective, alive and valuable only through the way it serves the development of other life contents. Money opens more options, but it does not enhance our essential ability to choose between them.

As I argued earlier, what it does through its emphasis on quantitive assessment and acquisition is to usurp the ways in which we confer value. The significance of money replaces the significance of things and of relationships. This implies that money will enhance real freedom only when it is grounded in essential freedom which is able to evaluate the multiple goods of human life. The other option is that those other human goods, those other life contents, will be stunted whenever money is treated as an end in itself. This is what has happened in modern society. 'Money, as the ultimate economic instrument, has turned into the ultimate economic goal. It has imploded in on itself as mammon.'[26]

An example which brings together the earlier point about non-reciprocal relationships and obligations and this latter aspect of freedom, illustrating the move from money as an instrument to money as a goal, is the one I started with in Chapter 1. It is the contrast between two City Republics in sixteenth-century Italy: Venice, where private citizens were fairly wealthy but the state was extremely wealthy, and Genoa, whose citizens had enormous private wealth in an impoverished state. I suggested that the reason for this was that Venetians traded in goods and Genoese in money. I can now begin to give reasons for that claim.

Trading in goods is complicated, especially over long distances. You have to look for co-operation and employees within adjacent groups since this sort of trade, of its nature, imposes bonds. Elaborate physical and relational infrastructures are required which are predicated on continuity and the quality of relationships. These cannot be built and sustained on a purely individual basis. A heavy commitment is required from others around oneself, with the need for at least some communal provision. With money, however, the relational nature of the transaction has changed from one which required close and continuing links within a specific community to one of impersonality, independence and differentiation. Its owners are able to detach themselves from groups which are perceived as heavily restricting their freedom. It enables the independence of the individual from the group. It emphasizes individualization and autonomy; the ability for individuals to refer primarily to their own beliefs, values and preferences in conducting their own existence and, indeed, to fashion those ideas for themselves.

The individual will then develop the tendency and feeling of independent importance and distance in relation to the social whole. Money itself constitutes the best embodiment of the very notion of private property and its possession is intrinsically connected with the notion of choice, of elective conduct. Possession of money loosens the individual from the unifying bonds of other economic and social relations. She will tend to relate to the social whole as one power confronting another, since she is free to take her money and set up business relations and co-operation

26. Dodd, *The Sociology of Money*, p. 49.

wherever she likes. She may then pragmatically constitute or join other groups of a different nature, membership of which commits and controls her energies to a much smaller extent. The prime example of this came with the invention of the joint-stock company. This was one of the most effective cultural formations in that it was now possible for individuals to participate in associations which have an objective purpose they want to promote and enjoy, without that connection implying any commitment on their part. Money makes it possible for people to join a group without having to give up any personal freedom. With the joint-stock company the stockholders were united solely in their interest in the dividends to such an extent that often they did not even care what the company produced. Nevertheless, there was the assumption that, at least at one remove, *something* was being produced. These investments created employment, goods and services. Now, however, that is increasingly neither the case nor even the intention. The growth of capital in itself has become the priority.

Some Initial Implications

The evil of the idolatry of money has been a constant theme in Christian teaching. An unsubstantiated identification of attitudes towards money as idolatry can easily be dismissed as merely quaint, a throwback to archaic imagery that no longer speaks to us. Simply repeating the call to give God the first place in one's life is of little use if the hearer does not believe in God. What this analysis provides is an explanation of how a mature money economy not only facilitates but perhaps even *requires* that ido-latrous attitude. Money can lure us into believing that the only values which exist are those which we ourselves attribute. If we yield to this notion this replaces the religious imperative to look beyond our own designations of 'value' for *real* value. This can, in the end, leave us insensible to the goodness and graciousness of God.[27] Without an explanation of how money does this, it is difficult to decide clearly what appropriate countervailing actions or attitudes are needed.

For example, this explanation clarifies the reasoning behind the requirement that economic activity be relativized by demonstrating the mechanism whereby money can become the central and absolute value which prevents the appropriate autonomy of other spheres. Money, by usurping other forms of value and other criteria for evaluation, leaves no 'space' for those values and criteria. The money value which we assign to things may so obscure their real or intrinsic value that we can end up doubting that there is such a thing as intrinsic value at all. This would suggest that some, at least, of the criticisms of specific forms of economic

27. Gay, *Cash Values*, p. 18.

activity (for example, capitalism versus command economy) may have been aiming at the wrong target. I am not suggesting that different economic systems do not display different shortcomings which need to be criticized. Rather I am suggesting that at times Christian reflection has been too concerned with symptoms rather than with causes. For example, *Centesimus Annus* says 'insofar as [capitalism] denies an autonomous existence and value to morality, law, culture and religion ... it totally reduces man to the sphere of economics and the satisfaction of material needs'.[28] This analysis would suggest that it is not merely capitalism which does this, but rather how money functions within a mature money economy. Capitalism may be the economic system which displays this feature most clearly, but it does so because it is the system in which these features of money have developed most fully.

The reductionist anthropology towards which this quotation points is another link between Christian reflection and an analysis of money, in that both address the depersonalization and the attenuation of the reciprocity of human relationships. The analysis of how money unites people while excluding everything personal and specific helps us to focus on some of the mechanisms which feed this aspect of contemporary society. It helps to explain the paradoxical fact that people express an ever greater awareness of the need for intimacy, for relationships which sustain and nurture, for their dignity to be respected, whilst simultaneously constructing ways of working and trading which undermine those desires.

Modern and postmodern life is distinguished above all by its disconnected character. The discussion on how money structurally obligates distance in relationships is significant for the Christian emphasis on the inter-connectedness of the human person. An analysis of what a mature money economy does to the reciprocity inherent in the exchange relationship gives more analytic rigour to what is usually a descriptive enunciation of the undermining of our awareness of this inter-connectedness. This undermining of our awareness explains in part why there has been an increasing Christian emphasis on the virtue of solidarity. That insistence acknowledges the need for an ever heavier counter-weight to the increasing fragmentation and distancing of relations and depersonalization which money obligates. Once more, a clearer articulation of the mechanism enables the possibility of identifying appropriate countervailing action.

The ways in which the freedom which money confers can become disconnected from real freedom has many resonances with Christian thought. One line of enquiry would be to juxtapose the implications of this analysis and a Christian approach to consumerism. Another would be to amplify the discussion of what constitutes essential freedom. There are

28. John Paul II, *Centesimus Annus*, n. 19.

also extensive implications for a better understanding of money and the understanding of power/empowerment. There is a tendency to treat money in a polemical way which does not account fully enough for the ambiguity present in power/empowerment. This flows from an unnuanced treatment of how money is actually perceived and used, of how it interacts with individualism and social relationships, and of the institutional environment and informational networks money requires. Regretfully, these lines of enquiry are beyond the scope of this present work.

Summary and Conclusions

The preoccupation of monetary theorists with the material or functional characteristics of specific monetary forms or instruments has tended to be misleading. This is because, in both classical and Marxist analysis, money has tended to be characterized as a commodity which is produced and sold like any other. However, by definition, money's most characteristic features are not those which it shares with other commodities, but those it does not. It is not consumed but either re-exchanged or hoarded. Other commodities may fluctuate in their relationship with each other, but money is a stable pole contrasting with the constant movements and fluctuations of the objects it represents in exchange. It therefore provides a constant standard by which they can be valued, an abstract intermediary through which they can be exchanged.

This mediation of exchange is, however, only possible on the basis of other social factors such as trust embodied in guarantors, the largest of which is the central political power. State validation of money is typically seen as an economic function. But it is much more than that, as the discussion of trust makes clear. The circulation of paper money proves that transactors accept and hold money. This can be seen to be not because of its intrinsic value as a commodity, but because of guarantees regarding its future re-exchangeability. Trust in money's abstract properties is, by extension, trust in the agencies responsible for monetary administration. The validating role taken by the community is not just a technical, legal question, but is also symbolically important. It is here that one can begin to see the basis of the legitimacy of moral claims by the *Lebenswelt*. Although functionally differentiated, the economy is radically dependent upon the wider society. Perhaps the most concentrated manifestation of confidence in the socio-political organization and order is the feeling of personal security that the possession of money gives.

However, a challenge to this stage of affairs is becoming apparent. In the opening section of this chapter I referred to the way in which forms of money mutate. Consider now the phenomenon of 'air miles'. These have no tangible existence, yet they are able to buy material goods and services. A similar phenomenon is 'loyalty points' give by some stores and super-markets which, again, can be exchanged for products provided by the card issuer. Although they are not tied to a sovereign currency and are untaxed (perhaps untaxable), these are forms of money – but now under the control of commercial organizations. There is a sense in which these companies are in line with Hayek's proposal that money be denationa-lized.[29] This phenomenon is likely to increase, posing the problem of how the fiduciary function is to be fulfilled. Furthermore, it initiates a new form of economic power struggle, based around the question of who will have control of the creation and distribution of money.

Yet although money's guarantors are, at least for now, socially and politically located, its *function* is not, since it is 'the purest reification of means, a concrete instrument which is absolutely identical with its abstract concept; it is a pure instrument'.[30] The reification of means and exchange relationships is highlighted in the view of the world of circula-tion and exchange of commodities, money and people as one of dynamic flux. With it comes the presupposition of calculability which reduces personal qualities to quantities. Indeed, the reification of exchange rela-tions as manifested in mature money-exchange relations is a presupposi-tion for calculation itself. The consequences of a shift from person–person or person–thing relations to thing–thing relations are immense.

Exchange is not merely an economic phenomenon. It is also a social and cultural phenomenon, with interaction or reciprocal effect at its centre. Society can then be seen as 'a constellation of interactions, as dynamic, individual and supra-individual, as a system of internal relations'.[31] This contradicts the subjectivist presuppositions of a marginal utility theory of consumption. As it is based on the maximization of individual utilities, it requires for its plausibility a host of assumptions concerning rational-choice models of human behaviour. I argued in Chapter 3 that these models are anthropologically inadequate, and lack both predictive and explanatory power.

Whenever and wherever money is used, it is not defined by its properties as a material object, but by symbolic properties. As money in con-temporary society becomes even less a material substance and increasingly symbolic, for example, the encoding of monetary holdings into electronic traces on a computer's memory, its intrinsic properties – mobility, transportability, potentiality, dynamism – become more obvious. These qualities are linked to the ideal of unconstrained freedom and empower-ment, unlimited possibilities for its use, being co-extensive with the idea of

29. Hayek, *Denationalisation of Money*.
30. Simmel, *The Philosophy of Money*, p. 211.
31. David Frisby, *Simmel and Since: Essays on Georg Simmel's Social Theory*, 1992, p. 97.

economic empowerment in itself. It is an ideal, something which is never reached in practice. Nevertheless, that ideal is at the centre of the concept of money as a symbolic medium. Hence the desire for money, the decision to work for it, save it, hoard it, accept it for payment even for things which, perhaps, should not be sold. In this aspect, Ellul is correct when he speaks of our passionate engagement with money.[32]

It is true that other economic instruments are associated with these activities, but such association is, at best, partial. Only money is synonymous with them. It is this symbolic feature which distinguishes money, makes it what it is, enables assumptions about its re-use in the future to be made. But such a conceptualization of money comes at a cost: to the economy itself, to society in general and to the individual, as money becomes a more and more exclusive and commanding social power. The universalization of money, caused by the expansion of the money sphere, means that money is used in transacting a growing number and variety of economic relations. Thus an increasingly large variety of social relations become transacted through the medium of money: 'use values' disappear and are replaced by 'exchange values'. It is this feature, with the accompanying development of the markets for land and labour, which was so central to the historical transformation of the market[33] discussed in Chapter 2.

In many ways Simmel anticipated some aspects of postmodernity. As the specific contents of life have been turned into expressions of money, so it has become possible to rearrange them endlessly. Life itself becomes experienced as a random collection of commodified values and meanings which we can arrange and rearrange as the fancy takes us. Inevitably we come to the (perhaps unacknowledged) realization that if meaning and value are so malleable to our whims, they cannot bear much weight, and certainly cannot support us. Our world-view becomes thinner and more brittle, so that we are left with the sense that life has no inherent meaning and no value goes beyond money value.

The ever increasing dominance of monetary evaluation, and the disregard of values and emotions, lead to '[a] preponderance of means over ends [which] finds its apotheosis in the fact that the peripheral in life, the things that lie outside its basic essence, have become masters of its centre and even of ourselves'.[34] This inversion of means and ends is seen most clearly in money due to its instrumentality. Its greatest significance is in its ability to give access to other things which alone can directly satisfy human need. But money does this so well, opening so many possibilities, that it itself becomes the object of our desires, ambitions and wants, thus

32. Ellul, *Money and Power*.
33. Polanyi, *The Great Transformation*.
34. Simmel, *The Philosophy of Money*, p. 482.

acquiring a powerful hold over our passions. Money 'is the absolute means which is elevated to the psychological significance of an absolute purpose ... Money is the secular God of the World.'[35]

35. Simmel, p. 238.

Chapter 7

THE FINANCE SECTOR: AN INITIAL OVERVIEW

The finance sector is generally regarded as a highly (perhaps the most highly) developed working out of free-market principles. It follows that the finance sector will be marked by the same limitations to ethical claims as the free market as a whole. The analysis of money suggests that it will be equally marked by the commodity in which it trades. The purpose of this chapter is not to provide a substantive discussion of particular questions; that comes later. It is to show the centrality of finance to the workings of the free market, and to explain some of its most distinguishing features. This provides the basis of a more systemic analysis of the sector and the ethical questions it faces. The following chapter explains the main features of the derivatives market. This is the part of finance which has grown more than any other. I have separated it from the main sector to help those unfamiliar with it to understand how it works and the issues it presents.

Discussion of morality in the finance sector tends to fall into two distinct types. The first focuses on the sheer size and complexity of global finance and its potential destructiveness. The figures are so far outside our experience that it is a struggle to imagine them. Everett Dirksen, a US Senator, famously remarked, 'a billion here, a billion there, and pretty soon you're starting to talk serious money'. Well, the turnover of the finance sector can be measured in trillions of dollars per day. The speed at which the sector operates is likewise hard for the ordinary person to grasp. So important is speed that one financial institution spent US$35 million on its computer system in order to gain access to the Tokyo stock exchange two seconds quicker than its rivals. Even a cursory examination of the consequences of how global finance operates reveals features which are potentially destructive. But having done that, one can be left thinking 'so what?' Such treatments tend not to be constructive, and are more likely to leave the reader feeling either helpless in the face of such complexity or, in the face of calls to overturn the whole finance sector and the free market, rather cynical about the likelihood of anything happening.

The second type is more typical of mainstream business ethics. It tends to look at illegalities such as insider trading or money laundering and the activities of individual practitioners or firms. The micro-focus usually adopted by business ethics has meant that many of the sector's specific characteristics have been overlooked.[1] Many of the ethical issues of the sector do not arise from the actions or intentions of individuals, or even of individual firms, although these are of course important, but from the operation of financial markets as a whole. The treatment of issues within the finance sector as if each one were discrete is one of the reasons why ethical reflection in this area has remained unconvincing for many people. A theological approach, however, encourages systemic analysis as well as the evaluation of individual acts. I will be discussing the position of the sector within society and its purpose in order to show why the sector merits particular ethical attention. This will show the high level of inter-connectedness of issues, and avoids an over-compartmentalized approach. To assist the reader some terms are defined in a glossary. They are also explained either within the text or, where that would be too cumbersome, in a footnote.

One complicating factor for financial ethics is in identifying what constitutes the finance sector. I am using a deliberately broad definition, covering all dealings involving financial flows. Activities which involve the exchange of goods and services are, therefore, excluded. These dealings in financial flows usually involve a financial intermediary. However, similar transactions which take place directly between 'productive' firms are included. Thus the finance sector brings together nearly everything which passes through financial markets or intermediaries.

The Purpose of the Finance Sector

Just as it is necessary to examine the purpose of business in general, so it is vital to examine what is the purpose of the finance sector. This exam-ination cannot be restricted to what are, mistakenly, deemed to be purely technical matters. Our technical choices are not value-free and often contain unexamined ethical implications. The deterministic assumptions of so many commentators lead only to a form of moral paralysis. It is illogical to be told by market theorists that the market economy grows out of and subserves human freedom, and then to be told that there is no alternative to following wherever the market leads.

One of the activities often cited as a major part of the sector's purpose is its social function of intermediation (that is, facilitating the flow of savings towards investment), and of risk management. Funds from a myriad of small savers, usually wanting low risk and easy access to their savings, are, through financial intermediaries, used to finance long-term, higher-risk

---

1. A notable exception is the excellent description of the intensity and circularity of pressures within the sector by McCosh, *Financial Ethics*.

borrowers. However, that traditional role has changed considerably. Financial innovation has led to credit institutions, particularly banks, initiating a process of *dis*intermediation. In order to spread their risk, these institutions have securitized their debts and loans. This has been done by getting the public, as well as other financial institutions, to invest in securities representing shares in a portfolio of previously granted loans. In the event of a default, the loss is not borne by the credit institution but by the security holder, whose asset collapses in value. This happened, for example, in mortgage-backed bonds in the UK and the USA in the 1990s.

Securitization is also increasingly used to finance acquisitions. Here it means that the purchaser offloads the risk of the transaction by selling bonds with the cash flow of the company being acquired used as security (collateral). It thus separates the debt from the company. Any loss caused by a decline in the value of the company, or its assets, is transferred to the banks and capital-markets institutions which bought the bonds, rather than being borne by the purchaser of the company. Proponents argue that this is a relatively low-risk method of financing deals. It is certainly low risk to those who buy the company. It is not clear how it is low risk for the bond-holders. The potential problem is that the full risk of such debt-structuring is usually not clear until something goes wrong, by which time it is too late.

This demonstrates both a significant shift in the identity of the risk bearer, and a shift from a bank-oriented to a market-oriented economy. It also points to a switch of investment funds away from the financing of production and into financial assets. In Chapter 5 I pointed to this as a significant change in attitude towards investment in the joint-stock company. Throughout the OECD, the contribution by financial markets to the financing of production has either stopped increasing or is actually falling. This means that the financing of production and trade is becoming of more marginal concern to financial markets as they become increasingly concerned with managing previously accumulated wealth. This conflicts with what has traditionally been seen as one of the most important functions of the stock market, that is, the optimum allocation of the supply of new capital.

Another aspect of intermediation is the creation and allocation of credit. When, say, a bank extends a loan it is not (usually) lending money it physically has on deposit from savers. If it is a healthy bank it is 'lending' money it will receive in the future from depositors and from the repayment of loans (this process is greatly helped by the non-physicality of money today). Therefore, the act of extending a loan leads to the creation of a deposit liability, either for the lending bank itself or for the banking system as a whole. Since bank deposits are the largest component of any nation's money supply, this means that the creation of credit is, in the most literal sense, the creation of money. While society can be neutral about the level of output of other goods and services, it cannot be neutral about the 'output' of banks, that is, the amount of deposits and advances which banks create.[2] There can be considerable tension between macro-economic policy objectives requiring a restrained growth in banking output, and microeconomic objectives such as stimulation of productivity within the banking industry. In addition to the moral implications of changes in the level of money and credit within an economy, there are also moral implications in banks' substantial power to influence the allocation of financial resources, and thereby real resources.

Intermediation also occurs through dealing houses acting as market-makers in the security markets. (The terms 'dealing house' and 'market-maker' are both fairly literal. Dealing houses are institutions which deal in assets; market-makers make markets by facilitating deals between differ-ent parties. If necessary, the market-maker will be one of those parties until another can be found.) One of the principal functions is the provi-sion of liquidity[3] to clients. Without such liquidity, markets cannot function. However, in a number of markets the spread (difference) between bid (buy) and offer (sell) prices is so small that such client-based business provides virtually no profit. This applies to the UK gilts market, the US Treasury market and the UK equity market. Because profits from providing clients with liquidity are inadequate to service the risk capital employed, dealers have to find alternative means of generating revenue, means which may give rise to ethical questions. A security house acting in a dual capacity, that is advising clients on what to buy and sell and also dealing on its own account (known as proprietary trading) can be faced with severe conflicts of interest. Instead of acting purely as agents of its clients, the house will take the best deals onto its own books. It may even deal against its own clients. There is also the case where a house has built up a large position (that is, a market commitment) in a share which it now considers a poor investment. How does the house unload it?

Multi-function houses generate profits from a variety of activities. Proprietary trading has already been mentioned. Research departments, needed to advise clients, also enable the house to take positions before the information is released to clients. This may involve dealing with clients only on one side of the market while that position is being built up (known

2. See, for example, Charles P. Kindleberger, *Manias, Panics and Crashes: A History of Financial Crises*, 3rd edn, 1996. He analyses over 30 market crashes. Each had a common pattern which included an increase in the money supply through an explosion of credit which led to the formation of a financial bubble.

3. A market is said to be liquid when participants can rapidly execute large-volume transactions with a small impact on prices, or when a position can be reversed quickly without significant cost from the payment of a bid–ask spread. Illiquidity is seen in wider bid–ask spreads, a small transaction size for which a quoted price is good, and market-makers withdrawing from the market.

as 'front running'). Variable prices are quoted depending on the nature or size of the counterparty (that is, the other party to the transaction with whom the house is dealing). Influencing the market through ramping the price (that is, buying a security to push up the price and then selling, hoping that there will be a time lag before investors react to the change in supply and demand) also enables profits to be taken. Without these profits, multi-function houses could not exist. There would then not be houses with the capacity to handle the large deals required by institutional investors. If the purpose of the sector includes providing services for all categories of client, does it follow, therefore, that the 'best interests' of such investors actually require that practices which on the face of it seem unfair should continue?

Some conflicts of interest, following the cases investigated by Eliot Spitzer, the New York State Attorney General, have been officially removed. One of the best known instances is that of Henry Blodget, a stock analyst who worked for Merrill Lynch during the technology bubble of the late 1990s. He was involved in Merrill's investment-banking business helping to bring Internet companies (and substantial underwriting fees) to the firm. His reports were used to recommend investments which he was denigrating in internal emails. Analysts are now barred from working on both sides of the business.

The 'Specialness' of the Finance Sector

Many books on business ethics do not discuss the sector, despite its size and importance. Those which do contain at least one chapter will typically look mainly at shareholder issues such as insider trading, hostile take-overs, and leveraged buy-outs. What this practice conceals is an implicit assumption that the finance sector is one sector among many. While it may have a particular range of problems, it nevertheless can be dealt with in the same manner, and from the same perspective as, say, the pharmaceutical or motor industries.

While it is clear that many aspects are common to all business enterprises, for example, the fair treatment of staff, pollution, whistle-blowers and so on, this assumption of commonality prevents a clear focus on the many ethical issues faced by the finance sector. I have already argued that the commodity which is traded, that is, money, already presents significant differences to other commodities. Even what may appear to be a similarity can, in fact, mask a profound difference. For example, transparency is seen as a virtue in any activity. It is needed so that others may know what I, the moral agent, have done. The complex nature of financial dealings, especially in the field of derivatives, has, however, become such that transparency is needed so that *I, the agent,* can know what I have done. It is not uncommon for experienced Corporate Treasurers to discover that the opacity of transactions carried out to manage risk leaves them without any clear understanding of the actual instruments they may hold, or their risk profile.[4] Even those issuing new financial instruments may only learn the true nature of their products in the pages of a High Court judgment, as, for example, Morgan Stanley discovered to its cost.[5]

Many of the ethical issues specific to the finance sector are the result of its position within the economy. This can be illustrated most clearly by looking at banks. There are four main systemic reasons why banks are generally considered special even within the finance sector. The first is their pivotal position within the sector. This is due to the fact that they are, for a substantial number of borrowers, the only source of finance, and because they manage the clearing and payments systems. The second arises from the potential for systemic instability (contagion, domino effect) resulting from bank runs. There is a much higher degree of inter-connectedness between banks than is found between companies in other industries. Consequently, the failure of one bank can directly cause immediate losses to other, inter-connected banks.[6] In addition the failure of one bank tends to undermine confidence in the system, leading to depositors withdrawing from other banks.[7]

The third reason, closely linked to the second, arises from the very nature of bank contracts. Liquid deposits are used to finance the acquisition of illiquid assets. Should it be necessary to sell on these assets, particularly if this needs to be done quickly, the seller is unlikely to get full value, as potential purchasers are unable to evaluate customer-specific information, and so will downgrade the value to compensate for unquantifiable risk. Even the mere fact of selling large assets can drive down the price, increasing further the possibility of insolvency. This may, in itself, turn a solvent bank into an insolvent one. The final reason arises from the presence of central banks as lender of last resort, deposit-insurance schemes and other safety-net arrangements. These in themselves may result in adverse selection and moral hazard[8] as banks may believe

4. Justin Welby, 'Risk Management and the Ethics of the New Financial Instruments', *Ethical Perspectives* 4.2 (1997), pp. 84–93.

5. Jonathan Kelly, 'New Products Open Banks to New Risk', *International Financial Law Review*, 24 June 1998, 24–25.

6. This was one of the causes of the intervention by the Federal Reserve following the collapse of the hedge fund Long Term Capital Management (LTCM) in September 1998. This will be discussed in more detail in Chapter 8.

7. Charles A. E. Goodhart, 'Some Regulatory Concerns', in *The Emerging Framework of Financial Regulation*, 1998, 213–54 (229–34).

8. In economic terms, 'moral hazard' is used to define anything which encourages risky behaviour by leading financial risk takers to believe that they will benefit from risky actions, while being protected from the losses. An example within the regulatory framework is deposit insurance for banks.

that they can adopt risky strategies as they will not be allowed to fail. Here banks have precedent on their side. Credit Lyonnais in France, and banks in Japan and South Korea, received significant support when they faced difficulties, indicating that 'too big to fail' may well be true. With the increase in banking consolidation through mergers and takeovers, the number of institutions which fall into the category of 'too big' is increasing.

The risks attaching to this area of the finance sector are not merely theoretical. Throughout the 1980s and 1990s many countries experienced significant banking-sector problems, with worse outcomes than in any similar period since the Great Depression. These problems were due to factors such as poor credit control, connected lending, insufficient liquidity and capital, and poor internal governance.[9] These can be termed the traditional causes of banking problems. In the period 1980–96 (therefore excluding the consequences of the economic crises 1997–98) 133 countries experienced significant banking-sector problems. Two classes of problems were identified: 'crises' (41 instances in 36 countries) and 'significant' (108 instances).[10] The impact of bank unsoundness on the real sector was analysed.[11] Negative results identified included high interest rates, reduced credit and sometimes a credit crunch, reduced growth and in some instances actual recession, disintermediation and a growth of non-bank financial institutions, and disruption to the payments system. Thus the designation of banking as 'special' is not misplaced.[12]

Further analysis of these banking-sector problems revealed that many of them, most notably those of Norway, Finland, Sweden and Eastern European countries (all 'crisis' situations) followed financial liberalization as did those of the United States (designated 'significant').[13] Davies, along with a significant number of other commentators, is firmly of the opinion that the levels of financial instability reached in the 1980s and 1990s are a permanent feature of liberalized financial markets, rather than a consequence of the initial adjustments to liberalized markets. This assessment raises important questions about the nature and desirability of liberalized markets which I will be examining in Chapter 9.

In Chapter 1 I argued that any evaluation of the goals and purposes of a sector needed to include the impact of that sector's activity on other sectors and society as a whole. This is particularly true of the finance

9. Charles A. E. Goodhart *et al.*, *Financial Regulation: Why, How and Where Now?* 1998.
10. Goodhart, *Financial Regulation*, table A1.1, pp. 17–30.
11. Goodhart, *Financial Regulation*, table A1.2, pp. 31–33.
12. For a wide-ranging collection of supporting studies, see Harald A. Benink (ed.), *Coping with Financial Fragility and Systemic Risk*, 1995.
13. E. Philip Davies, 'Financial Fragility in the Early 1990s – What can be Learnt from International Experience?', in C.A.E. Goodhart (ed.), *The Emerging Framework of Financial Regulation*, pp. 15–41.

sector because of its centrality. There is a range of perfectly legal activities which may, in certain conditions, become ethically questionable. These activities include speculation, over-easy credit – and equally its opposite, risk aversion. Risk aversion in this context is the reluctance to provide finance in the face of an economic downturn. The resulting loss of liquidity or high lending premiums may cause significant difficulties to otherwise solvent firms, as well as considerable disruption to financial markets.[14]

A further distinguishing feature of the finance sector is the nature of the business relationship within much of the sector.[15] This relationship requires a difference in ethical behaviour. Typically a business will take outputs from its suppliers, or create them itself in an 'ideas' company, and transform them into the desired inputs of its customers. This is an essentially linear process, which involves the business producing added value between two discrete groups at opposite ends of the value chain. This is not, however, always the case in financial institutions, which instead frequently have a more circular relationship. With some, such as pensions companies, a complete circularity is envisaged: those who 'supply' the contributions are intending to 'consume' the eventual product, the pension, and so have the nature of beneficiaries. It may be less complete with general-insurance companies: premium income is 'supplied' by those who may 'consume' the product if they successfully claim under their policy. The relationship is more complex with a bank. Its customers may either 'supply' its deposits or 'consume' its loans, in which case the process may be seen as linear. However, they may do both, so leading to the circular model.

This is not the only area of relationship complexity. Bank regulation treats depositors as if they were beneficiaries, with the banks as fiduciaries.[16] Management theory and shareholders, however, treat banks as a business. The conflicting models with their differing expectations lead inevitably to moral ambiguity. This confusion between the differing roles and expectations can also be seen in the attitude of the depositors themselves. They require – at least in western liberal economies – absolute

14. There have been two clear examples in the last few years. During the turmoil in the financial markets of August to October 1998, companies hoping to issue new stock found the market closed to all but the strongest. Demand for commercial mortgage-backed securities almost vanished, and liquidity so dried up that many markets effectively failed to function. Then after the collapse of share prices for Internet-based companies in 2000, Initial Public Offerings (IPOs) more or less dried up for a year and have barely begun to recover since. It may be many years, if ever, before the IPO market returns to the level of 2000.

15. Ian Morison, *Banking Ethics – What is Special About Banking and Finance?*, paper presented to the Finance and Ethics Group at the Von Hügel Institute, 1 March 1994.

16. That is, of, or relating to, a holding of something in trust for another. It implies a high degree of responsibility and certain obligations to others.

security (the assumption that depositors will always get their money back),[17] together with a high rate of return, involving shopping around to see who is offering the best deal. Some consequences of these complex and ambiguous relationships will be discussed in Chapter 9 which looks at volatility, the finance sector and non-financial institutions.

Another distinction between the finance sector and business in general is in the treatment of time. Part of the importance of financial markets lies in their function of harmonizing and adjusting the different temporal preferences within society. This enables long-term decisions to be taken and is effected through the management of deposits and the allocation of capital. This strategic nature of capital is one of the reasons why financial markets have to be treated differently from other types of market, even to the extent of attracting high levels of regulation. That is the price of social importance: power brings obligations, omissions are more serious and a bad example may have disastrous consequences.

The 'Positioning' of the Finance Sector

In Chapter 1 I raised the issue of the 'positioning' of business in general vis-à-vis society as a whole, while the preceding section has pointed to one aspect of the positioning of the finance sector within the economy. The centrality to which I adverted is without precedent. In a sense, the finance sector is the central nervous system of the economy. It directs real resources to end-users. It is clear that the developments of the last 25 years or so in the finance sector have provided the rest of the economy with a range of new products and markets with which to deal with the increasing uncertainties of global trade.[18] However, it is equally clear that this centrality has not been completely benign.

The consequences for the rest of the economy following excess volatility in financial markets demonstrate clearly the internationally exposed and politically consequential status these markets have achieved. With their extensive interlocking networks they show remarkable technological, institutional and social mechanisms in their operation. They are equally notable for their fragility, and the speed of destabilizing contagion. More subtle, however, has been the resulting imbalance to the productive sector

17. Although there is only a limited Deposit Protection Fund, so that in theory a depositor does not have absolute security, in practice this is not a consideration for the generality of depositors.

18. However, it should be noted that innovations in finance, as in productive processes, can shock the system and lead to overtrading. Financial innovations are often under-priced in order to have them gain acceptance, and hence overused. Overtrading in this context is not univocal. It may involve pure speculation for a price rise; an overestimate of prospective returns; or excessive gearing.

caused by the distraction away from productive investment by business towards the financial economy. This has distorted business's role in economic activity and perhaps given the financial function within firms too important a place. It can also cause a fatal change of strategy. For example, Enron shifted from the regulated transportation of natural gas to the unregulated energy-trading markets, under the impression that there was more money in buying and selling financial contracts linked to the value of energy assets than in actual ownership of physical assets. But more about Enron later.

The distortion of the financial function within firms can be seen, for example, in the changed function of Corporate Treasurers. Their principal task has been to raise the funds required to finance the firm, to invest surpluses as profitably as possible, and to protect the business from unnecessary financial risk. As awareness of derivatives increased, with the possibility of not only covering risk but also of generating income, the role required of the Treasurer has changed. It has become common for the Treasurer's performance to be compared with some form of benchmark, either that of other company divisions or outside. Instead of the role being one of enabling the company to undertake its business, it has become itself a measured profit-centre. If the company is under pressure it can be tempting to speculate in financial markets. The dangers of this can be seen from the many cases where this type of speculation has led to substantial losses.[19] This sort of speculation needs, of course, to be distinguished from those cases where, it is alleged, complex financial instruments were used as a means to perpetrate fraud. Again, Enron comes to mind.

Turning now to the finance sector's positioning vis-à-vis society in general, the picture is more complex, with significant questions about the ethical claim that the free market promotes freedom. In Chapter 2 I looked at the dependence of the free market upon non-democratic state action for its inception and growth, together with its requirement for immunity from democratic political pressure if it is to continue – particularly in a global context. Its relationship with the state is, therefore, highly ambivalent. The relationship between the nation state and the finance sector is one of the most crucial in the current stage of globalization. One consequence of the 24 hour operation of financial markets is that every major event is immediately converted into asset prices,

19. For example Procter and Gamble's dealings in interest-rate swaps resulted in losses of over $100 million in 1994. The loss of $1.2 billion by Metalgesellschaft in 1993/94 on its positions in energy futures and swaps was more complex. Although it was originally thought that these losses resulted from speculation, it was later established that the company was trying to hedge its position. Nevertheless, it demonstrates the risks for firms dealing in derivatives. It also revealed that the company's board and senior managers had not understood its hedging strategy. To show that nothing had been learnt, in 2004 China Aviation Oil had to seek court protection after losing $550 million trading oil derivatives.

currency-exchange rates and in-flows or out-flows of capital. Governments constantly watch the financial markets to gauge their response to political action, thus effectively leading to a reduced margin of action for governments. As commentators have noted, 'through continuous trading of currencies and government bonds, financial markets effectively dictate macroeconomic policy'.[20] Or again, 'because of fiscal crises, many European Union states raised interest rates to defend their currencies and sought to reduce government expenditure, notably for social and welfare programmes, *in large part to satisfy traders in the currency and bond markets*'.[21] There are questions about the role and dominance of the finance sector, and about its impact on the common good. Should the economy, and with it the finance sector, serve the needs of society, or society the imperatives of the market? This is to ask once more the question already raised several times: Is there to be a market economy or a market society? Do we want a society where all human activities and relationships are to be formed by and in compliance with the market?

The centrality of the finance sector within the economy, and the different type of business relationship it has, require that it receive special ethical attention. The pivotal position of the banking system in particular gives it great social importance. This centrality means that the sector's activities can have a far greater impact on the economy, and thus on society, than any other single sector. It is also a sector undergoing rapid change. Its traditional social functions of financial intermediation and risk management are being transformed by innovation, technology and globalization. It has provided the rest of the economy with new products and markets with which to deal with the uncertainties of global trade, yet its own activities have added to that uncertainty. This comes about from such features as speculative currency trading, price volatility in derivatives and the risk of systemic instability arising from highly geared acquisitions.

Several questions arising from this will be discussed in Chapters 8 and 9. Has the instrumental function of finance been lost, so that instead of serving the real economy, the finance sector has come to have too dominant a role, with finance trading as an end rather than as a means? Has the growth of a global financial system led to a dangerous decoupling of the system from the real economy and from society's ability to regulate it in any meaningful way? Given the amount of decoupling from national contexts, can questions concerning the legitimacy of moral claims by the *Lebenswelt* even be asked? This raises more than just the question of what

---

20. Jonathan Perraton *et al.*, 'The Globalization of Economic Activity', *New Political Economy* 2.2 (1997), pp. 257–77 (265).

21. Stephen Gill, 'European Governance and New Constitutionalism: Economic and Monetary Union and Alternatives to Disciplinary NeoLiberalism in Europe', *New Political Economy* 3.1 (1998), pp. 5–26 (9), emphasis added.

(if any) are the most appropriate forms of regulation for today. Questions about what is the most ethically appropriate understanding of efficiency are also germane, as one must ask: 'efficient for whom?' I have referred to the cutting back of social and welfare programmes to satisfy bond and currency traders. In effect, markets, not democratic processes, have determined what happens to programmes designed to promote equity. What are the appropriate criteria when balancing social programmes and economic efficiency?

Although externalities are usually thought of solely in relation to physical processes (for example, pollution) the finance sector also generates them. An obvious example is generalized instability caused by financial activity. This need not be confined to the economy itself. Stock-market scandals caused a dissolution of the Kuwaiti Parliament in the mid 1980s and increased political instability in India in the mid 1990s. There are also such features as the consequences of reckless lending being borne not by the financial institutions but by the poorest sectors of those countries to whom inappropriate lending was made, with punitive arrangements not shared by the commercial sector. How is this to be addressed?

I have alluded to the issue of power several times in earlier chapters. With the finance sector this issue assumes particular relevance, especially when coupled with the sector's combination of expert and exclusive knowledge. There are the obvious questions of the balance of power between the sector and the nation state and between it and both business in general and with certain sectors of business. The asymmetry of power is not always to the advantage of the financial institution. Within banking, for example, it varies by category of customer and the level of competition for a particular type of business. Nevertheless significant power does accrue. Among other consequences of asymmetrical power, the collective control of finance capital empowers banks in particular to define crisis and non-crisis situations, an ability which frequently produces a self-fulfilling prophecy.[22] Common participation in lending consortia reduces the number of non-participating competitors and fuses the interests of the participants. This does not necessarily produce a benefit for the client. In the securities market, control of information confers power. This can be used either for the efficient operation of markets or for classes of speculators to manipulate prices (insider trading). There are, however, other questions which the development of the finance sector raises. The economy is not only a place of exchange. It is also the place of political processes, of power struggles between different interests and different actors – firms, social groups and public authorities. The development of

---

22. This ability is in part shared by pension funds and unit trusts (mutual funds in the USA) via their ability to dump large blocks of shares.

the finance sector has changed the balance of the relations between different actors, and these changes have ethical import.

Summary and Conclusions

The range of ethical issues confronting the finance sector is far wider than the actions of individual moral agents which are usually considered under this heading. I am not minimizing the importance of individual action – the pursuit by one individual (Leeson) of his self-interested personal project was enough to bring down an entire bank (Barings). Levine and Milken caused the eventual collapse of Drexel Burnham Lambert through insider trading. It is easy to focus on cases of this type, giving a spurious impression that such individuals are typical. What is typical, however, is the impact on the sector of the assumptions of economic rationality discussed in Chapter 3. To this must be added the speed of monetary transactions, often requiring almost instant decisions, the complexity and uncertainty of transactions, and the expectations of short-term goals. It then becomes clear both that the character of the individual is crucial, and that the nature of the activity does not easily lend itself to moral reflection and judgment.

Nevertheless, such individual action cannot be the sum total of our enquiry. Without subscribing to a deterministic understanding of structures, it remains true that the context itself may provide a very high percentage of the explanation of why an issue came about. This can be in two main ways. The first, rather straightforward way, arises from corporate culture. Corporate culture and remuneration schemes have been identified as crucial factors on a number of occasions. This can be seen in, for example, various pensions mis-selling scandals. These were in large measure driven by the commission-based remuneration schemes used by the insurance companies, together with often lamentable levels of staff training. The link between remunerations schemes and the incentive to either illegal or at least questionable activity is never automatic. Nevertheless, it is a constant danger.

Insofar as authors have identified corporate culture as a significant factor in a wide range of businesses, the finance sector is similar to any other, although the sums involved are often bigger. It is an aspect which regulation seeks to cover by promoting sound practice and governance. However, regulators are limited, in that historically they have been seen as responsible for the conduct of financial agents and firms in the markets, rather than the markets themselves. Yet, as this chapter has shown, the second way in which context influences actions is precisely in the way that financial markets as a whole operate and impact on other sectors of society. Within this context, agents might well be acting legally and within regulations, yet still be engaged in activity which raises ethical questions. Regulation, however, is increasingly unable to reach significant parts of the sector's work. This is not just due to firms locating in lightly regulated off-shore centres. It is also because of the greater use the sector is making of outsourcing, frequently on a cross-border basis. Outsourcing has the potential to transfer risk, management and compliance to third parties who may not be regulated. It is difficult to see how the sector can be confident that they remain in charge of their own business and in control of their business risks. Although legal, the ethical questions are significant, because external service providers have the potential to lead to systemic problems. Problems associated with risk and systemic instability are discussed more fully in Chapter 9. Here I just want to point to the importance of considering how the market as a whole operates.

Standard business ethics does not address this wider aspect due to its micro-focus, extending at best from individual agent to individual firm. Many strands of theological reflection, on the other hand, have maintained that consideration of the structural dimension is of equal importance. In addition, that reflection has, unlike many free-market theorists, insisted that the relationship of the state to the market should be one which can ensure that markets remain instrumental, not determinative. Free-market ideology has a clear conception of the role of the market and of its relationship with society. Standard business ethics cannot engage with this vision because it has failed to address the question: 'What for?' With its individualistic focus it cannot counter the free market's potential to negate the social character of business. Christian theological ethics, on the other hand, precisely because it does have an overarching world-view, has sufficient 'weight' to engage in dialogue as an equal partner.

Chapter 8

THE DERIVATIVES MARKET

In this short chapter I shall be looking specifically at the derivatives market. Using the concept of the common good, I will show what the contribution of derivatives is and how they carry with them significant dangers. An increasingly important issue in financial management, exemplified particularly by derivatives, is the balance of risk against reward. Derivatives can generate enormous rewards for some. At the same time they represent an unquantifiable risk of such magnitude that the possibility exists for the global finance system to be destabilized. Having described the main features of the derivatives market, I will use the examples of Long Term Capital Management, Enron and Barings Bank to illustrate some of the problems.

A Contribution to the Common Good

Chapter 7 indicated some of the contributions of the finance sector to the common good. Traditionally, the sector has been seen as one which smoothed fluctuations in income and expenditure (accepted savings, made loans), inter-temporal imbalances (short-term savings, long-term loans; present savings, future income streams) and differing levels of risk aversion (between savers, borrowers, investors). This represents its inter-mediation function. Financial markets and institutions perform the essential function in an economy of channelling funds to those individuals or firms which have productive investment opportunities. Performing this function well helps ensure that the economy operates efficiently and promotes growth.

If these contributions are to be made, other requirements need to be met. These include a stable currency and orderly capital flows. By the sector's investment choices, it preserves the marginal efficiency of capital, so helping to ensure that scarce resources are allocated in the most productive way. Therefore investment based on economic fundamentals, rather than speculative froth, and sound long-term credit are also required.

The sector contributes to the common good through a variety of mechanisms, not all of which can be examined here. My focus will be principally upon new financial instruments – commonly referred to as derivatives. This choice flows from their ubiquity, often unsuspected by the general public,[1] their importance in the US and UK finance sectors, and their contentious nature arising from the scale of risk which they carry.

The growth of derivatives has been one of the principal financial innovations of the last 30 years. They are not a new concept – simple forms were known to the classical Greeks. What is new is their range, complexity, hybridization and customization, made possible by computer technology. A derivative is a contract whose value is derived from the prices and volatilities of other financial securities (called the underlying asset or security). It does not require any investment of capital in these underlying assets. As a contract between two counterparties to exchange payments based on underlying prices or yields, any transfer of ownership of the underlying assets or cash flows becomes unnecessary.

The principal economic function of derivatives is to facilitate the transformation of risk through the transfer of exposure to these risks among counterparties. By allowing the different components of risk embodied in financial assets to be unbundled and traded separately, these risks are redistributed between agents and economic sectors. This allows economic agents to tailor their exposures more closely to their investment or funding preferences. For example, an oil company investing in a new well is faced with risks on exploration, extraction, oil price, interest rates and exchange rates. These can be separated out so that the oil company keeps the risks on which it has expertise (exploration and extraction) and sells the others through hedging.[2] Derivatives, by expanding opportunities for risk sharing, are therefore a highly efficient means of hedging and trading risk exposures. This does not mean that risks in the aggregate are transformed, only that they are assumed by those most willing to bear them. Risk exposures are transferred; at the macro-level they are not eliminated.

Typically a derivative might trade at one-tenth, or even one-twentieth, of the cost of using the underlying cash-market security. These lower transaction costs and limited cash demands of derivatives allow a trading of risks which otherwise might not have been contemplated. The ability to hedge unwanted risks through the use of derivatives while retaining others may, at the margins, promote investment which would not otherwise

---

1. For example, flexible fixed-rate mortgages are all derivative based.
2. Hedging: the protection of an open position to minimize risk; for example, to try and cover potential losses by betting that derivative prices will move the other way as well. A position where this has not been done is called unhedged, and is a riskier position to maintain.

occur. In addition, by providing a smooth transition across currencies and across widely different regulations, tax rules and institutional practices, corporations may invest more easily. Again, therefore, derivatives may promote marginal investment, that is, investment which would otherwise be too marginal to consider. In normal circumstances, derivatives generally contribute to greater liquidity in the markets for underlying price risks. By creating demand for underlying securities that would otherwise be thinly traded, investors pay a reduced liquidity premium. It follows that dealers' abilities to use derivatives to manage the market-risk exposures of their inventories better should enable them to provide finer spreads (a smaller difference between bid–ask prices) to their customers.

These considerations show that derivatives can make a valid contribution to the functioning of financial markets. These markets, in their turn, can make a positive contribution to the common good. Derivatives are one of the most flexible and efficient means of transforming unwanted financial risks through the transfer of exposures among counterparties. They can facilitate investment which might otherwise be too expensive or cumbersome to undertake. The popular perception that derivatives have little merit, often fostered by newspapers, is erroneous. This is not to say, however, that they are without major defects, defects which can seriously undermine their contribution to the common good. These will now be outlined.

Destabilizing Features of Derivatives Markets

Some episodes of illiquidity are normal and unavoidable features of market dynamics. These episodes are a response to periods of greater than normal uncertainty about future prices, perhaps because of uncertainty about a change in interest rates. Political uncertainty also plays a part. For example, the Colosio assassination and the uprising in Chiapas increased general uncertainty in the Mexican financial markets, contributing to the financial crises of 1994. The liquidity issues I shall be discussing here are of a different order and magnitude. A major cause for concern over derivatives is their potential contribution to a systemic crisis (that is, a financial disturbance which causes widespread disruptions elsewhere in the financial system). This concern arises from two notable features of derivatives markets, that is, their lack of transparency[3] and the

---

3. This has two principal meanings. The main one is high levels of asymmetrical information, that is, one party to a financial transaction often does not know enough about the other party to make accurate decisions. The second meaning is that derivatives are opaque because of their inherent complexity, with dynamically changing risk profiles, and because there are very few disclosure rules. For example, there is no need to disclose liabilities arising from derivatives in the balance sheet.

market's structure, both of which can impact severely on liquidity. In addition they facilitate leverage and risk.

The lack of transparency means that market participants do not have adequate information on the size of firms' exposure to market and credit risk,[4] so increasing the potential for misjudgments. This is partially because these risks are not disclosed on company balance sheets and are not made available to credit-rating agencies. This makes it far more difficult for outsiders to assess the potential risks to which a company is vulnerable. Even in normal trading conditions it is difficult for outside investors and policy-makers to evaluate the risks borne by individual institutions and the broader markets. Therefore, when a price shock occurs, its effect on a counterparty with a large position cannot be assessed by others with any degree of certainty. Uncertainty about a firm's creditworthiness can suddenly and severely affect that firm's standing in the market. This leads to a denial of funding and trading access as creditors back away. This can be the case even with solvent institutions, exacerbating any liquidity problems and frequently having knock-on effects in other sectors of the market. For example, a foreign investor facing liquidity problems or difficulty in hedging exchange-rate exposures may liquidate its underlying position in a country's equity and bond markets.

Because the lack of transparency applies not only to individual institutions but also to the scale and distribution of aggregate risk exposures in the market, the result of credit uncertainty can spill over. The risk is then that problems at one firm are incorrectly assumed to apply to other firms with similar activities. Even without uncertainty generated by price shocks, uncertainty about aggregate positions and hedging demands can lead to misjudgments. Market participants may base their risk management strategies on incompatible assumptions about the robustness of market liquidity. This can cause shocks to be amplified or transmitted across markets.

If it is difficult for experienced market professionals to determine the true risks of a particular instrument or market condition, how much more so for the non-financial corporation which has bought the instrument (the end-user). The fact that certain instruments are deemed too risky for all investors (the 'sophisticated investor' test) is itself eloquent testimony of the dangers. But even outside such categories, as I noted in Chapter 7, it is often extremely difficult for non-financial corporations to monitor the new

---

4. Market risk: the risks brought about by changes in market conditions, for example, price, volatility, bid–ask spreads. Credit risk: the risk that a counterparty will not live up to its financial obligations. Derivative credit risk is different from loan credit risk because the amount at risk is dynamic and reflects changing prices and volatilities of the underlying asset.

exposures involved in the instruments they have bought. The attempt to do so requires considerable investment of the business's resources.

The second major feature of derivatives markets, which can cause severe liquidity problems leading to a potential destabilization, is their structure. The market-making function supporting liquidity in many segments of the market is performed by a relatively small number of institutions. This concentration leads to less resilience of market liquidity to shocks than would be the case if it were more widely dispersed. When an erosion of liquidity occurs, price volatility increases and market participants' ability to manage their exposures is impaired, increasing their vulnerability to price shocks even further. This effect was seen in the aftermath of the collapse of LTCM.

Some arbitrage transactions[5] span multiple markets, particularly in their funding and hedging components. Executing these arbitrages often requires the dynamic rolling of positions[6] which in turn depends critically on market liquidity and market access. An inability to roll these positions could force the unwinding of the arbitrage position and transmit shocks across the markets involved in the transactions. In times of stress the close linkages of the markets and concentrations of market-making institutions increase the scope for disturbances to be quickly transmitted between markets. Again, this was seen following the collapse of LTCM. A further effect of the concentration in the market-making function is that credit exposures among derivatives dealers are also high. Inter-dealer exposures which are large in relation to the firm's capital could exacerbate contagion risk and could inhibit the market's ability to absorb large price changes.

These two factors, lack of transparency and market structure, may, separately, affect the ability of financial markets to perform their functions of risk transformation and capital allocation. Lack of transparency can lead to highly destabilizing erosions of liquidity as market participants misjudge levels of risk. The growth of options markets and the spread of associated dynamic hedging strategies may increase the risk that an initial price change in underlying markets could be amplified by positive-feedback effects.[7] Likewise, the market linkages engendered by derivatives transactions which straddle various market segments could cause an initial price shock to travel further and faster than in the past. When the two operate simultaneously, their effects are mutually reinforcing. When

5. A trading strategy exploiting tiny price differences of two similar instruments which are traded in different markets. The trader simultaneously buys the cheaper instrument and sells the more expensive substitute.

6. To roll: to replace an existing position or transaction with another similar position. Rolling over: the closing of a position in an expiring contract and the simultaneous opening of the same position in a later-expiring contract.

7. Positive feedback: the processes that amplify price changes in a market, causing an initial price change to be followed by further changes in the same direction.

joined by the consequences of a third market feature, they can overwhelm the market. That third feature is the use of leverage and the presence of Highly Leveraged Institutions (HLIs).

Leverage as a term can be used to describe several related phenomena. Its most basic, equal to the term 'gearing', is the ratio of borrowed money to a firm's or an individual's assets or cash in hand. For example, when someone buys a house, he or she might put down £10,000 deposit and get a mortgage of £100,000. That is a leverage ratio of one to ten. Leverage also describes the multiplied effect from a small change in prices on profit (or loss) or the value of a position. It can also describe the ratio between the amount an investor deposits as an upfront payment (known as initial margin) and the notional amount of exposure he or she gains. For example, a share is trading at £10 and an option on the share at £1. The option gives the investor ten times leverage. HLIs are defined as 'large financial institutions that are subject to very little or no direct regulatory oversight as well as very limited public disclosure requirements and that take on significant leverage'.[8] Many of these HLIs are hedge funds. The starting point for understanding hedge funds is that they do not hedge; rather they do the opposite. In normal usage to hedge is to reduce risk by laying off a bet. Hedge funds make bets. They are not regulated in the same way as conventional funds; more than half are off-shore, although it is not possible to be too specific because no one knows exactly how many hedge funds there are. Most estimates are that by mid-2005 there were about 8,000 funds managing US$1 trillion. Although not all hedge funds are highly leveraged, and other institutions may also have some or all of the attributes of an HLI, the best known HLI is almost certainly Long Term Capital Management.

The trading strategy which caused LTCM's problems was based on convergence of exchange rates ahead of European Monetary Union. The mathematical model LTCM followed assumed relative market tranquillity. If certain bond yields relative to US Treasuries widened, it predicted that market forces would correct the differential and yields would inevitably begin to converge. As spreads began to widen in early 1998, LTCM bought long corporate and foreign bonds at the same time that it sold short Treasury instruments.[9] In August 1998 Russia defaulted on its debt repayments, causing turmoil in the foreign-exchange markets. This led to a 'flight to quality', principally the Deutsche Mark and US dollar. The

---

8. Basel Committee on Banking Supervision, *Sound Practices for Banks' Interactions with Highly Leveraged Institutions*, 1999, p. 3.

9. To buy long: to agree to buy an asset in the future on the premise that its price will rise higher than the contracted priced. To sell short: to agree to sell an asset not yet owned on the premise that its price will go down. When the time comes to hand over the asset, the trader expects to be able to buy it for less than the price at which he or she has agreed to sell it.

spreads widened, rather than narrowed, and LTCM found itself on the losing end of both sides of key investment decisions.

As their contracts deteriorated, their initial margin quickly became inadequate and they were faced with increasing 'margin calls', that is, demands for more cash or collateral to guarantee performance on these contracts. LTCM was, however, very highly leveraged indeed. At its peak it was running positions which were worth more than 200 times its equity capital. Its scramble to unwind its positions, coupled with its need to liquidate assets to meet margin calls, meant that it was selling into a falling market, magnifying its losses and further undermining its ability to meet margin calls. It also reduced the value of assets held as collateral by its creditors. Yet even if these assets had held their price, due to leverage they were totally inadequate to meet LTCM's commitments. Their creditors, none of whom seemed aware of the extent of LTCM's risk exposure, were faced with huge losses. This, coupled with the almost total drying up of liquidity in the market, threatened to bring about a systemic crisis. The US Federal Reserve had to step in and organize a rescue.

I will be discussing some of the implications of all this later when looking at risk distribution. Here it is sufficient to note the reality of the dangers posed by lack of transparency, both to creditor institutions and to the market in general; the consequences of liquidity erosion and spillover into other markets; the dangers of high leverage ratios and the speed at which seemingly sound positions can reverse into enormous losses. The danger of the systemic crisis in September 1998 can hardly be overestimated.

One problem associated with derivatives stems from the same source as a benefit. The increased ability to separate and trade risks means that some counterparties can assume riskier positions more readily than in the past. The type of trading that LTCM was conducting was believed to be low risk. Even if it had been, it is necessary to keep in mind that most trading is a zero-sum game, that is, if one party has made a profit, the counterparty has made an equal loss. What made LTCM stand out so dramatically was not just the size of the losses, or the number of creditor institutions caught up in the fallout. It was that these events, according to all the models available, were simply not supposed to be able to happen.

Since LTCM, calls for greater disclosure, so as to increase transparency, became more pronounced. One result was the issue by the Basel Committee of a range of measures for banks' dealings with HLIs.[10] Another was the report from the Financial Stability Forum with guidelines for hedge-fund managers.[11] Despite all the increased regulatory attention to the relationships between banks and HLIs, significant problems remain, as was shown in May 2005. Rumours that a major hedge fund (or possibly

10. Basel Committee on Banking Supervision, *Sound Practices*.
11. Financial Stability Forum, *Sound Practices for Hedge Fund Managers*, 2000.

several) were on the brink of collapse sent bank shares tumbling. This suggests that the market, at least, does not think that banks are sufficiently insulated from the investment policies of funds to whom they lend. What happened is that a number of US funds bought long debt bonds in General Motors and then supposedly hedged their position by selling shares short in the same company (on the basis that the expected down-grading of General Motors debt to 'junk' would reduce the share price). Two things went wrong with their strategy. The first is that share prices rose on news of a speculative bid for a large block of General Motors shares. The second is that the hedge funds had failed to realize that a downgrade to junk would force many debt holders to dump their investments, as they are only allowed to hold investment-grade bonds. This caused the price to collapse. Like LTCM they were on the losing end of both sides of their investment decisions. The bonds had to be bought for a higher price, and shares sold for a lower price, than each were then trading at. Despite some improvements noted by regulators, trading in derivatives by hedge funds and others remains high risk. The regulatory initiatives, however, also miss out on another significant problem. Which is where Enron comes in.

While LTCM lost a few billion dollars, Enron not only wiped out $70 billion of shareholder value, it also defaulted on tens of billions of dollars of debts. Although Enron was known as an energy-trading company, it had in fact evolved until it was, at its core, a derivatives-trading firm. In his testimony before a US Senate Committee, Frank Partnoy[12] explained the complicated ways in which Enron had used trading in derivatives to cover up its losses in all its other activities for three years, and then how that same trading imploded when the technology bubble burst in 2000, leading to its bankruptcy in 2001. One of the points he stressed was that companies, like Enron, which trade in derivatives are unregulated. Warning signs were not picked up by what he termed 'the gatekeepers' – that is to say, institutions such as auditors, law firms, banks, securities analysts, independent directors and credit-rating agencies. Some of Enron's employees were lying systematically about their profits and losses on the derivatives trading operations. Simply put, Enron's reported earnings from derivatives seem to have been more imagined than real.

Lying employees leads us into the final example, that of Barings Bank of London. Nick Leeson was a trader based in Singapore who appeared to be generating enormous profits from his derivatives trading. It seems that systematic violations of proper procedures were allowed to continue; as long as the profits continued to be earned no one reined him in. His

---

12. Frank Partnoy, *Testimony at Hearings before the United States Senate Committee on Governmental Affairs*, 24 January 2002.

problems stemmed from his trading in derivatives based on the Nikkei Index in Japan. All went smoothly until the Kobe earthquake caused the Index to fall and his positions promptly went into negative. He tried hiding the losses in fictitious accounts, but eventually the true situation became clear. Within a short time Barings Bank was bankrupt and was sold for £1.

Summary and Conclusions

This assessment is only interim (and therefore very brief); a fuller evaluation will come in the next chapter. Derivatives have undoubted common-good features. These include the separation of different components of risk, portfolio diversification and gains in the efficiency of the international allocation of capital, with increased investment at the margin. Derivatives are not unique in being risky forms of investment. Neither is speculation *per se* a bad thing. Most major economic developments were at one time speculative. The development of railways is the classic example. The question is: 'Do the benefits outweigh the dangers?'

One of the things which links all the examples I have discussed is the impact of unexpected events: Russia defaulting on its debts, the end of the technology bubble and an earthquake. This point will be taken up in more detail when looking at risk in the next chapter.

Chapter 9

RISK, VOLATILITY AND 'GENOA TENDENCIES'

In Chapter 6 I described some of the consequences of trading in money using the example of Genoa. Among other features, I referred to the ways in which the relational nature of the transaction becomes one which leads to impersonality, independence and differentiation. The owner of money develops a particular view of freedom and of investment. These are what might be termed 'Genoa tendencies' in our economic life.

A major example of such tendencies is the rootlessness of the finance sector, stemming from the ways in which money enables independence at the cost of community. While economies are becoming increasingly de-territorialized, money can ignore national boundaries with even greater ease, so that trading in money has become the dominant transnational economic activity. I will be discussing some aspects of this rootlessness in this chapter.

The 'Moral Hazard' of Volatility and Risk

In economic terms 'moral hazard' is used to define anything which encourages risky behaviour by leading financial risk takers to believe that they will benefit from risky actions while being protected from the losses. For example, someone who takes out insurance against theft may become more careless about security knowing that the cost of any loss will be borne by the police, the insurance company and other premium payers. Banks are well aware of the dangers of moral hazard with loans, where the borrower uses the loan for a different project which is riskier than the one approved, but which offers potentially higher rewards. However, reflection within the perspective of particular goods which do not contribute to the common good reveals a significant area of moral hazard which has been overlooked by the literature. This is the moral hazard of volatility and risk management itself.[1] This volatility both arises from and is a

1. For example, Daly's excellent analysis of volatility, its causes and transmission mechanisms to the real economy makes no reference to the issue of moral hazard. Kevin James Daly, *Financial Volatility and Real Economic Activity*, 1999. Mishkin's analysis gives prominence to moral hazard, but only in the classical sense of information asymmetry between borrower and lender and bank-deposit insurance. Frederic S. Mishkin, *International Capital Movements, Financial Volatility and Financial Instability*, 1998.

contributory cause of the systemic financial fragility which has been evident on many occasions in the last 20 years.

Early symptoms can be seen in the boom in the international market for bank credit during the 1970s and its collapse by the early 1980s. Loans to less-developed countries are probably the best-known example. October 1987 saw the London and Wall Street stock markets crash. In 1989 Japan's stock-market bubble collapsed. The European exchange-rate mechanism collapsed in 1992–93. The bond market crashed in 1994. East Asia went into turmoil in 1997. In 1998 Russia defaulted on its debts and the consequent unwinding of highly-leveraged positions almost caused systemic failure. Each of these events caused great volatility in exchange rates, interest rates and market rates for a wide range of securities. Each of them had different proximate causes. Yet, viewed from the perspective of moral hazard, each was rooted in the same market conditions of risk-prone transactions.

During the 1970s and early 1980s the growth in international bank credit was matched by the transformation of the financial markets into an expanding international security business, one which by the mid-1980s had moved significantly away from traditional bank activities and into others which were not industry related, with risk-prone business the chief source of financial intermediation. As returns on capital could only be maintained by the creation of debt, financial institutions sought outlets beyond industry, and financial flows became increasingly dissociated from the real sector. Low growth rates of gross domestic products in OECD countries led banks into business such as corporate mergers, acquisitions and property transactions, areas where the rate of returns were not proportionate to the risk taken. Speculation, involving a high degree of risks in the economy, generated the demand for a substantial part of financial flows in OECD countries.[2]

Following the breakdown of the Bretton Woods exchange-rate regime, two oil-price shocks and the de-regulation of financial markets, new forms and institutions for financial intermediation emerged, often in response to market uncertainty rather than to real activity. The poor growth record in the real sector created a situation whereby the finance sector could only grow by generating business within its own activities. Money was increasingly dissociated from any direct connection with real economic activity.[3] Risk-prone business soon became the chief source of financial

2. Sunanda Sen, 'On Financial Fragility and its Global Implications', in *Financial Fragility, Debt and Economic Reforms*, 1996, pp. 35–59.

3. For example, only about 10% of foreign exchange transactions are needed for traditional trade.

activity. Off-balance sheet activities[4] were innovated which, being off-balance sheet, make the overall risk exposure of financial intermediaries more difficult to assess by the market or by the supervisory authorities. Such activities offer derivative financial instruments such as warrants, asset-based securities and over-the-counter (OTC)[5] transactions. Demand for these products has grown enormously so that by December 2004, the notional value of OTC derivatives alone was US$248 trillion.[6] Since the major part of the demand for financial activities was related to market-based uncertainties primarily originating in the finance sector (for example interest- and exchange-rate fluctuations) the situation reflects a paradox whereby finance can only survive through its own turbulence.

Simmel's analysis of the nexus where means and ends are so intertwined that logically one does not know which comes first helps us to understand this present feature of the finance sector. Discussion of its contribution to the common good pointed to the sector's role as a true intermediary with its function of temporal smoothing, maturity transformation, reduction in transaction costs and risk transformation. Now, however, the sector is increasingly a means for the real economy to gain protection against the activities and uncertainties generated by the sector itself.

Cross-border Capital Flows

I will shortly be arguing that derivative risk imposes a particularly large risk burden on certain groups and sections of society. To justify that claim I will indicate briefly one further aspect of capital markets. This section will deal with the issue of speculative capital flows, that is, capital mobility dissociated from economic fundamentals. This links with the points raised about destabilization leading to contagion and with the moral hazard of volatility. It illustrates a way in which the finance sector, by adhering to the free-market model, works against the common good.

There has been a long-standing presumption within western economic orthodoxy that the case for liberalizing capital account transactions is essentially analogous to that for liberalizing trade. Liberalization of capital markets enables increased international integration of financial markets, bringing undoubted long-term benefits. These include opportunities for portfolio-risk diversification and consumption smoothing through borrowing and lending. Investment at the margin can be

---

4. Off-balance sheet: Banks' business, often fee-based, that does not generally involve booking assets and taking deposits. For example, trading of swaps, options, foreign exchange forwards, stand-by commitments and letters of credit.

5. OTC transactions are customized financial instruments which are traded off-exchange.

6. BIS, *OTC Derivatives Market Statistics*, May 2005.

increased due to the ability to invest in riskier, but higher-yield projects.[7] By increasing the access of foreign banks to a domestic financial system, the efficiency of the intermediation process between savers and borrowers is raised. This lowers the cost of investment.[8] But there are significant short-term costs attached to high degrees of financial openness.

Chapter 7 referred to the connection between financial-market liberalization and banking crises. There are structural reasons why economies at an intermediate level of financial development may actually be destabilized by full liberalization.[9] It is increasingly accepted, by both well-respected academic economists[10] and senior central banking officials,[11] that bouts of generalized financial instability are likely to be characteristic of deregulated financial systems. Research also demonstrates the links between liberalization, volatility, instability and contagion.[12]

Serious concerns for policy-makers have been raised by the magnitude of the capital flows recorded by some developing countries in recent years when coupled with abrupt reversals and the ensuing contagion effects. The Mexican crisis (1994) led to widespread financial instability in Latin America. The collapse of the pegged exchange-rate mechanism in Thailand (1997) resulted in currency turmoil in Asia. Research demonstrates that these effects are the result of shifts in market sentiment rather than shifts in economic fundamentals,[13] and that interest-rate volatility magnified an initial exogenous shock and contributed to contagion.[14]

Agénor and Aizenman,[15] like many other commentators, were prompted by the crises in Mexico and Asia to reconsider the costs, benefits and sustainability of the liberalization and integration of world-capital markets. By focusing on capital flows, the financial system and the supply side of the economy, they were able to evaluate welfare losses under financial openness. These losses were shown to be higher under financial openness than under financial self-sufficiency. When volatility of interest

7. Maurice Obstfeld, *The Global Capital Market: Benefactor or Hindrance?*, 1998.

8. Pierre-Richard Agénor and Joshua Aizenman, *Volatility and the Welfare Costs of Financial Market Integration*, 1998.

9. Philippe Aghion, Philippe Bacchetta and Abhijit Banerjee, *Capital Markets and the Instability of Open Economies*, 1999.

10. For example, Barry Eichengreen, *Towards a New International Financial Architecture: A Practical Post-Asia Agenda*, 1999.

11. For example, Murray Sherwin, Deputy Governor of the Reserve Bank of New Zealand, 1999.

12. For example, Olivier Loisel and Philippe Martin, *Coordination, Cooperation, Contagion and Currency Crises*, 1999.

13. Barry Eichengreen and Ashoka Mody, *What Explains Changing Spreads on Emerging-Market Debt: Fundamentals or Market Sentiment?*, 1998.

14. Pierre-Richard Agénor and Joshua Aizenman, 'Contagion and Volatility with Imperfect Credit Markets', *IMF Staff Papers* 45 (1998), pp. 207–35.

15. Agénor and Aizenman, *Volatility and Welfare Costs*.

rates is introduced into the equation, these losses were magnified. Any existing distortions were also magnified by large inflows of capital.

Putting forward the orthodox economic view, Eichengreen argues that changes in technology will work to increase international capital mobility, limiting the capacity of governments to contain market pressures at an acceptable political cost.[16] He accepts, among other things, that there will be speculative attacks against currencies and major capital inflows and sudden reversals which are not grounded in economic fundamentals. Although this may be a matter for regret, his technological and economic determinism leads him to the conclusion that this is an inevitable trade-off in order to gain the presumed benefits of international investment.

There are different components of capital mobility. For example, foreign direct investment,[17] in general, has little or no destabilizing effect.[18] What appear to have major destabilizing effects are short-term bank lending and foreign-exchange OTC instruments.[19] Not all aspects of these highly complex financial features can be dealt with here. I will continue to focus on OTC derivatives because of their proven involvement with destabilization and their deep implication in the moral hazard of volatility itself.

Ethical Considerations

My main focus of analysis will be risk. I have already drawn attention to a number of risk features inherent in derivative trading. These include the difficulty, indeed the near impossibility, market participants have in gauging either their own true risk exposure or the exposure of other participants. Derivatives have quantifiable benefits but unquantifiable risks. In part this is due to lack of transparency and complexity, together with the dynamic nature of the risks which can spill over into many markets. This is compounded by the market structure and the moral hazard of volatility, whereby the financial sector can generate more business and make bigger profits if assets have a volatile price.

The *effects* are not, however, confined to market participants. The non-financial sector of business bears increased costs in having to buy protection against volatility and must divert resources to managing risks –

16. Barry Eichengreen, *International Monetary Arrangements for the 21ˢᵗ Century*, 1994.

17. Usually defined as foreign acquisition of shares in domestic firms when the shares acquired exceed a certain fraction of ownership, usually 10–20%.

18. Aghion *et al.*, *Capital Markets*.

19. Estimates usually suggest that around 80% of foreign exchange transactions are round trips of seven days or less. A 'round trip' is the practice of buying and then selling the same investment on the futures market, or vice versa. Many round trips are completed within a day.

resources which are not then available for their core business. I will be expanding that point shortly. Whole economies can be destabilized by speculative cross-border capital flows, often in the form of derivatives, together with speculative attacks on currencies not driven by market fundamentals. The analysis in the following sections will have three strands: risk measurement, risk distribution and risk evaluation. I will be rejecting as inadequate the assumption of the financial sector that risk is purely a technical, value-free matter. I also reject the assumption that risk is a professional issue alone. Rather, it is a public issue.

Risk Measurement

Risk is central to financial markets. It can be the nature of the contract, as for example with interest-rate risk if it is a debt claim. Or it might be because the ability of the counterparty to perform their contractual obligation becomes impaired. The relationship between the risks taken and the expected return is defined by the risk–reward trade-off, and calculated by risk–benefit analysis. Any discussion of risk must address the problems of measurement which have tended to be treated in abstract, absolute terms. In the non-technical literature, especially at the time of LTCM's collapse, this shows itself in the impression that there was no systemic risk prior to the introduction of derivatives. Even a cursory glance at history shows that this was not the case. The systemic risk exposure of derivatives must be evaluated relative to the risk exposure of the alternative financial structure they replace. On the other hand, the technical literature, with its assumption of value-free analysis, also ends in abstract absolutes.

Risk–benefit analysis is presented as factual, objective, scientific. Yet it is not, and cannot be, value-free because it is values which determine what will count as harms and benefits, and how much such harms and benefits will count. Furthermore, different people can (within limits) appraise identical risk differently because appraisal will depend crucially on the structure of beliefs, anticipations and expectations regarding the case in hand.[20] Far from being objective, the figures about probabilities that are put into the calculation reflect the appraiser's level of confidence that the events are likely to occur.

Measurement contains normative elements. These include the judgment that a possible outcome is adverse and hence its possibility is identified as a risk; how conservatively to estimate possibilities; how to frame such risks, that is, whether in terms of probability of favourable or adverse outcomes; and what comparisons and alternatives to represent in

20. Kriston Shrader-Frechette, *Risk Analysis and Scientific Method*, 1985.

characterizing the nature and magnitude of the risk(s). There is a tendency to prefer variables which can be quantified and ignore those which cannot. Quantifiable variables are not necessarily the most significant and to concentrate on them is to beg the question as to what impacts ought to be evaluated. The IMF and BIS, among many others, have called for ever greater reliance on financial institutions' own in-house risk models[21] as a method for risk management by major market participants. These models are seen as a significant pillar in moves to ensure orderly markets. However, such an approach leaves some of the deeper issues unexplored.

Risk measurement has become ever more technical, with the development of models based on Value-at-Risk (VaR).[22] These models give a spurious impression of exactness with their use of mind-numbing algorithms (an algorithm is a step-by-step problem-solving procedure with a precise set of rules). Yet even with sophisticated VaR models, it has proved difficult to predict levels of risk. These models rest on multiple predictions of probability theory. The positive benefits of the use of probability are enormous. For example, life, health and fire insurance would be impossible without it. Many bridge designs, along with a myriad other engineering feats, would never have been evolved. Yet the reliance on probability is fraught with danger. By definition, it builds on past events and the amazing stability of key events over many years. Yet these stable relationships can dissolve.

For example, for decades the world price of oil was regulated by western oil companies. No one imagined that OPEC would dominate the world energy scene and destroy the price assumptions. Similarly, the yield relationship between equity and bonds in the USA remained stable for over 80 years, until the early 1970s when their traditional relationship reversed and bonds were revealed as risk investments. No one predicted this would happen because, although predictable, it was unimaginable. If human beings cannot imagine it, how is a computer program to do so? No one's risk model included the serious consideration of a major national state defaulting on its loans. Yet Russia did. Or, to reverse the predictable/unimaginable argument, a major Japanese earthquake is imaginable. It remains unpredictable. The effects of the Kobe earthquake on the Nikkei Index destroyed Leeson's market positions.

Broad diversification is often used to justify large exposure in untested areas. However, diversification is not a guarantee against loss, only

---

21. For example, Basel Committee, *A New Capital Adequacy Framework*, 1999.

22. VaR summarizes the expected maximum loss over a target time horizon within a given confidence interval. The time horizon will normally correspond to the longest period needed for an orderly portfolio liquidation. VaR relies on the volatilities of assets and the correlation between them; in effect, the uncertain relationships between many uncertainties. VaR is calculated assuming 'normal' market conditions. It is an educated estimate of market risk.

against losing everything at once. Risk models tend to confuse probability with timing. They assume that an event with low probability is therefore not imminent. Furthermore, chaos theory alerts us to the fact that even very small deviations from multi-levelled probability calculations can have far-reaching consequences. In addition, the assumption that all risk probabilities can be determined accurately is false. There are inaccuracies caused by modelling and measurement errors or assumptions. There are events which simply are not amenable to analytic techniques, such as calculating the probability of human error or illegal activity such as Leeson's. When these features are added together, it can be seen that while useful, VaR models remain strictly limited, an educated guess.

The use of VaR models is meant to protect capital. However, the more these models are used, the greater the turbulence introduced into the market. This is because the models are deeply affected by volatility. Less volatile markets give a lower VaR, implying that for the same apparent level of risk, the financial institution can acquire more assets. However, if volatility increases, VaR rises by at least a proportional amount. Following the model, the institution must sell some of the assets, causing markets to fall further and volatility to rise. This leads to yet more selling. This is what happened to markets in the crisis of 1998. Regulators demand that price information be fed into VaR models on a daily basis. However, this can mean that shocks are amplified, because institutions know immediately how much their positions have been affected. Thus derivatives can cause a vicious circle. Because of their complexity, it is hard to do anything except rely on VaR models. Yet these models can increase the volatility which makes the derivatives so complex in the first place. Models which are meant to protect capital can cause a firm to dump assets precisely when the markets are least liquid, thereby eroding capital.

Risk measurement may also give an illusory impression of control. Yet derivatives do not eliminate risk; at best they are assumed by those most willing to bear them. There are subtle ways in which attempted control, by creating a false sense of security, compromises coping ability. The classic example is the *Titanic*. The new ability to control most kinds of leaks led to the under-stocking of lifeboats, the abandonment of safety drills and disregard of reasonable caution in navigation. LTCM, by their reliance on mathematical models, showed the same sort of phenomenon. They assumed that their models gave them control over their risk exposures, leading them to assume far riskier positions than they otherwise would, and to neglect adequate consideration of their high-leverage position. They were therefore vulnerable to the unexpected. As Ravetz, a philosopher of science, reminds us:

> Risks are conceptually uncontrollable; one can never know whether one
> is doing *enough* to prevent a hazard from occurring. Even after a hazard

has occurred, one is still left with the question of how much more action would have been necessary to have prevented it, and whether such action would have been within the bounds of 'reasonable' behaviour.[23]

Measurement of risk in the financial sector, therefore, is ethically far from being unproblematic. Measurement itself contains largely unexamined normative judgments. VaR models can themselves feed into destabilizing volatility and can erode capital. They can also, paradoxically, lead to riskier behaviour.

Yet hidden beneath these risk models is a more subtle, but powerful, feature. Simmel's analysis of the 'quantitive' orientation with its emphasis on calculation[24] resulting from the way in which reality is reduced to a monetary formulation, is highly suggestive here. The hegemony of computational methods of risk analysis leads increasingly to a computational morality. When allied to the loss of reciprocity in the exchange relationship,[25] this furthers the bias whereby it becomes acceptable to believe that people not only can, but ought to, use and exploit each other as they use and exploit any other natural object. Money, by becoming the measure of all activity, and by becoming an end rather than a means,[26] moves to the centre of our ethical deliberations. It is money which is to be preserved, enhanced, nurtured and striven for. Increasingly, there is no other goal which is so all encompassing, so all consuming. It becomes an idol. It therefore becomes increasingly difficult to factor in other goals and values which might be at risk. This in turn strengthens the bias towards measuring only quantifiable variables, and measuring them in monetary terms. We are back once more to the beginning of the circle.

Although at one level the models used by the finance sector are immensely sophisticated, their normative components have been overlooked. Also overlooked has been the way in which they reinforce a computational morality which values only what can be measured in monetary terms. Their sophistication masks large areas of uncertainty which are not sufficiently allowed for when calculating the actual risk present in the system. The models used also introduce more uncertainty in the market by increasing price volatility. By encouraging a false sense of security they can undermine more prudential attitudes. Finally, risk models only measure risk in monetary forms. Perhaps one might argue that it is precisely money which is at risk, and so it is right that that is what

---

23. Jerome R. Ravetz, 'Public Perceptions of Acceptable Risks as Evidence of their Cognitive, Technical and Social Structure', in Meinolf Dierkes, Sam Edwards and Rob Coppock (eds.), *Technological Risk: Its Perception and Handling in the European Community*, 1980, pp. 45–54 (47), emphasis in original.

24. Simmel, *The Philosophy of Money*, pp. 278–79.

25. Simmel, p. 457.

26. Simmel, p. 431.

is measured. However, a great deal more than just money is at risk. Furthermore, it is only risk to the financial institution using the model which is measured. Again, a great deal more than just financial institutions are at risk and this is an inadequate definition of the risk-bearers.

Risk Distribution

A second major concern with risk–benefit analysis is that its utilitarian basis only considers the aggregate risks and benefits, without considering the justice of their distribution, that is, who will gain the benefits and who will bear the risks. In Chapter 2 I argued that one of the major limitations to the usual ethical claims for the free market is that 'justice' is confined to those who are already participants in the market, and takes no account of distributive justice. In this instance, the 'market' in question is even more strictly confined to those who participate in the financial markets. Some of the risks of derivatives are borne by market participants (loss of profit on a contract), but by no means all of them, nor necessarily the most long-lasting. Risks resulting from an activity may be wholly or largely borne by some people/groups, while the benefits are shared equally, or enjoyed entirely, by persons other than those at risk. I will be discussing an example below. When those bearing the risk are antecedently worse off then those who benefit, the position is even more ethically questionable. Risk is measured in order to safeguard market participants. The question is: 'is that enough?'

Free-market proponents see the market as having a superior capacity to secure an optimal allocation of goods and services. They dismiss moral notions of distributive justice as hopelessly subjective, stressing the unrivalled structure of productivity incentives implicit in private property institutions. Ross, however, argues that justice does not refer to the production of the greatest sum of good, but to the right distribution of good.[27] There is a criticism of the utilitarian bias in economic thinking similar to the criticism made of Pareto optimality. The present state of affairs sanctions the use of derivatives and the distribution of risk/benefit because of the enormous wealth which *may* be created. It is predicated on the assumption of three things. Firstly, an increase of (monetary) wealth is always to be preferred and the greatest increase in (monetary) wealth is to be preferred most. Secondly, the distribution of risk is either morally neutral or outweighed by the creation of monetary wealth. Thirdly, externalities are of no concern to the market.

In general, worries within the finance sector about derivatives seem to centre almost exclusively around the notion that defects may lead to

27. W. David Ross, *Foundation of Ethics*, 1939, p. 319.

market conditions which would inhibit wealth creation or cause wealth loss. This is the tone of the BIS documents on Capital Adequacy and on banks' relationships with HLIs. It is also a refrain running through the speeches of Alan Greenspan and other central bankers. Wealth creation or loss is the only criterion. While it is true that this is an important criterion, it is not true that it should therefore be the only one. Such a position is inadequate.

Ethical issues, however, arise in the potential conflict of individual rights and public risks, between my 'right' to invest my money how I will so as to create wealth, and society's interest in maintaining stable economies and protecting the poor. Analysing the finance sector in the way this chapter has done, especially as regards the moral hazard of volatility, enables us to discern an instance of where a particular good (the sector's increased profitability, an individual institution's greater market share) militates against the common good. It is not just the direct participants in the markets who are affected – indeed, as LTCM and the Asian crises demonstrate, they may well be the ones who are least affected. What happens in the markets can have sudden, unpredictable and unavoidable consequences for a great many others.

A vivid illustration was provided by the financial crisis in Asia in 1997/98. Michel Camdessus, then Director of the IMF, is credited with describing this as the first financial crisis of the twenty-first century. What he was doing was acknowledging that the Asian crisis was different from earlier crises. Previously the IMF had assumed that at the core of any crisis were failures in macro-policy, primarily monetary and fiscal policies. What Asia presented was essentially a crisis of the *private* sector. Large-scale public funding was raised for rescue packages which were used mostly to repay private foreign investors, so facilitating their escape from investments which had turned sour following the speculative currency attacks of other private investors. In effect, investors avoided sharing in the downside risks associated with their investment choices. With LTCM it was again private investors who were bailed out.

Christian reflection, on the other hand, would put greater emphasis on considerations arising from the wider common good and solidarity. It cannot ignore what happens to the poor when markets go into turmoil. A speculative attack on a currency can halve the value of a farmer's crop before he harvests it, or drive an exporter out of business. A lifetime's savings can be wiped out. A rise in interest rates can fatally inflate the cost of holding stocks for a shop-keeper. Of course, effects are not limited to just individual lives. Whole economies can go into decline, with the poorest sections often the worst affected, especially in any subsequent fiscal-restructuring regime, which usually involves cutting social welfare, education and health programmes. Perhaps commodity prices, on which export earnings may depend, fall because the economies of major consuming countries go through a recession. Or the banks have suddenly decided that, due to increased risk exposures elsewhere, they will not lend a country any more. Or simply contagion overwhelms them. As Mervyn King, then Deputy Governor of the Bank of England observed, speaking of recent crises:

> These crises have created millions of victims, whose circumstances and aspirations were totally unrelated to financial markets. In Korea unemployment tripled, in Indonesia several years of economic growth were wiped out leading to political instability and similar results have been visible in other parts of Asia as well as Latin America.[28]

Any reflection on risk distribution would be trivial if it shirked the consideration of the distribution of power in relation to the pattern of risk incurred. History seems to suggest that we are less unhappy about technological hazards transposed to Third World countries than about having them sited in our own country. It is significant that the distribution of derivative risk has been weighted towards those same countries (the 'emerging markets'). Would the financial markets view derivative risk differently if it had been, say, US or UK citizens who were among the 'millions of victims'? Given the geographic spread of the risk-bearers, it must at least be asked if the unconcern of the markets is at all related to the fact that the West has the economic and political power to export its financial risk elsewhere, particularly as it was western institutions which were not only the ones bailed out, but also the ones which directly benefited from the financial distress. It was a condition of IMF aid in the Asian crisis that the recipient countries committed themselves to selling off their indebted companies to US corporations and to opening up their financial markets to US banks.

The virtue of solidarity discussed in Chapter 4 requires us to have the same concern about these risk-bearers as if they were citizens of our own country. Their condition cannot be viewed with equanimity or with distancing mechanisms such as references to 'the discipline of the markets'. Consent and compensation are normally associated with the moral acceptance of risk. Where there is no consent and no compensation, it is highly questionable that it is moral to impose risk. Without consent or compensation these 'millions of victims' have had to bear the costs of mainly western investors' gambling. Ignoring the distributional effects of our actions simply allows the most powerful and articulate groups affected by the action to impose or avoid the outcome which suits them most. This phenomenon usually goes under the heading of exploitation.

At the corporate level, businesses, seeing their equity plummet when stock markets collapse, are unable to raise new funds. However, the

28. Mervyn King, speech at the Federal Reserve Bank, 9 September 1999.

corporate costs of risk and volatility are not confined to times of crisis. Short-term program-trading, such as portfolio insurance[29] and index arbitrage, may create volatility and uncertainty in markets originally designed as a means by which corporations could raise capital for the pursuit of long-term goals. The need to protect itself against this volatility and uncertainty involves the corporation in considerable outlays. The companies do not have the option of being able to take avoiding action. All action to resolve risk creates risk and in financial markets, inaction is also the choice of a particular risk profile. To invest reserves or leave them as cash are both risk choices. To use option strategies in foreign exchange creates many risks; not to do so creates others. Here we have an example of the ambiguous relationships between the finance sector and its customers mentioned in Chapter 7.

The understanding of the common good I have been presenting identifies here a conflict with particular goods. I referred earlier to the considerable resources which a non-financial end-user must devote to the monitoring of its derivative position. These resources include managerial time and energy, IT resources and so on. Without their use, the end-user will be unable to understand, monitor and control the effects of opacity and volatility on its core business. These resources are not then available for what was described in Chapter 4 as the business's common good, that is, the production of useful goods and services efficiently and sustainably. Thus, there are three clear conflicts of particular goods between non-financial corporations and financial intermediaries. The first, as discussed in Chapter 8, is the difference of perspective between the holders of stock for hedging purposes and those holding stock for long-term investment. The second is generated by the finance sector's dependence upon volatility, a feature against which the non-financial sector must guard itself. The third arises from the diversion of resources by non-financial end-users to cope with ever more sophisticated instruments which increase the particular good of profits and market share of the financial intermediary.

Some of the costs to the business may be almost intangible. Chapter 7 referred to the change in ethos in the Treasurer's role, with Treasury being increasingly seen as a profit-centre rather than a cost-centre. There are also the intangible changes in general corporate ethos as financial risk absorbs increasing amounts of managerial attention. A high-risk ethos can become part of the organization system which eventually permeates all areas. The willingness to take risks is part of a healthy entrepreneurship, but only when it is understood, managed and an integral part of the business's core activity. The risks of highly complex derivatives frequently

---

29. A form of hedging that uses Stock Index Futures contracts and index options to limit the downside risk of holding a diversified portfolio of common stocks.

do not pass that test in a non-financial corporation and can destabilize its underlying corporate ethos and function.

Ethical distribution of risk is normally associated with free and informed consent. It might be argued that the governments of crisis countries had given consent on behalf of their citizens by allowing their financial markets to become more and more integrated in the global economy. When considering this, we need to keep in mind the observation that when two parties are in very unequal positions, mutual consent does not guarantee fairness. Given the asymmetry of economic and political power, it is questionable whether, even with perfect information on the risks involved, such countries could be said to have freely chosen to assume the risks. When one considers the IMF imposed conditions for aid, it would be even harder to suggest that consent to still greater liberalization was given 'freely'.

As for 'informed' consent, if market practitioners cannot be sure of the extent of the risk, how are others to know? These arguments apply *mutatis mutandis* to non-financial firms faced with increased uncertainty originating in the finance sector – uncertainty which generates so much of the finance sector's profits. Again it is questionable whether they give free, informed consent to the risks they run. Judging by the fines imposed on Bankers Trust over the derivative losses sustained by Procter and Gamble, there would appear to be, at least in some cases, legal and regulatory questions about this as well as ethical ones.

The risks and volatility associated with the widespread use of complex derivatives are not merely technical issues. Neither can their destabilizing possibilities be considered as purely an intra-market affair. Uncertainty and volatility increasingly affect us all. The sector which traditionally enabled long-term planning of income and expenditure has now become the source of increasing uncertainty and instability. The moral hazard of volatility leading to greater risk-taking increases still further the risk burden borne by others. Whereas some can find ways to cushion or protect themselves, others cannot. When skill, effort, determination, initiative and hard work can be vitiated so quickly, then faith and confidence in social and political systems inevitably fades, as does respect for ethical values. Thus the contribution of derivatives to systemic risk, dependency-producing turbulence, economic and political destabilization and the redirection of resources away from real production raises ethical issues which affect the wider society. It is this which justifies the discussion of risk in a wider forum than just the financial community, a contention which I will examine in the next section.

Risk Evaluation

In determining whether some risks are acceptable there is a need to go beyond the generally recognized duty of non-maleficence. The standard of due care is met when the goals the agent pursues are significant enough to justify the risks imposed on others. But as well as asking: 'For what ends?' it is also necessary to ask: 'Acceptable to whom?' and 'How is acceptability to be arrived at?' Is it to be determined by expert opinion alone, or is there a role for lay opinion?

One preliminary point needs to be dealt with before turning to such questions, and that is: are we, with derivative risk, dealing with a risk to a private good or a public good? The discussion on risk distribution has shown that it is a portion of the 'public' which bears an involuntary, uncompensated risk. The IMF,[30] among others, sees currency stability as *public* goods. Yet the risk models used by financial institutions assume that it is a private good which is at risk. To the contrary, exchange rates between major currencies have the character of public goods for the world economy. Wide swings in the dollar–euro and dollar–yen exchange rates, for example, have a destabilizing impact on countries who have large export markets to Europe, Japan and the United States. This could be seen in 1997 when the appreciation of the US dollar contributed to the collapse of those Asian currencies which maintained a formal or informal peg to it. Or again, in 2005 the United States exerted considerable pressure on China to revalue its currency because of trade imbalances between them.

An implication of Simmel's analysis of the fiduciary nature of money has relevance here when considering the destabilization of currencies. Simmel rightly maintains that trust is essential for the effective functioning of money within any society. If that trust in money is damaged or undermined, money may continue to function as a means of exchange and a store of value. The risk is that we will damage and undermine all the other forms of trust in authority and in the social institutions and relations which are essential to bind a society together. Christian analysis, because it rejects the atomistic individualism of the neoclassical model, cannot be indifferent to such risks to social cohesion. This strengthens still further the case for exchange rates to be seen as a public good as well as the case for questioning the morality of speculative currency attacks.

The next issue is what role to assign to expert opinion. One of the noticeable features of the finance sector is its possession of expert and exclusive knowledge. This may well contribute to the sector being seen by many as 'ethic resistant'. This is because the combination of knowledge

30. Michel Camdessus, in a speech opening the IMF Research Conference 'Key Issues in Reform', 28 May 1999.

which is both expert and exclusive can lead to the apparent exclusion of others in any discussion about the activities upon which that knowledge bears. This in turn can give the appearance of any justification of that activity being little more than the creation of an alibi through the sector's power and isolation from discourse in the public forum. In discussing the role of expert opinion we need, however, to draw a very clear distinction between evaluations of risk magnitude and evaluation of risk acceptability before considering whether expert or lay opinion is the better.

Clearly experts have a greater knowledge and understanding of particular risk probabilities and magnitudes. Some might argue, therefore, that as their knowledge is more reliable, it is experts who are most able to make rational decisions about risk acceptability. This position reflects the *de facto* situation with derivative risk, but it has major problems. The first problem is reflected in the discussion above on risk measurement. Measurement of derivative risk is neither exact nor objective. This weakens the claim of expert knowledge, although obviously it does not eliminate it. The second problem is that it is difficult to accept the disinterestedness of those judging the acceptability of a risk when they are the ones who receive the benefits but are not the ones who bear the greatest risk. The presence of expert and exclusive knowledge disenfranchises the very persons likely to be risk victims.

The third problem is that, although it is true that society in general has less accurate knowledge of risk probabilities, that is beside the point. Even if risk estimation were objective, the determination of whether a risk is acceptable is not. It is determined by our perceptions and constructs, sensitive to specific assumptions about measuring preferences, determining social choices and quantifying risks, costs and benefits.[31] Decisions about risk acceptability are less a function of knowledge of risk probabilities than a function of the value attached to avoiding potentially catastrophic consequences and to obtaining benefits from taking some risk.[32]

An interesting and vital point emerges from Schrader-Frechette's researches into risk, risk perception and risk acceptability. She was investigating environmental risks, but her observations have a wider applicability. A key feature of lay, as opposed to expert, opinions on risk acceptability was that it hinged, not on the level of *probabilities*, but on things such as an inequitable (as opposed to equitable) distributed risk and on the severity of consequences in the unlikely event that an accident were to occur. Thus lay opinion was based on different *values* than the opinion of experts. With the finance sector's evaluation of derivative risk, the measurement of probabilities is uncertain, the distribution of risk is

31. Mary Douglas and Aaron Wildavsky, *Risk and Culture*, 1982.
32. Kriston Shrader-Frechette, *Risk and Rationality*, 1991.

disregarded and the severity of consequences is unknowable beforehand. Experience after the event, however, shows that consequences can be very severe indeed. It would not be surprising, therefore, if lay opinion on the acceptability of derivative risk differed from that of the expert financial community.

This is only important if lay opinion has a legitimate claim to have its voice heard. For risk distribution to be ethical there has to be consent in some form from those who bear the risk. This implies that the risk-bearers have, in some way, been involved in the debate on its acceptability. This is one clear reason for the legitimacy of the claim of lay opinion to be heard. Here we touch again on an issued raised in Chapter 4, that is, how is the *content* of the common good to be arrived at? Subsidiarity requires that the content cannot be imposed top-down, whether that top-down is from government or from a technocratic elite. Until now the debate on risk has largely been within the financial community itself, either market participants or regulators. It has been viewed as a professional issue, that is, those in the sector look to their peers for determination of what is and what is not acceptable risk. The argument here, however, is that it is not a professional issue. It is a public one due to the risk to a public good, its scale and its distribution. There are useful analogies which can be drawn from other areas of risk.

Until about the early 1970s, the traditional engineering approach to risk was the one just described. Engineers would look to their peers and would see risk evaluation as a professional issue. However, as public awareness of health and safety decisions changed, the willingness to delegate the decision-making authority over risk decisions began to erode. Now, public participation in risk decisions, and particularly in the value judgments that determine the acceptability or non-acceptability of risk in a particular context, is recognized as essential. Safe engineering is now a public issue.

An even closer analogy to derivatives can be drawn from biotechnology. It too has quantifiable benefits with, its critics assert, unquantifiable risks. The change in status of, for example, genetically modified organisms from being a professional issue to being a public one has been exceptionally rapid. In line with Schrader-Frechette's analysis, much of the lay concern hinges around the severity of consequences, as well as the distribution of risk/benefits in connection with such features as, for example, seeds with 'terminator technology' and the consequences to future generations and to bio-diversity. All these are seen by many as public issues, and calls from the scientific community that they be the ones to decide whether the risks are acceptable are unlikely to be heard. The time for such scientific paternalism has now passed.

Such paternalism has its parallel in the expert and exclusive knowledge of the finance sector, and it is as inappropriate there as it was in, for example, the nuclear, medical and biotechnology sectors. However, changing derivative risk from being a professional issue to being a public issue faces formidable difficulties. Among these difficulties must be included the complexity of the issue and its highly technical features. This will make it very hard indeed for ethicists to bring the issue to the public forum because there are at present comparatively few ethicists with a detailed knowledge of finance. Here a further comparison with genetics may be appropriate. Just as ethicists had to learn the language and concepts of biotechnology and genetics in order to engage meaningfully with, for example, gene therapy, so ethicists will need to enter the language and concepts of the finance sector.

Earlier discussion has pointed to some of the other formidable difficulties. How are the risks to be quantified so that they can be evaluated truthfully? Is it even possible to quantify them? How are we to decide whether or not free and informed consent to the risks exists? How, if the risks are deemed acceptable, can they be equitably distributed? The present decisions on risk are expressed in monetary terms. An appeal to a wider set of values must face the fact that there are some things on which one cannot put a monetary value, for example, justice, participation in the decision-making process, stability and other social values. Yet if there is to be a genuine debate on risk acceptability we must find a way of incorporating these features into our analysis. There is real and symbolic value which attaches to how we make decisions. Derivative risk is an area where the principles of subsidiarity and solidarity can make a significant contribution to that 'how'.

Summary and Conclusions

At the heart of this discussion is the rootlessness of money. It was a significant contribution to the condition of Genoa which I described at the very beginning: that is, a City Republic where individuals were enormously wealthy, but the state was, comparatively speaking, impoverished. A contemporary parallel can be drawn through the structure of international investment. The aspect of rootlessness has to be evaluated by weighing up the benefits of capital mobility, which are considerable – much inward investment has brought many benefits. However, not all capital flows are of this kind, nor even with productive investment is there necessarily a long-term commitment. Great pressure is exerted on governments to improve corporations' profitability, otherwise capital will be withdrawn. This is most typically seen in the de-regulation I have referred to, but also by the manipulation of tax laws which ensure that little, or even no, tax is paid. The evasion of tax means that any concept, however minimal, of the social obligation of ownership is also evaded. The tackling of tax avoidance and evasion is one of the central aspects of morality in finance, yet governments are afraid that capital will flee to areas of lighter tax enforcement, so nothing major is undertaken. Part of the evaluation of this rootlessness is an assessment of the balance of reward and loss associated with risk.

Risk assessment is generally made up of three steps: risk identification, risk estimation and risk evaluation, that is determining whether a given risk is acceptable or ought to be acceptable by society. I have argued that the first phase has been, at best, partial. While risk arising from lack of transparency, market structure and leverage are receiving increasing prominence in the financial community, the risk arising from the moral hazard of volatility has been overlooked. Risk estimation has been mis-presented as being objective. Its presentation has continued the fact/value dichotomy discussed in Chapters 2 and 3. This mis-presentation has allowed the values which are present to operate unexamined. I have also argued that the VaR models used to estimate risks have, in fact, added to the risk by increasing volatility and undermining more prudential attitudes.

Following a discussion of the inequitable distribution of risk, with the risk-bearers being largely non-financial firms and the 'millions of victims' in crisis countries, the final section focused on risk evaluation. I argued that derivative risk should no longer be seen as a professional issue but as a public one. The possession by the finance sector of expert and exclusive knowledge has so far not facilitated debate in the public forum, and few ethicists are yet equipped to deal with the technical complexities of the issues. Finally, I argued that both subsidiarity and solidarity are required if the evaluation of these risks is truly to incorporate the common good.

I have not tried to examine all ethical questions arising from derivatives, but have focused on the scale of the risks, the speed at which they can cause systemic crisis, the way in which they not only transfer risks between agents but also increase the total risk within the system and the way risk is distributed. Taken together, these can seriously undermine the common-good function of the financial sector. There are also the conflicts they set up between particular goods both in terms of resources diverted away from production and in the differing consequences of volatility for the non-financial and finance sectors, with the latter exhibiting moral hazard following the fact that so much of the sector's profits depend upon continuing volatility.

The multi-layered complexity of derivatives is a significant contribution to their risk. The long roll-call of large firms and investment funds which have incurred substantial losses using derivatives suggests that many users either do not understand or do not appreciate the risks involved.[33] Insofar

33. For example, Orange County, California: $1.5 billion; Showa Shell Sekiyu: $1.5 billion; Metallgesellschaft: $1.2 billion; China Aviation Oil: $550 million; Procter & Gamble: $157 million; Glaxo: £110 million.

as many of these users were financially sophisticated, it may also suggest that some instruments are intrinsically dangerous. There is a need to explore much further the twofold question arising from this. The first part concerns the finance sector. What are the ethical constraints on the development and marketing of ever more sophisticated instruments? Are these intrinsically valuable or so complex that no client can use them and adequately monitor the new exposures involved? Do they serve the client or do they arise from the moral hazard of needing to maintain volatility so as to maintain profits? The second part concerns non-financial end-users. Contrary to popular mythology, managers are not paid to take risks. They are paid to know which risks are worth taking. When considering the purchase of such instruments, will the result be a more focused core operation or is the firm seeking to lay off the proper risks which managers should take? What are the tangible and intangible resources taken up by their use? Arriving at answers to these questions will go some considerable way towards ameliorating the negative aspects of derivatives.

The key ethical claims of the free market are justice, efficiency and freedom. Using the concept of the common good, I have identified ways in which the functioning of derivatives markets works against those claims. The way in which risks are distributed across society, including geographical distribution, with the non-financial spheres bearing a disproportionate burden, is incompatible with a Christian understanding of justice. Efficiency is undermined by the diversion of resources and corporate focus within non-financial businesses. Efficiency is also undermined by the resources needed to monitor risk within financial institutions and the erosion of capital caused by model-induced volatility. Chapters 2 and 7 identified ways in which the finance sector constrains democratic process and choices. The political and social consequences of capital flight and price volatility can be added to that analysis.

It is neither necessary nor possible to ban all derivatives. Doing so would not abolish risk or destabilization and would deprive the market of the positive features they have. What I have argued in relation to risk evaluation is that risk should cease to be seen as a professional issue and become instead a public issue. To achieve that, ethicists will need to engage in the task of entering the language and concepts of the finance sector, as was done with genetics in order to present the issues to a wider public (this book is a contribution to that task). This may seem a very modest proposal in the face of the scale of risk which derivatives pose, perhaps even disappointing. Some Christians will want a denunciatory blast against 'structures of sin' and demand 'a prophetic call'. However, what I am arguing here is that Christians have often moved too quickly from the description of human and institutional failure to solutions in the categories of biblical revelation or Christian theology. What is required is a *partnership* between all those involved. The public debate has not yet reached the stage where choices can be resolved – at least not if one wishes to apply the principle of subsidiarity in arriving at the content of the common good. In this chapter I have sought to make it possible for us to get a clearer view of the state of affairs which troubles us. At this stage, one of the principal tasks of ethics is to identify the questions and bring them to public attention. It is to struggle to disentangle technical and economic complexity, and assert that narrowly conceived economic criteria alone are inadequate as rules for evaluation.

Another important task for ethics arising from the analysis here is to examine questions concerning the paradoxical nature of our relationship to risk. One the one hand, derivatives help promote a high-risk ethos. On the other hand, their growth points to a deep desire to control and, if possible, eliminate risks. Yet all investments and all loans are risky, because they are based on educated guesses about the future, rather than certain knowledge of what will happen. The search for a risk-free life is a nonsense doomed to failure. Prudence does not mean the avoidance of all risk. An ethics of risk management is required which incorporates both prudence and courage without recklessness.

Chapter 10

REGULATION AND THE PROBLEM OF INTEGRITY

While the character of the individual is crucial, the way markets operate as a whole is also ethically important. Operations at a systemic level, that is, risk, financial instability and the possibility that finance's *instrumental* function has been eroded, have now been discussed. That discussion used the framework of the common good. This chapter will use personalist ethics as a way of focusing on the actions of the individual institution and individual agent. This will be through an exploration of how personalist ethics can contribute to the achievement of regulatory objectives for the sector.

Discussion of regulation is often grounded in an analysis of how regulation impacts on economic efficiency.[1] Depending on the writer's particular viewpoint, there will be a reflection on how regulation does, or does not, increase moral hazard; on whether government intervention in general is, or is not, welcomed; on whether certain well-known scandals demonstrate the need for external regulation or demonstrate the need for a greater market discipline[2] which is being hampered by regulation. These are undoubtedly important issues. However, concentration on these has tended to leave a range of other equally important aspects relatively neglected. These include such issues as rules versus the moral character of the agent; the making of judgments in situations of moral complexity; corporate responsibility versus individual responsibility and problems arising from the *combination* of new forms of organization, evolving social systems and new technologies, which have transformed the context and scale of human action.

---

1. For example, Franklin R. Edwards, *The New Finance, Regulation and Financial Stability*, 1996.
2. Market discipline: the market, through the price mechanism and the choice of counterparty, will reward 'good' behaviour and punish 'bad' behaviour.

The Purpose of Regulation

Regulation (the establishment of specific rules of behaviour), monitoring (observing whether the rules are obeyed) and supervision (the more general oversight of a firm's behaviour, for example, external supervision to reinforce internal controls) in the finance sector, while concerned with the control of monopolistic power, are more about ensuring systemic stability and consumer protection. Recognizing that consumers of financial services are a heterogeneous group, regulation differentiates between the retail market and the wholesale market. The systemic dimension enters because, as I showed in Chapter 7, the social costs of financial problems, especially in the form of contagion effects, can easily exceed the private costs of institutional failure. This is particularly true of banks.

High social costs of private failure are not limited to the finance sector of course. The extra, unacknowledged, factor at work in the sector is the fiduciary nature of money itself and the ways in which the central political power is implicated in its use and preservation. This introduces an additional level of social concern and helps to explain the sometimes irrational public demand for high levels of regulatory knowledge and intervention. For example, comments in the press following the failure of Barings' Bank implied that the Bank of England (which carried out the regulatory function then) should have known more about Barings' business than its own management did. Allied to this is the underlying fear that the commodity (money) which has become the central value and organizing principle of so much of life is under threat.

Regulation does not, however, aim at total stability. Alan Greenspan (Chairman of the Board of Governors of the US Federal Reserve System) summed up the aim of regulation as 'designed to limit – not eliminate – the risk of failure'.[3] Thus, public-policy arrangements do not eradicate the incentive for clients of financial institutions to exercise due care. Regulation cannot eliminate all possibility of consumers making the wrong choices in financial contracts. Regulation of the finance sector is a huge and complex area of study. It also varies between countries. I am not foolhardy enough to think of covering the subject in any detail. What I want to look at, however, is the person who is regulated. That person, his or her suitability, is what underpins regulation in all jurisdictions.

It is most easily spotted in UK regulation because unlike, for example, the USA, all regulation is carried out by one body, the Financial Services Authority (FSA), and much of the detail hinges on the existence of the 'Approved Person'. Only such an individual is authorized to perform particular (extensively defined) controlled functions in particular firms.

3. Alan Greenspan, 'Remarks before the Independent Community Bankers of America National Convention', 11 March 2005.

That authorization can be withdrawn if the FSA considers the individual to be no longer fit and proper to perform the function to which the approval relates.[4] The FSA has three sets of key factors which it will take into account when assessing fitness and propriety. These are (a) honesty, integrity and reputation; (b) competence and capability; (c) financial soundness.[5] The purpose of these regulations is to ensure that only fit and proper persons are engaged in controlled functions in the sector. Although regulations in other jurisdictions vary somewhat in their wording and emphasis, this characterization of the suitable practitioner is one which would be sought anywhere.

In this chapter I will be looking at how personalist ethics can contribute to this concern with the individual practitioner. Before turning to the details of such a person, however, I want to discuss factors which have a particular influence on some attitudes within the finance sector. I have claimed that an analysis of how money operates enables a clearer understanding of underlying features within the finance sector. I will now use some elements from that analysis to identify some of the mechanisms which bear upon financial practitioners.

The 'Detached' Agent

In discussing the fiduciary character of money, Simmel drew attention to the social requirements needed before 'such a delicate and easily destroyed material as paper [can] become the representative of the highest money value'.[6] Now money is even more ephemeral. Often it is no more than electronic traces on computer memories, guaranteed data streams. Because of its very abstractness, its existence only as a function and symbolic reality impacts heavily on those who trade in it. There is the often heard remark, 'Money isn't real. It's just shifting noughts on a computer screen.' Or again:

> I could step forward and with just one wave of the hand buy or sell millions of pounds' worth of stuff. And it was just stuff: it wasn't bread or milk or something you could use if the world came to an end. My products were notionally called Japanese Government Bonds, or futures or options, but nobody cared what the hell they were. They were just numbers to be bought and sold. It was like trading ether.[7]

This inability to conceptualize accurately what one is trading in has profound consequences for how one trades. This abstractness, together

4. FSA, *Handbook*, Chapter 10, www.fsa.gov.uk.
5. FSA, *Handbook*, 'The Fit and Proper Test for Approved Persons (FIT2)'.
6. Simmel, *The Philosophy of Money*, p. 172.
7. Nick Leeson, with Edward Whitley, *Rogue Trader*, 1996, p. 101.

with the sheer size of many of the trades, combine together into something which the human mind cannot adequately grasp.[8] It is not surprising, therefore, that trading in money becomes disconnected from an ordinary sense of reality, and dealers end up thinking of money as 'stuff', 'ether', 'noughts on a screen'.

Accounts of the financial markets such as *Liar's Poker*[9] and *F.I.A.S.C.O.* undoubtedly sensationalize, but nevertheless do capture attitudes which can develop in those who deal not only with 'abstract' money, but also with the further abstractions of derivatives. At what one might term the 'bread and butter' end of retail banking, where the client can be seen within a more human scale, such attitudes are far weaker. However, with the growth of online banking and ATMs, the ever-expanding use of credit cards rather than individually negotiated loans, and the cost-cutting pressures to reduce the branch structure of retail banking, anonymity and impersonality are increasing here too.

The analysis of money and the modern understanding of freedom in Chapter 6 described the ways in which money enables more numerous, more diverse and yet, at the same time, more anonymous networks of relations. Money creates a certain style of life because it 'has provided us with the sole possibility of uniting people while excluding everything personal and specific'.[10] This anonymity within the exchange relationship which money engenders is further heightened in financial markets. The ethics of the finance sector used to be encapsulated in the phrase: 'My word is my bond'. It relied almost exclusively on intangibles such as reputation, personal transactions with known counterparties and the frequency of repeat business. Now, however, one of *the* defining characteristics of contemporary financial markets is precisely their impersonality. In a way which is only now beginning to spread elsewhere with e-commerce, trading in financial markets is carried out over telephone lines, screens and other forms of 'distancing' technology. Thirty years ago, people working in the City of London and Wall Street knew the names of their clients and often many of their personal details. Now a deal is done on screen or over the phone with someone, possibly on another continent, whom the dealer has never met and is never likely to meet. Again this adds to the disconnectedness from ordinary reality.

A further aspect of Simmel's analysis of money and freedom is relevant here. He describes how money enables the individual to distance herself from the group and live by her own beliefs and preferences. When associated with the strong impetus to disconnectedness brought about by the

---

8. For an account of the emotional impact of these large trades, see Frank Partnoy, *F.I.A.S.C.O.: Blood in the Water on Wall Street*, 1998.

9. Michael Lewis, *Liar's Poker: Two Cities, True Greed*, 1989.

10. Simmel, *The Philosophy of Money*, p. 345.

abstractness of money and the impersonality of financial markets, it is not surprising that disengagement is the result. This leads to the notion of freedom as the ability to act on one's own, without outside interference or subordination to outside authority. This tendency seems to be operative whenever a 'rogue' trader is identified (usually when things go spectacularly wrong, as they did with Leeson). This notion of freedom is strengthened yet further by the widespread ideals of power, dignity and efficiency as typifying the identity of a free agent. This disengaged identity, with its attendant notion of freedom, tends to generate an understanding of the individual agent as metaphysically independent of society. This characterization of the economic agent as one who is socially independent is at the heart of the free-market model. Any dependency between the individual and society is seen in causal terms (for example within social-contract theory) rather than touching our very identity. Insofar as financial markets are viewed as the nearest thing we have to a truly free market, this characterization of the agent will be further endorsed. Thus money, social ideals, the financial markets and economic models combine to give a unified image of the disengaged, socially independent agent. One consequence of this is to give authoritative weight to a view of freedom as lack of external constraint, so increasing the reluctance to accord external regulation a strong place. What it exalts is a quite unreal model of self-clarity and control.

The Cynical Agent

At the same time, however, control is eroded by another feature of the way money influences us. I have referred to the way in which money reduces both the highest and lowest values into one value form, that is, money value itself. This places all values on the same level, regardless of their inherent differences. Everything and anything can be bought or sold for money; perhaps even *everyone* can be bought and sold this way. This gives rise to what Simmel identified as cynicism and the blasé attitude. The cynic notes that those who have the money can buy the finest, most ideal and personal goods. At the same time, it is seen that even the most worthy person cannot have those goods if the necessary money is lacking.

> The nurseries of cynicism are therefore those places with huge turn-overs, exemplified in stock exchange dealings, where money is available in huge quantities and changes owners easily. The more money becomes the sole centre of interest, the more one discovers that honour and conviction, talent and virtue, beauty and salvation of the soul are exchanged against money and so the more a mocking and frivolous attitude will develop in relation to these higher values that are for sale

for the same kind of value as groceries, and that also command a 'market price'.[11]

Another consequence of the levelling of all values – although very different in its expression – is the blasé attitude caused by a loss of feeling for value differences. All appears grey and dull, not worth getting excited about. Seeing the same phenomenon of everything and everyone as being open to purchase destroys all possibilities of their enjoyment. This flat and grey quality of experience accounts for the emergence of a kind of craving for excitement, for heightened stimulation and for 'extreme impressions'.[12] Obviously not everyone is affected to the same degree, but there is a well-known phenomenon within the finance sector of thrill-seeking, the buzz of doing extraordinary deals, the adrenalin rush sought in a risky trade. What is sought, almost above all, is stimulation in whatever form comes to hand. 'The search for mere stimuli in themselves is the consequence of the increasing blasé attitude through which natural excitement increasingly disappears. This search for stimuli originates in the money economy with the fading of all specific values into a mere mediating value.'[13]

This presentation of the financial practitioner as being particularly at risk of being detached, cynical and blasé leads to an important question. How determinative are these pressures? I have mentioned on several occasions corporate culture and its strong influence. Are we dealing here with such a strong culture, such a strong influence, that no more can be said? I would argue that we are not. With its insistence on our embodiedness, personalist ethics takes the position that we are neither completely free nor completely determined. Its anthropology sees human action as falling somewhere between behaviourism and voluntarism. Behaviourism reduces all human action to forces outside the person's control. Voluntarism disregards our embodied nature and overlooks the importance of perceptions, beliefs and previous actions for explaining our current activity. Our freedom is not unlimited. Because we are finite, embodied creatures, biological, social and historical forces shape and constrain us in profound ways. On the other hand, neither are we completely determined. Our action is not solely the product of forces external to personal choice, even when those forces operate from within strong social structures. Such structures are not forces of nature. They are the sum total of factors created by concrete acts of individuals which reinforce one another. Therefore although they may be difficult to overcome, they can be changed, they can be removed. It is within these institutional forms that the regulatory regime must try to achieve its objectives. More than

11. Simmel, p. 256.
12. Simmel, p. 257.
13. Simmel, p. 257.

this, however, needs to be said, and I will be looking at the interplay between the individual and the organization in the next chapter.

The Problem of Integrity

The requirement of probity for financial practitioners is found in all regulatory regimes. Although not all mention integrity explicitly, it is implicit; yet it is deeply problematic. I will continue to refer to the FSA requirements for clarity's sake, but it is applicable far wider than just the UK. The criteria for an Approved Person pose a problem for mainstream business ethics which, whether utilitarian or contractarian, are essentially act-based theories. What is significant about the fit and proper criteria is their inclusion of elements of the evaluation of *persons*, or inner traits of person, rather than just acts. To describe an Approved Person is also to describe that person's virtues. We need to keep in view the whole of the moral act, from intention through action to consequences. If we do that, we can see that virtue is not reducible either to the performance of acts independently identified as right, or to the disposition to perform such acts. This is because there is more to a virtue than just having a disposition to act in the right way. One cannot, therefore, examine the characterization of the Approved Person by an analysis of right and wrong acts and subsequently define what is meant by the virtues mentioned in terms of a conceptual or causal connection to such acts. Such an approach would be reductionistic, in that it would be insufficient to capture the nature of virtue. This, however, is precisely the approach taken by the FSA (and implicitly in other jurisdictions).

The Approved Person regime is, in effect, an acknowledgment that ethical behaviour in the finance sector is not strictly rule-governed. This is an interesting admission on the part of a rule-setting body! There can be no complete set of rules sufficient for giving a determinant answer to the question of what an agent should do in every situation of moral choice. Yet the regulatory regime is attempting to hold together in a single framework detailed, clear rules of obligation *and* a characterization of the virtuous Approved Person. By delineating behaviour which it deems to be incompatible with integrity, it seeks to strengthen the virtue by rules. Generally speaking, virtue-based business ethics is unable to encompass both, due to the polarization of an ethics of virtue as an alternative to an ethics of obligation.[14] This is a false polarization.

14. For a rejection of any link between rules and ethics, see Sternberg, *Just Business*; Edmund L. Pincoffs, *Quandaries and Virtues: Against Reductionism in Ethics*, 1986. It is not just virtue-based *business* ethics which rejects this link. Much of Martha Nussbaum's writings argue that practical wisdom and rules constitute alternative, as well as rival, standards of right action. For example, *The Fragility of Goodness: Luck and Ethics in Greek Tragedy and Philosophy*, 1986.

In social ethics there cannot be certitude. There are, perhaps, certain general norms, but moving from the general to the more particular and specific involves the use of practical reason to deal with contingent acts. The more one descends to the specific, the greater the possibility of contingent circumstances entering the picture, leading to a greater possibility of exceptions in moral truth and obligation.[15] It follows that rules do not exclude the need for virtue. Indeed, their very existence *requires* virtues such as practical wisdom and judgment. Thus practical wisdom is a pivotal concept if one wishes to avoid the polarities of law and virtue. It is necessary to hold in tension both rules and virtues, and see virtues as integrally connected to moral rules without being reducible to them. This provides a framework which can encompass financial regulation. There can be dialogue, rather than an aprioristic rejection of rules as a valid contribution to ethics.

The inclusion of integrity in the FSA's criteria raises a number of important difficulties. The first difficulty is the assumption that we all understand the same thing by the word 'integrity'. The FSA is aware that this is not necessarily the case. In *An Ethical Framework for Financial Services*,[16] the FSA stated that it wants to establish a clear, shared understanding about what integrity means in practice. The literature reveals that there is indeed no single understanding of what integrity is, nor how it functions. For example, De George, writing specifically on the subject of integrity and business ethics, presents it as little more than a synonym for 'ethics', but with the add-on of going beyond the minimum requirement. It is a quality which his ahistoric business practitioner just has.[17] With Rawls the emphasis is not so much on moral integrity as psychological integration.[18] Taylor stresses the importance of consistency,[19] while Sutherland, because of doubts based on the work of Parfit about the unity of the self, dismisses the need for having consistency at all.[20]

The second difficulty comes with the assumption that the nature of integrity can be determined by the type of behaviour which indicates its lack (because the FSA will withdraw recognition of the Approved Person if they perform certain acts) and the implicit corollary that refraining from these acts indicates the presence of integrity. In other words, it promotes an understanding of integrity (a virtue) as reducible to acts. I have already suggested that this is an erroneous characterization of virtue. Even

15. Aquinas, *Summa Theologiae*, I–II, q. 94, a. 4.
16. FSA, *An Ethical Framework for Financial Services*, 2002.
17. Richard T. De George, *Competing with Integrity in International Business*, 1993.
18. Rawls, *Theory of Justice*, pp. 519–20.
19. Gabriele Taylor, *Pride, Shame and Guilt*, 1985.
20. Stewart Sutherland, 'Integrity and Self-Identity', in A. Phillips Griffiths (ed.), *Ethics*, 1993, pp. 19–27.

allowing for the differences in accounts of integrity, it is generally accepted that it can only be specified in relation to the wholeness of a human life, the wholeness of a person. Integrity, I will argue, is the virtue of having a morally unified self, and it is difficult to see how it can be explicated by reference to dispositions to perform particular acts or to a simple disposition to avoid others.

This is not to underestimate the FSA's operational difficulties here. Failure to conform to the fit and proper criteria can be the basis for disciplinary action whose penalties include fines or loss of authorization to work in the finance sector, both for individuals and for corporate entities. Therefore the FSA must be able to justify such disciplinary action in a fair, open, juridical context. It *must* specify examples of behaviour which could lead to such action if its procedures are to be transparent and avoid uncertainty. However, the understanding it promotes of what is integrity is reductionistic and runs the risk of being self-defeating.

A further difficulty is that integrity clashes with the utilitarianism underpinning economic rationality and free-market ideology. To return to a theme discussed in earlier chapters – the way in which the person is conceptualized within ethics is not a theoretically neutral concept. It will shape what is considered morally important and what can be left aside. Utilitarianism presupposes a concept of the person in which present desires, which are the source of one's actions, can conflict, where pursuing one desire can interfere with the fulfilment of another. It expects discrete choices and decisions, and opportunistic behaviour. It may require something of an agent which she thinks no one of integrity could do. Bernard Williams makes integrity the focal point in his criticism of utilitarianism. He argues, among other things, that utilitarianism constitutes an attack on personal integrity by dismissing as unimportant the deeply held commitments from which arise a person's most significant actions.[21] A further criticism, which Williams does not make but which can be drawn from his argument, is that utilitarianism requires us to allocate value to the objects of our concern and care in proportion to their values as assessed from an impersonal point of view. But if I do that, they may no longer bear the value that *I* place upon them, and so no longer reflect my commitments.

Integrity, on the other hand, presupposes a different concept of the person, one where it is necessary to ask: what is the meaning of an action in the context of the person's life, what is the relationship of the action to the person's moral integrity? Integrity obliges us to take account of those features specified in the discussion of the elements of personalist ethics, in particular, that the agent is an integrated, historical subject, able to act

21. Bernard Williams, 'A Critique of Utilitarianism', in J.J.C. Smart and Bernard Williams (eds.), *Utilitarianism: For and Against*, 1973, pp. 77–150, especially pp. 108–18.

according to conscience, freely and responsibly. We also need to give adequate weight to the ways in which social structures and institutions help shape the person's identity and conceptions.

The recognition of these different ways of viewing the person raises two important issues. First, does the clash between these two characterizations of the person bring us back full circle to the view that business and ethics are mutually exclusive? Utilitarianism, because it specifically goes against the concept of integrity, will not be able to form people of integrity. To accept free-market ideology as the basis of business ethics, therefore, is to have sold the pass. The considerable number of practitioners in the finance sector who espouse free-market ideology will, therefore, be placed in an incoherent and unsustainable position vis-à-vis integrity. Contractarianism is no better placed. All that Rawls, for example, requires of his moral agents is rational, self-regarding calculation during the choice of the principles of justice. Nothing more than that can safely be inferred about the moral agent. Rawls defined the person as someone who can be 'a fully cooperating member of a society over a complete life'.[22] Given the variety of possible societies in which a person might have to co-operate, it is not clear what this description can contribute. It also begs the question of whether those who are so severely physically disabled or mentally disordered as to preclude being 'fully cooperating members of society' are to count as persons. It is difficult, therefore, to see how this approach will help the realization of integrity.

The resolution of this tension between integrity and business lies in part in what one sees as the purpose of business. If the wider view of the purpose of business which I have outlined is accepted, then much of the tension dissolves. By no means all, however. It is clear that defining what the purpose of business is does not ensure that any particular firm falls within the definition. It may well be that a person of integrity could not work in a particular firm and maintain that integrity. But that merely illustrates the need to distinguish between a particular business and business in general. There is also the empirical point that people of integrity are to be found in business. By definition, they have found a way of being business practitioners without compromising their integrity. A further defence against the view that they are incompatible lies in how one conceives the *telos* of one's life, particularly the *telos* of the life of one who is a business practitioner. This will be developed later.

---

22. John Rawls, 'Justice as Fairness: Political Not Metaphysical', *Philosophy and Public Affairs* 14.3 (Summer 1985), pp. 223–52 (233).

The Non-dualistic Nature of Integrity

The view of integrity which I am going to propose emerges naturally from the perspective of personalist ethics. Chapter 4 noted that personalist ethics arose as an explication of the phrase: 'the human person integrally and adequately considered'. I have just suggested that integrity can only be specified in relation to the wholeness of a human life, the wholeness of a person, and that integrity is the virtue of having a morally unified life. It is too simple to assume that a life where personality integration has occurred is thereby a life of moral integrity. However, integrity should not be seen as a shorthand general term for moral perfection. One may be virtuous without possessing integrity. Contra Aristotle, it is simply not the case that someone who has one virtue has them all. I may, for example, be honest, courageous, loyal and kind, but utterly lacking in sound practical judgment. (This does not have to mean, as many writers suggest, that I have the opposite vice. In this particular example I may lack sound practical judgment because I have low intelligence.) There are many moral heroes who in some senses are also morally problematic. Francis of Assisi's asceticism was unconstrained by temperance; St Catherine of Sienna was probably anorexic; Martin Luther King was an adulterer. Moral heroes can, in fact, be deeply paradoxical. The very qualities which most people would find morally questionable – hedonism, avarice, an ability to maintain convivial but purely instrumental relations with others – were precisely the qualities which put Oskar Schindler in a position to save thousands of Jews. All of these examples had deep flaws as far as virtue goes. Does this mean that Martin Luther King, for example, lacked integrity? The following discussion will show that he probably had it, but that answer may only be possible from within the Christian tradition with its realistic acceptance of failure, its acknowledgment of false starts, mistakes and the need for new beginnings.

The proposal that integrity can only be posited in relation to the wholeness of a life has two meanings. The first is in the sense of a life that is integral and which precludes dualism. The second is the more straightforward sense of all of a person's life. The first dualism which is precluded is that which would separate the inner from the outer, reflection from action. It is here, and only here, that action and integrity become one. Reflection which enabled the agent to discern the right course of action but which did not lead to the actual *doing* of the action would be sterile. The point of disciplined moral reflection is precisely to enable the person to act in accordance with a reasoned grasp of the exigencies of human nature. With integrity there is a coincidence of motive, intention and action. At its heart is a refusal to deceive oneself about one's motives, intentions and interests. Integrity, therefore, requires a self-knowledge which has been tested and developed. Obviously a refusal to deceive oneself about one's motives is not necessarily linked with moral behaviour. I may be very aware that my desire to perform a particular action is rooted in, for example, envy or a thirst for revenge, and refuse to delude myself into thinking that there is some motive such as justice present. Self-knowledge is a necessary but not a sufficient attribute of integrity.

Accepting the importance of self-knowledge reveals that some parts of the finance sector are faced with a very particular problem. Self-knowledge does not come easily or quickly. It takes time and requires experience (and here the first meaning of the wholeness of life starts to blend with the second). It points to a journey of experience and learning, not to a mere intellectual puzzle that one solves. A certain clear-sightedness is needed, as well as emotional balance, if one is to be able to stand back from the dominant market ideology which maintains that motivations other than personal-wealth maximization are irrational. As this is the paradigm of financial theorists, financial practitioners are particularly exposed to it. It is rare to find these qualities well developed in young adults. Yet these are increasingly the employees in many of the occupations covered by the Approved Persons regime. Given the current employment practices of the sector, it is difficult to see how firms can ensure that only people of integrity are, for example, traders. This is not to suggest that young traders will necessarily be lacking in honesty, truthfulness, diligence and other worthy qualities. What they are far less likely to have is a strong sense of integrity which will enable them to resist the enormous pressures to, for example, cut corners in order to maintain performance figures.

The second dualism precluded by integrity is the dualism between feelings/emotions and reason. This view stands in contradistinction to Kantian forms of morality which draw on this dualism precisely to exclude feelings and emotions. Our emotions are not grounded in an intellectual judgment about what is good or bad for us. We frequently find ourselves desiring what we know to be bad for us and disliking what we know to be good for us. However, emotions can also draw us, on the basis of pleasure or pain, towards what is truly good or to avoid what is truly harmful. It is only a small step to say that our emotional response needs to be directed by our reason if we are to see what is truly good or harmful for us and act accordingly. Hence the dualism of emotions and reason into which the reality of the person as embodied spirit seems to lead us.

However, if the concept of integrity as a unified living of our lives is true, such a dualism is false. There is a need for more than just rational powers to be involved in integrity. There must also be, as feminist ethics has insisted, an integrity of the emotions. Any ethical approach which relies too much on reason, and does not adequately incorporate the affective, will be inadequate at accounting for and nurturing true integrity. This is because such a theory cannot explain the motivational power of emotions, or acknowledge the fact that motivation and value must come together. However, a correct balance is needed. If feelings become central then the consistency which integrity requires becomes almost impossible. The subjectivity of daily life and the transitory nature of many of our feelings do not provide a firm foundation for the ethical life. But feelings are, nevertheless, an essential part of human life, and ethical theory and practice must deal with the whole person. Failure to attend to this aspect of our lives does not mean that we operate by reason alone. Rather it tends to be the case that our emotions affect us in unexamined ways. It is a major criticism of business ethics that it has ignored the impact of emotions on our behaviour. This is true even of virtue-based business ethicists such as Solomon, Freeman and Dobson. This is particularly surprising in light of Aristotle's view that to be a good person one must have the right emotions.

Such an integration of the emotions so that they are in harmony with our reason is, like self-knowledge, only arrived at after a long struggle. Indeed, for most of us that struggle will continue, at least to some degree, all our lives. Nevertheless, in and through that struggle, over time we move towards an ever greater integrity. Again, therefore, it is necessary to ask if the employment practices of the finance sector are helpful in this regard. But more than this, it is necessary to ask which emotions are actually encouraged by the sector.

The earlier discussion on the detached agent suggests that one emotion is a sense of power. Consider Leeson's remark that 'with just one wave of the hand' he could buy or sell millions of pounds worth of assets. He, like the protagonists of *Liar's Poker* or *F.I.A.S.C.O.*, came to believe, at least for a time, that what he wanted to do he could do. While he was on a roll he felt almost omnipotent. Leeson knew that as long as the profits continued to accrue, no one would seriously question him. As both his case, and various scandals concerned with the mis-selling of pensions, insurance policies and other financial products show, in a results-dominated culture you do not challenge those who are producing what is demanded. Simmel alerts us to the ways in which money seems to empower by subsuming within itself so many forms of power previously located in other social institutions. Yet this power is without any real sense of responsibility because of its disconnectedness from a sense of reality. The emotional engagement with others is lacking, and so the values associated with engagement are also absent.

Furthermore, it is a power which moves easily into anxiety. Pay, status, even the job itself, are dependent upon meeting ever more stringent performance targets. Extreme competitiveness can be engendered both within an institution (who will get the biggest bonus this year?) and between institutions (outperform Firm X or lose the business of Fund P). Our competitor easily becomes our threat, and few of us are at our best when we feel threatened. Illusions of power, anxiety, competitiveness and insecurity are all potent emotions. At the very least they are difficult to bring into harmony with our reason. When they are reinforced by the way that jobs and remuneration packages are organized – particularly where the basis is 'you eat what you kill' (that is to say, remuneration is calculated according to the amount of fees you generate) – for many people it becomes impossible. This is not to suggest that such individuals will all become dishonest, but these emotions may well affect judgment, the willingness to make perhaps unjustifiably risky investments, to cut corners, to do what has become known as 'gambling for resurrection'. What they will not do is enhance integrity, and the sector must ask itself which behaviour it *actually* wants, rather than just theoretically signs up to. What it cannot coherently do is, through its employment practices, promote economic rationality with its emphasis on personal-wealth maximization as the only valid motivation, and then be surprised if some of its employees fail to develop integrity.

These emotional aspects connect with the description given earlier about cynicism and the blasé attitude, especially the seeking of stimuli. A leading addiction clinic placed advertisements in a London newspaper targeting successful City professionals who seemingly thrive under pressure, but in fact turn to drink to cope. A spokeswoman for the clinic referred to the 'culture of youth and machismo in the City. Admitting you're struggling is forbidden. The "eat what you kill" culture lives on and it doesn't allow for personal weakness.'[23] This initiative stemmed from what doctors reported as a steady rise in alcoholism referrals from City workers caught up in the high drinking culture found there.

The third dualism which is precluded is that between propositional knowledge and evaluative knowledge. Here propositional knowledge refers to intellectual knowledge as we ordinarily speak of it. It has a certain objectivity, a certain independence from the knower. Being universal in character, it prescinds from individual circumstances and differences. Because of its objectivity it is easily communicable to others. Evaluative knowledge, on the other hand, has to do with quality rather than with quantity. It deals with the goodness or beauty of a thing, with its value. Inasmuch as value does not exist 'out there' by itself, it is not universal but profoundly concrete and personal. It is a particular way of knowing the individual existing thing with which we interact in an experience of judging it to be good or bad, beautiful or ugly. We go out of ourselves and attach ourselves to the value that we find in the object. The distinction between these two types of knowledge is pivotal for ethics. The Approved Person must have both types because the key factors used by the FSA include integrity *and* competence and capability. Again the

23. Reported in 'Priory Clinic Targets City High-flyers who Need Drink to Cope', *The Independent*, 5 April 2005, p. 15.

finance sector is faced with particular problems. The sector is highly technological in character. With its use of such means as econometrics, financial models and highly complex algorithms for measuring risk, it emphasizes a view of the economy which is 'objective', efficient and quantifiable. We are confronted with a bias in favour of propositional knowledge. This bias is then greatly strengthened by the nature of regulation and the attendant compliance culture.

The ideal agent who seems to be envisaged by the notion of the compliance culture is one who has amassed the greatest knowledge of many detailed rules and follows them. It is to make compliance equivalent to propositional knowledge. Certainty has been given a prominent position. Yet all that compliance tells us is that there is conformity to regulations. It tells us nothing about the characters and qualities of those complying. The relationship between ethical theory and practical decision is complex, not linear. It is brought about not by simple deductive inference, but by judgment. If there is to be room for moral judgment (and without moral judgment there cannot be moral integrity) regulation must to some extent be under-determined, with rules open to alternative applications in the light of differing circumstances and forms of self-perfection. Therefore regulation has to leave room for individual judgment if integrity is not to be crowded out. It may be that the rules will have to be applied with a slightly lighter hand than regulatory regimes normally envisage if they are not to conflict with the fostering of integrity.

Simmel's analysis of the move to quantitive assessments is helpful here, and helps to explain the complex mechanisms whereby the objectification of reality has become, for many, the model of the agent's relation to the world. Our rationalist ambition is to turn practical reflection as much as possible into calculation. As Taylor points out: 'The bent of utilitarianism has been to do away with qualitative distinctions of worth on the grounds that they represent confused perceptions of the real bases of our preferences which are quantitative'.[24] Regulation, because so much of it deals with quantitive forms of measurement, reinforces this, which helps to explain why utilitarian calculus sits relatively easily with regulation. External regulation and supervision have traditionally taken the form of establishing quantitive standards in the form of ratios for factors such as capital, cash reserves and large or connected loans and transactions. Despite the place given to Approved Persons, this quantitive approach is still extremely important, and is the sole technique in recommendations by the Basel Committee[25] (the international body which establishes high-level standards of banking supervision, based in Basel, Switzerland).

24. Charles Taylor, *Human Agency and Language: Philosophical Papers I*, 1985, p. 17.
25. Basel Committee on Banking Supervision. For example, *A New Capital Adequacy Framework*.

Yet ethical judgment most often turns on qualitative assessments, for example, an evaluation of desires. Regulation may, therefore, of its very nature, actively inhibit the development of more nuanced approaches to ethics and development of character. This is because cases of ambiguity, by their very nature, do not come neatly pre-packaged and labelled as falling under a particular principle. A compliance culture, with its emphasis on certainty and clarity, may be unhelpful in that it does not engender the evaluative aspect which enables the recognition of what is morally significant in the agent's perception of the situation. It may not enable the agent to give appropriate weight to what is not specifically covered by the regulation, particularly non-quantitive aspects. Finally, it will not empower the agent to seek the most appropriate and fullest description of the act. Without such a description, it may be hard to recognize that a particular action is morally significant. We require pro-positional knowledge to help us marshal the facts of the case accurately. But when the exercise of our free commitment brings us to the moment of decision, we are not deciding among facts. We are deciding among values. The quantitive approach will not help us here. It is the work of evaluative knowledge.

The final dualism to be rejected will only be briefly alluded to here, as its implications will be explored in the next chapter. This last dualism is the one which opposes self to others. This is a false opposition. I have already argued that there is no *necessary* reason why my interest cannot include the interests of others. The argument here goes deeper. Integrity requires holding a clear sense of oneself as a unique person of worth (dimension 8 of personalist ethics) and also of the 'other' in their complexity and value. It requires self-respect and self-esteem as well as respect, sympathy and esteem for the other, understood precisely as other but in relation. This follows from the understanding of the person as a relational being who only becomes an 'I' in relation to a 'Thou' and as one who is a social being. It begins to shade into the virtue of solidarity, but is not subsumed by it, because it includes such goods as friendship, intimacy and parental love. It is, thus, partial, but it is also impartial in that it is not limited just to those who are close to us. Following Aquinas, virtues of self-care and care for others are distinct but equal qualities of character which enable one to act with integrity towards all of one's concerns.

Summary and Conclusions

Regulation may be viewed as a mechanism whereby the concerns of society are brought to bear upon a particular activity. The regulation of 'fit and proper' persons is concerned mainly with external verifiables. Indeed, it is obliged to be. But if financial institutions are to be confident in their compliance with the regulations, then they cannot be indifferent to those features of character which build up towards these external manifestations. Whether they wish it or not, the question of virtue has come into their calculations. Concepts such as the integrity which the FSA requires of Approved Persons cannot float freely in the air. They must be rooted in the moral character of the agent. They must also be rooted in the institutional forms and employment practices of the sector. The institutional form of the community in which the person finds herself may militate against an adequate exercise of integrity, indeed may specifically prevent it. Further aspects of these institutional forms will be examined in the next chapter.

The discussion of integrity in this chapter has been highly selective. I have made no attempt to cover every possible aspect. Instead the objective has been to focus attention on certain aspects of integrity which have particular relevance to the finance sector. These aspects have been shown through looking at the problems of a non-dualistic life in a situation which encourages a detached identity, and cynicism or a blasé attitude. Chapter 4 argued that the self-realization of moral good through work puts in question certain personnel practices. This claim has been illustrated by a number of difficulties arising from the employment practices of the finance sector.

Pure or perfect integrity is probably an ideal which is seldom fully realized. Certainly for most of us our integrity is a matter of degree rather than all or none. It is both a process and a result. This conclusion follows from seeing that integrity is arrived at only through the convergence of a number of processes. One is the gradual overcoming of various dualisms, a process which takes time and experience. It is a unification which is not simply the assembling into a whole of what had been previously disconnected. Rather, with this unification we see a fullness and flexibility which is more than that resulting from numerical addition. The next chapter takes this deeper by looking at ways in which this unifying can be personally appropriated.

Social structures and institutions help shape the person's identity and conceptions. However, personalist ethics holds that social matrices are not radically determinative. Nevertheless, pervasive social conditioning is a reality which, particularly with the young, can have a determinative effect on our activities. How the firm as an institution conducts itself will, therefore, have a powerful influence. The unhelpful employment practices discussed include the youth of many employees, some of whom are put into positions which can generate illusory feelings of power, but which also provoke deep anxiety. Career and remuneration structures which enhance feelings of competitiveness and insecurity add to the mix of potent emotions. Again the relationship between the individual and the institution is an issue which will be taken further in the next chapter.

Chapter 11

THE INDIVIDUAL, THE SECTOR AND THE COMMON GOOD

This chapter will bring into clearer relationship a number of themes I have been discussing. These include how the particular goods of the individual, and the intermediate bodies of the firm and the sector, are related; how this connects to the common good of the wider society; and the issue of identity. I shall often be using the term *telos*. This is a Greek word meaning 'end' and, like the English word, can refer to the final point of a process or to a purpose or goal. Kotva proposes *telos* as shorthand for the concept of the meaning of human life, what is most worthwhile aiming at in life, the supreme Good.[1] It is in this wide sense that I shall be using the word.

Integrity, Freedom and Identity

I have suggested at several points that there is tension between free-market ideology and integrity. The main points of that tension lie in integrity's requirements. Integrity requires history, both past and future, commitment and a *telos*. The market does not. In the market, time is compressed into an ever narrower present. What you have done, what you have achieved, is largely an irrelevance. The maxim: 'You're only as good as your last deal', has itself been eroded, so that what matters is the deal you are currently making and the deal that is on the horizon. It is your choice as a consumer *now* that is crucial. Your past choices matter only as a very general guide to present behaviour. Each present choice is really a discrete one, as novelty in choice is highly valued. Advertising slogans such as: 'The new you!' or 'Re-invent yourself', reveal that some aspects of the market are predicated on a discontinuity with present perceived identity. These slogans imply, as I have already suggested, that an existing identity can be discarded and a new one created (immediately?) by consumer choices. As for your future choices, they only impinge to the extent that they are objects of present calculation. Permanence, in this

---

1. Joseph Kotva, *The Christian Case for Virtue Ethics*, 1996, p. 17.

perspective, is at best an irrelevance, at worst something to be positively discouraged.

It would seem, then, that commitment, perseverance, constancy, all words associated with permanence and integrity, are not axiomatically valuable to the market. The market claims to serve our freedom, but here we can see another instance of how the freedom it suggests is at odds with a deeper understanding. I have already referred to the question of the balance between freedom and determinism. Freedom, in this perspective, does not equate with whim or unpredictability. Indeed, one might well suppose that anyone acting in a generally unpredictable or inconsistent way was lacking in freedom, in that such a person is easily blown off course by passing considerations or random events. Rather, a free subject will act in accord with relatively stable values and attitudes. The freedom proposed by the market is predicated precisely on changing values, wants, needs and desires.

This does not deny the reality of behaviour which arises from biological and environmental factors. This is because the human person is embodied, with a personal and socio-cultural history. There are many 'givens' which constrain the individual. These givens include past actions of the agent and systemic features of the environment within which the agent must work. But it is necessary to insist that there is an area of our lives in which we have sufficient freedom to deliberate and choose between possible actions in a manner which shows consistency and commitment.

This understanding of the free subject points to a vital component of integrity. There is a vital connection between who we are, that is our identity, and what we do. I am not going to describe in detail the philosophical debate about what constitutes personal identity over time. That debate centres on three broad accounts of how I know that I am the same person over time. The first account is the physical criterion where identity consists in the obtaining of some relation of physical continuity, typically bodily continuity or brain continuity. The second is that of psychological continuity, that is, overlapping memory chains, or memory together with other psychological features. The third is the mixed criterion which holds that the best account of a person's identity will make reference to both physical and psychological continuities. In my view the last version is most persuasive. Our embodiment captures something of our deepest notions about what makes for the same person over time in our usual circumstances. Our mental life and physical events cannot really be described in impersonal or identity-neutral terms. Experience requires subjects. A particular headache has to be had by someone. The memory of writing this particular sentence can properly only be mine. In discussing identity in Chapter 4, I pointed to the importance of identity over time, with responsibility and commitments (both from the past and to the future) as important features. Without this notion, it is difficult to see how we can continue to hold trans-temporal moral notions such as responsibility for our actions, personal commitments, or be especially concerned about the fate of some future person just because that person is me. Within regulatory regimes it is always the case that disciplinary action will only be taken if an individual is judged to be personally culpable. Such a stance requires an account of integrity in line with the one proposed here.

Integrity and identity are in a dynamic relationship with each other. This relationship implies that there is a substantial, coherent and relatively stable set of values and principles to which one is genuinely and freely committed. It is this combination of freedom and commitment which characterizes the identity of the morally mature individual. Such a commitment is underpinned by a conception of ourselves as historical beings. A human life can only be understood in terms of past, present and future. At the beginning of life the prospects for the future usually play a larger role than constraints from the past. Towards the end of life, it is commitments already made which tend to be more important than future prospects.

Our identity, our commitments, and therefore the precise requirements of everyone's particular integrity include the many social roles we have. Among these there is the identity we assume as employees of *this* firm in *this* industry. The precise colourations of our role as producers will come from the particular corporate culture in which we find ourselves. This is so even if we are at odds with the firm. My role may then be 'disaffected trader' or 'disheartened compliance officer'. However, when identity is seen in terms only of the roles we occupy, it is not surprising that we feel ourselves to be fragmented. We have multiple roles. What is to unify them? While our identity may be in part made up by our being both producers and consumers, we are more than this. The *telos* of human life is not exhausted by these features. To accept that these are all there is, is to accept the market's self-evaluation of being all that we need, that economic activity is the sum total of our lives. I have already proposed one way of seeing that such a claim is utterly inadequate in Chapter 4. If the points made about identity over time are accepted it follows that this is another reason why the claim of the market to provide an adequate conferral of our identity must be rejected. The form of this market-conferred identity is precisely one of dis-continuity, of discrete actions and choices.

Without 'meaning' (and here intended as some 'end' of our life) we drift. It is useful to recall here Simmel's analysis where he describes what happens when we lose the end and substitute the 'means' of money. What should be a means, a tool, becomes instead the end of our endeavours. But it is inadequate as an end, and implodes in on itself. We produce (work) in order to consume. Production is seen only in an instrumental way and its potential as a means of self-realization is negated. Our role as consumer is never enough. It is without stability and lacking in sufficient content. If my purchasing power decreases, who am I? If I cease to produce, who am I? These questions reflect the felt experience of many people. The question is: 'Is that experience all that there is, all that there can be?' 'Does it in effect sum up the whole of reality, the full potential?'

In the business context neither Christian nor other religious conviction can be presumed. There needs to be a way of responding to these questions which is accessible and satisfactory irrespective of our religious beliefs. It needs to be one which accords with religious convictions without, at the same time, excluding those who do not share them. The next section will argue that having an adequate *telos* for our life enables us to overcome this fragmentation. It unites our roles across time and serves as a guiding principle in our choice of actions. It unifies our desires, and enables us to maintain an appropriate balance before the demanding, but ultimately limiting, view of our identity proposed by the market.

The Telos *of Integrity*

The criteria for an Approved Person in essence does not ask: 'What shall I do?' but rather: 'How should I live?' This is not a question about the immediate. Neither is it a question about what I should do now or next. Rather it is about a manner of life. Christian ethics, when it is being most true to itself, is not about the evil to be avoided; it is about the good which is to be done. It asks us to respond to the question of how we should shape and live our life as a whole, so that one's life will not be judged to be a failure. One way into answering that question is to look at how the dreams we have for our life shape our understanding, our striving. These help us to construe what we can be and how we can or should act so as to achieve that. Arthur Miller, in *Death of a Salesman*, captures the human dilemma when he has Biff, the son of the salesman Willy Loman, say of his father that because he had the wrong dreams about himself, he never knew who he truly was, and therefore had not known what his life could have been.[2] With great poignancy, his lament shows us the tragedy of a life that was wasted. Biff is only able to escape the same waste by his decision to reject the false dream his father tried to impose on him. We are left to imagine the future waste of his brother's life because of his refusal to do the same. Similarly Martin Luther King's 'I have a dream' points to the power of the concept of 'dream' – in his case not the dream for an individual life, but for a social life; not just the manner of life for an individual, but the manner of life for a nation. In this sense, 'dream' can act as a potent non-technical alternative for *telos*. It shows us that having a dream means

2. Arthur Miller, *Death of a Salesman*, 'Requiem'.

being attached to ideas about ourselves, attached to aspirations which accord with that dream, attached to means which bring us closer to these aspirations, the fulfilment of that dream.

It is necessary to stress this point because of impoverished understandings of what is involved in an adequate *telos*. I have just suggested that a *telos* requires that we are attached to means which bring us closer to the aspirations contained in the fulfilment of that *telos*. Yet Petrick and Quinn, in their contribution to the respected and influential *Sage Series on Business Ethics*, take a very different position. They discuss eudaemonistic teleology which they define citing Aristotle and Aquinas. Yet despite their sources they then make the extraordinary claim that a eudaemonistic teleology means that managers 'implicitly accept the dictum "All's well that ends well" regardless of the means used to produce the results'.[3] It is difficult to see how a disregard for the means used can equate with integrity; the means used must express the values contained in the end towards which the action is aimed, otherwise that end is subverted.

Within a teleological framework such as the one I am suggesting here, 'being' implies 'becoming', and becoming implies the appropriation of a good which enables moral existence. It is not enough simply to be, simply to exist, because existence requires the transcendence of the self into the good by which existence is defined (dimension 6). To exist is to become something more than I am now. It is only when the *telos* is identified that we can identify the kind of attachments by which we are brought into being, which form the identity of the person we could be, with the life we could have. To be is to be for something, and the *telos* represents what that something is. In the language of Aquinas, all choice requires attraction towards a desire for some object which is intelligible in the light of some feature of the human good. This object, this *telos*, must be one which is capable of guiding our practical reason. It must present itself to us as something to be pursued, nurtured, maintained and respected.

So what *telos*, what dream for our life might there be? As the example of Willy Loman demonstrates, without being psychotic, I can still consistently hold to a stunted or mistaken version of the good for myself. A staple of ethical discussion is that there is no generally agreed 'end' of human life, no universally accepted definition of the good life. When we seek to define the good life, we tend to reject, as an imposition, compliance with a pattern which antedates our own will. We wish to originate the pattern ourselves. Anything else seems to be a restriction on our freedom to originate the pattern ourselves, and that dishonours our dignity. As my analysis in the previous chapter showed, practitioners in the finance sector are more likely than some others to resist the imposition of an external

3. Joseph A. Petrick and John F. Quinn, *Management Ethics: Integrity at Work*, 1997, p. 49.

authority because of the influence of the institutional forms within which they work. By extension, it is unlikely that they would accept some externally formulated and imposed *telos*. Can there be some worthwhile *telos* towards which the financial practitioner can aim which will give a sufficiently coherent *telos* to unify action while respecting plurality?

When considering *telos*, there is a difference between the *telos* for humanity, that of this particular person, and that of this particular type of person, for example, a financial practitioner. All of these are clearly related, but retain important distinctions. For the purposes of this discussion we need to retain as central the fact that a *telos* will always be relative to a way of life and to the character of those for whom that way of life expresses, in some sense, who they are. It cannot simply be an expression of a principle which comes into play irrespective of the person's way of life. Neither can it simply result from events external to that person's way of living.

As a community, the finance sector has, through its extensive involvement in consultations with the various regulatory regimes under which it operates, affirmed its adherence to certain ends. This involvement could be considered an example of subsidiarity working to help arrive at the content of some particular aspect of the common good. It illustrates that subsidiarity can increase a sense of responsibility and foment co-operation instead of conflict. However, one must also bear in mind the danger of 'regulatory capture', that is, that organizations and people write their own rules of conduct. It is a difficult balance to attain, and will always need to be the subject of continual scrutiny if the right balance is to be kept. These ends to which the sector has given assent are what type of market it wishes to be, and what type of person should operate in it, the 'Approved Person' (or equivalent) who must exhibit certain virtues. Chapter 7 has identified further aspects of the sector which form part of its *telos*. Its intermediation function and the way in which, through its allocation procedures, it helps ensure productive investment and preserves the marginal efficiency of capital, locates its *telos* within that of the wider economic sphere. Given the understanding of the purpose of business established in earlier chapters, and the centrality of the finance sector, the *telos* of an individual financial practitioner must include a very broad social element.

This links with the non-dualistic nature of integrity which rejects a false incompatibility between my good and the good of others. An adequate *telos* will not only focus on the individual. It will need to incorporate concerns of respect and sympathy for those who are not, in any important sense, closely connected to the individual. In other words, any conception of an adequate *telos* requires a social dimension. It cannot be one based on atomistic individualism. For persons of integrity, the well-being of others will be a central concern in the meaningfulness of their own lives. Thus, a *telos* which confers coherence and meaning for those working within the finance sector must reflect the sector's social purposes. It must be ample enough to confer coherence and meaning to the individual practitioner, understood as one whose way of life, by definition, has enormous social implications. The self does not dominate in this understanding of the *telos*, but neither is it ignored.

The wider context provides a *telos* which can be incorporated into the life of an individual without stunting it. It is compatible with the view of human flourishing indicated in the detailed discussion of personalist ethics and basic goods. There was described a view of work as one means of self-realization, a means of moral growth, of becoming. (This is not to ignore the reality that for many work is experienced as demeaning, dehumanizing. This, however, points to the need to strive to improve work, rather than to dismiss it as without worth.) It requires the notion of commitment and the dynamic relationship between the good of the individual and the wider good. The concept of the common good, which embraces both social and personal, means that one's own good can only be adequately construed in the context of some wider good, participation in which bestows meaning and purpose on one's life. The *telos* of the firm's well-being is not enough. Even when extended to the whole of the finance sector by the individual being committed to the type of market envisaged by the regulations, it is still inadequate. It must be located in the 'purpose' of the sector, as discussed in Chapter 7, the sector's 'positioning' and the general 'purpose' of business which I have been proposing. Anything less will be too small for us.

However, it must be recognized that this may still be insufficient to provide a unifying *telos*. The youth of many employees presents some difficulties. Our willingness to ask what our life means can be avoided as long as we do not acknowledge our mortality. If we think we are going to live forever (and emotionally that is how it appears in our youth), there is little need to worry about the shape and meaning of our life as a whole.

A deeper reason why it may be insufficient is because, just as we are more than consumers, so we are also more than producers. While our work is a very important vehicle for our becoming more human, it is not the only one. Our life is wider than our job, our identity richer than just one role and the firm should not demand, openly or manipulatively, that we invest more of ourselves than the job requires. Again employment practices come to the fore, with the sector's demands for long hours and total commitment. If the sector wishes to employ people of integrity, this implies employing people who have achieved a certain balance in their lives. The precise balance will vary from individual to individual, but a person of integrity will, by definition, be one who gives adequate attention to other parts of his or her life, to other appropriate commitments. These other commitments will, in turn, be helping to nurture and form the person of integrity. Without them it is difficult to see how such a person will, for example, resolve the dualisms I have discussed. It follows that what the FSA in particular has legislated for is impossible if the only context is that of its sphere of work and influence. It has prescribed something which the sector *on its own* cannot deliver. For the FSA and other regulatory regimes this may be an unpalatable conclusion, but that does not change the conclusion.

Who we are, where we are going and how to get there are vital questions in our lives. The world is not simply made up of 'facts' with an occasional ethical dilemma thrown in. Rather our life-world is permeated with ethical import, thoroughly coloured by what ought to be. Contra free-market ideology and atomized individualism, the *telos* of human life, while always intensely personal, is not a private affair. It is only within communities of practice and virtue that the discernment, struggle and acquisition of our end is to be accomplished. 'It is always within some particular community with its own specific forms that we learn or fail to learn to exercise the virtues.'[4] Our nature is historical, finite and embodied. We cannot simply *will* ourselves into becoming a certain sort of person. Specific relationships, policies, practices and actions all have an influence. Failure to attend to any of these influences is to deny facets of our nature. In the next section I will highlight some of the ways in which the financial firm, as one of the institutional communities within which the agent is located, can be an important influence.

The Individual and the Institution

In Chapter 2 I argued that because the market operates within a complex social framework, it draws on values which are external to itself, such as truth, trust, honesty and obligation. These non-economic values are essential to the market. I raised the question as to how these values were to be fostered within the business environment itself. I suggested there that reliance on self-interest was self-defeating in that the increase in self-interest could, over time, move the moral perspective of participants away from those values which support the market, thus undermining the background conditions essential to its operation. Integrity is a case in point. It is built on, and presupposes, a wide range of values. These values include a form of self-interest, but it is not the self-interest presupposed by the market, which only acknowledges economic rationality. Integrity is a virtue which is at least difficult, and perhaps impossible, to understand within that model of rationality.

It is surely the case that the primary responsibility for prudent and ethical management of a firm rests with that firm and not with the

4. MacIntyre, *After Virtue*, pp. 194–95.

regulatory body in whose jurisdiction it falls. Therefore regulation, if it is operating well, will reinforce, not substitute for, the responsibilities of the management. Such responsibility will include ensuring compliance with regulatory requirements, but the firm needs to go beyond that. All compliance does is demonstrate that written procedures are being followed. It cannot be safely inferred from the existence of a compliance officer that the firm is acting to high ethical standards.

Some very influential works on virtue ethics have lacked an explicitly social or community dimension.[5] This has not generally been the case in virtue-based business ethics precisely because it refers to virtuous behaviour in a social setting. However, just where one would expect direct linkages between the individual and the institution, for example in Solomon,[6] the discussion slips straight into questions of social responsibility and the corporation as moral agent;[7] as part of the wider community with its own culture;[8] and a brief reference to corporate-role identity.[9] More than this, however, needs to be said.

Virtue ethics in general and virtue-based business ethics in particular do recognize the importance of community. Some form of community (which need not, as it usually is in the discussion of virtue ethics, be the family or a geographical location) is needed if individuals are to become capable of morality and sustained within it.[10] Within complex forms of communal life (and the finance sector is one such) we learn the lived way of virtue which requires forms of perception, morally relevant descriptions of situations, habits of action and the relevance of certain considerations. It is only if there is some reasonable level of congruence between articulated requirements and actual behaviour that we can be sustained in our morality by these communities. There is a necessary link between virtue and action. If one wishes to explicate a virtue, say courage, one will almost inevitably use paradigmatic examples of courageous action to demonstrate what is meant. It is not the case that we can just intuit that a virtue is there. It is always demonstrated by the way a life is lived. It is a pattern of behaviour, an enduring trait of character which inclines the agent to act in one way rather than another. But integrity cannot be seen in quite the same way, often because its outward manifestation is an action displaying another virtue. One cannot see the quality of integrity as virtuous – or even understand what the quality is – except by living examples, by seeing what might be called mentors. Such a mentoring role requires moral

5. For example, Phillipa Foot, 'Virtues and Vices', in *Virtues and Vices and Other Essays in Moral Philosophy*, 1978, pp. 1–18.
6. Solomon, *Ethics and Excellence*.
7. Solomon, pp. 131–35.
8. Solomon, pp. 145–52.
9. Solomon, p. 161.
10. See, for example, Stanley Hauerwas, *Community of Character*, 1981.

leadership. Moral leadership, in contrast to manipulation, charisma or demagoguery, helps us to find our better motives. It impresses upon us moral truths which perhaps fear or self-interest narrowly construed might cause us to ignore.[11]

The finance sector might thus be seen as acting somewhat in the manner of a 'localized' community, as proposed by MacIntyre.[12] He, however, would tend to disagree. His analysis of work and the goods internal to it leads him to the conclusion that once productive work had moved outside the household, it was 'expelled from the realm of practices with goods internal to themselves'.[13] It is unlikely, therefore, that he could readily accept a work community as a localized community. Furthermore, MacIntyre does not see these localized communities as necessary components of a good society, but rather as alternatives to contemporary society.

Part of MacIntyre's position arises from the way he perceives 'external' goods, such as money, as being somehow less worthy than goods internal to practices.[14] He neglects positive external goods, together with the virtues and communities which promote them. This goes some way towards explaining his pessimism and his conviction that moral renewal cannot occur except from the survival through the barbaric age of relatively self-contained communities which are unconnected to a wider society.[15] However, I am arguing that work holds within itself the possibility (not the certainty) of self-realization, and that *through* work we can become more human. Therefore the particular working community can make a positive contribution to how the good life is articulated. Furthermore, because the concept of the common good articulates the concept of intermediate bodies and the role they can have, it avoids the questionable moral ghetto that MacIntyre seems to be proposing with his localized community.

Integrity, in the context of a community, is a multi-level phenomenon. There is the widely recognized fact that trust, and consequently trustworthiness, is necessary for efficiency. Without trust the costs of trading become unduly high. Persons with integrity are more trustworthy than those without it. Despite this, acting with integrity is not a cost-minimizing strategy. It is, however, of a kind which is to the firm's longer-term advantage. For example, integrity helps sustain the community. Knowing that our colleagues are doing something difficult or worthwhile makes it

---

11. See Lawrence Blaum, 'Community and Virtue', in Roger Crisp (ed.), *How Should One Live? Essays on the Virtues*, 1996, pp. 231–50.

12. MacIntyre, *After Virtue*, pp. 238–45.

13. MacIntyre, p. 211.

14. MacIntyre, for example pp. 176, 181.

15. MacIntyre, p. 245.

easier for us to believe that we too can do it. This, however, is not simple conformity. Conformity assumes either no or very weak independent motivation to translate conviction into action. Conformity is characteristic of what is known as the 'moral chameleon', one who simply takes on the morality of the dominant person(s) in the group.

It should not be assumed, however, that integrity will always sustain the community in some non-conflictual way. Certainly Pincoffs' thesis that the virtues are qualities enabling persons to function well within some form of common life[16] has broad-brush merit. However, as MacIntyre argues,[17] genuine virtues are dysfunctional to any but the best forms of common life. There is the possibility of there being 'forms of social and political life in which the practice of the virtues is at revolutionary odds with those forms, so that one can only be virtuous by being in systematic conflict with the established order'.[18] In line with his general pessimism, MacIntyre perhaps overstates his case a little. Nevertheless, he is right to argue that the situation both can and does arise. It therefore cannot be presumed that virtues will have the functionality ascribed to them explicitly by Pincoffs and implicitly by writers such as Solomon who seek to establish a virtue-based business ethics.

If integrity is to be fostered and preserved by the institution, there has to be a certain mutuality. The institutional forms are not neutral, and failure to attend to their influence can result in the situation outlined by MacIntyre. In discussing various dualisms, I pointed to the motivational role of emotions, and there have been references to the need for commitment both there and in this chapter. It is necessary for these two aspects to be in harmony if integrity is to be adequately nurtured and sustained. Where they are in harmony, the firm benefits. General experience in business shows that where there is a long-term commitment by employees to their firm and a concern for the fortunes of other employees, especially by managers, long-term entrepreneurial solutions to problems are more likely to emerge. This confirms the argument that as free, responsible subjects, economic initiative involves the person's self-realization through work. It also illustrates the reality of particular goods contributing to the firm's common good. Even in a strictly commercial sense, firms where employees see each other as rivals, or at best impersonally, may well be less effective than firms where they have a strong commitment to each other and to the common good of the firm. It is,

16. Pincoffs, *Quandaries and Virtues*.
17. Alasdair MacIntyre, '*Sophrune*: How a Virtue Can Become Socially Disruptive', in Peter A. French, Theodore E. Uehling, Jr. and Howard K. Wettsein (eds.), *Midwest Studies in Philosophy*, Vol. XIII: *Ethical Theory: Character and Virtue*, 1988, pp. 1–11.
18. MacIntyre, '*Sophrune*', p. 7.

therefore, in the interests of the firm to foster long-term commitments as a means of enabling effectiveness as well as integrity.

Again the employment practices of the sector militate against this. I have already referred to the ways in which the structure of remuneration, status and job security can exacerbate negative emotional strains. Long-term commitment is unlikely to occur in an atmosphere of illusions of power, anxiety, competitiveness and insecurity. If the firm has instituted good screening processes for the selection of staff with high ethical standards, this may, paradoxically, worsen things. Darwinian pressures in working conditions will not allow such employees to exercise their integrity and they will leave. Furthermore, the sector is marked by regular waves of large-scale redundancies. These are not only with, for example, branch closures by retail banks, but also follow consolidations or downturns in the sector such as those which follow financial crises. There are also dealers leaving in their early thirties with burnout, and whole investment teams leaving to join another employer. These two groups in particular are simply not concerned with the longevity of the firm.

The sector needs to address these features if they are to retain the older employees who have matured sufficiently to have a real quality of integrity. Not only are they needed by the firm now, they are also needed for the firm's future. Without them, the firm will lack the role models and mentors needed by newer employees. Integrity is a form of human capital. It can be squandered, left idle or actively produce more and so accumulate. Neither will the sector retain staff if the results-dominated culture still refuses to challenge behaviour even when it is, or appears to be, producing high profits. Failure to challenge will not only allow another Leeson to emerge. It will also contribute to the risk culture which I described in the last chapter.

Summary and Conclusions

Chapter 1 raised the question of how, if at all, moral claims on business behaviour can be made by the *Lebenswelt*. It was suggested there that such claims must respect the relative autonomy and functional competence of business, and at the same time prevent the disintegration of society into unrelated, mutually exclusive fragmentation. The requirement of integrity precisely fits these criteria. The relative autonomy and functional competence of the finance sector are respected by virtue of the fact that the integrity of the financial practitioner can only be adequately construed if it is orientated towards an appropriate *telos* which gives full recognition of the sector, its tasks, purposes and positioning within society. Fragmentation is avoided by the very nature of integrity which must bring into harmony the desires, aspirations, social roles and values of the person. But it is not an unproblematic requirement. Perhaps from an operational point of view, the FSA would have a simpler life if it had only prescribed virtues such as honesty, truthfulness and diligence, rather than integrity. The FSA is to be commended for setting its sights higher, but it has brought into being the difficulty of juridically prescribing a state which cannot be juridically demonstrated.

Taking the discussion from the last chapter further, I have suggested an understanding of freedom and identity which is considerably fuller than those proposed by the market, and a *telos* which enables both the unification of the life of the agent and the achievement of the purposes of the sector. The process of a deepening commitment to a relatively stable set of values and principles enables us to appropriate in a personal way a *telos* for our lives. This *telos*, this dream, helps form the identity of the person we could be, with the life we could have. This view of integrity allows for false starts, mistakes and new beginnings. As Newman is often quoted as saying, 'to live is to change, and to be perfect is to have changed often'. The process of integrity, therefore, points towards, helps bring about, and manifests both to ourselves and to others, a becoming into the person we were created to be.

Career and remuneration structures can hinder the sustaining power of a community in which commitment to other employees and to the firm itself is an important means of nurturing integrity. When coupled with Darwinian pressures to perform, it becomes clear that these practices do not enhance the processes by which integrity is fostered and sustained. Moral integrity is a necessary condition for the health of society (and as such is an example of the way in which a healthy understanding of self-fulfilment and the common good are interwoven). It is, therefore, necessary to work simultaneously for the conversion of hearts and the improvement of structures. Such an improvement will not necessarily follow on from simply listening to the ever louder public calls for compliance. As the discussion of propositional and evaluative knowledge suggested, compliance, while good, in itself tells us nothing about integrity. Rather, the sector needs to appreciate the extent to which it bears a responsibility for providing institutional forms within which integrity can flourish.

It makes no sense to talk about developing the virtues unless we also understand human agency as a means of developing character. Moral growth is the transformation of the self from seeking satisfaction to seeking values. Virtue presumes that we are self-forming and determining agents. Paradoxically, it may be precisely the form of identity outlined at the beginning of Chapter 9 which opens the door to an acceptance of integrity. In that section I suggested that a consequence of the combination of money, social ideals, the financial markets and economic models is to heighten the reluctance to accord external regulation a strong place.

One feature of integrity is that it is self-imposed and self-accepted, and thus it can legitimately be presented as giving due place to autonomy. This, together with the self-determinacy of the agent in the account of integrity I have presented, may well make it more attractive to the self-image of financial practitioners and therefore more likely to be accepted.

In Chapter 2 I argued that ethical investigation in some domain of human activity requires a reflection on the goals of that activity in the light of the ultimate goods of both individual human life and community. In other words, it must give due weight to the 'for-the-sake-of' relationship. While the micro-focus adopted by mainstream business ethics prevents such an investigation, personalist ethics, if it is to be true to itself, cannot neglect either aspect of this investigation. If a *telos* represents a certain kind of life, the *telos* is not something to be achieved at some future point, but in the way our whole life is construed. To be one thing instead of another, I have to act in a particular way. By my actions I make myself the person I am, and by my actions I do things for good and for ill in the world. I am both subject and agent, and through the pursuit of an appropriate *telos*, I bring together both my personal good and the good of society.

Anything less than this wider understanding of what an appropriate *telos*, what an appropriate 'for-the-sake-of' relationship might be, is ultimately stunted. If it is seen as purely within the private world of the individual, it will not have the power to unify all the agent's social roles. Neither will it be able adequately to express work as a means for self-realization. If it is seen only as located within the individual firm then the agent may, for example, cut corners in order to secure business or profits for 'his' firm. If it is just the sector, then there is the danger of the sector's *telos* operating in such a way that the good of the wider society and non-financial firms is subverted. In Chapter 1 I suggested that a significant criterion for ethically evaluating a particular sphere is in relation to its reasonable values, constrained by how it impacts on other spheres. Chapters 8 and 9 applied this criterion and showed that the danger to the sector's *telos* is a very real one. The *particular* good of the finance sector can operate in such a way as to subvert the *common* good.

Final Word

Through what I have termed 'Genoa tendencies', money, in and of itself, has a power and symbolic place which goes far beyond a simple mechanism for purchasing things. It has assumed a centrality in our ways of thinking and relating which is so pervasive that we often scarcely notice its effects. Money is 'the absolute means which is elevated to the psychological significance of an absolute purpose'.[19] As such, it shapes the market in a way that trade in other things does not. It enables us, as individuals and as institutions, to disengage ourselves from particular places and communities. It has fundamentally changed the ways in which objects are valued. It has become (if I can be excused the pun) the common currency of the economic discourse which increasingly shapes our entire social life.

This may all seem to be verging on the deterministic. At times the sheer weight of what *is* can seem overwhelming. How often do we hear a speaker, seeking to refute another's point, begin with the phrase: 'The fact of the matter is . . .' Yet a critical understanding of the present can provide a path for imagination to open up new possibilities. The institutional features I have been describing are not like the law of gravity. They are human constructs, the result of human decisions, and so can be changed. 'When the power of given present facts is challenged as we come to see the present situation as the issue of contingent processes and choices, we gain resources for new decisions, and openness to new stages of process. We learn to act and to hope.'[20]

One approach to doing this (and it is only one – others are needed as well) is to seek a richer understanding of the moral identity of agents in the finance sector. Without a strong framework within which to act, we do not have a free agent, but one who is in the grip of an appalling identity crisis.[21] Without a framework, such a person would have no real orientation from which to judge issues of fundamental importance. This touches on the very notion of identity. Part of the answer to the question: 'Who am I?' will be those identity-conferring commitments over time by which I sustain the values which guide moral choices. Those values will define the ground on which I stand, and the overall shape I wish to give to my life. This is one reason why, even in the midst of pluralism, we need to address questions of 'the good'.

I have done this through an exploration of what moral integrity and *telos* might mean for the financial practitioner. This has been integrated into the *telos* of the sector which, in turn, has been inserted into a conception of the common good. It is self-defeating to try and separate out into neat compartments what is personal and what is structural. There is a constant interplay between them which is an inevitable part of what it is to be human. I want to end with a quotation from Nicholas Lash which sums all this up.

> What it is and what it means to be 'human' is never finally, definitively given or achieved. It is, rather, continually to be sought, in practice and

19. Simmel, p. 238.
20. Rowan Williams, *Resurrection*, 1982, p. 31.
21. Taylor, *Sources of the Self*.

in theory, in action, reflection and suffering, in the precarious, costly, unending quest for reconciliation between the constitutive elements of human experience. In God, the elements are reconciled in the stillness of his unity. And in our sharing of that stillness shall be our peace.[22]

22. Nicholas Lash, *Theology on the Road to Emmaus*, 1986, pp. 156–57.

GLOSSARY

Arbitrage: a trading strategy exploiting tiny price differences of two similar instruments which are traded in different markets. The trader simultaneously buys the cheaper instrument and sells the more expensive substitute.

Buy long: to agree to buy an asset in the future on the premise that its price will rise higher than the contracted priced.

Counterparty: the other party to a transaction. For exchange-traded futures and options contracts, the counterparty is usually the exchange itself. For over-the-counter (OTC) instruments, the counterparty is generally a financial intermediary such as a major commercial investment or merchant bank, or a securities company.

Credit risk: the risk that a counterparty will not live up to its financial obligations. Derivative credit risk is different from loan credit risk because the amount at risk is dynamic and reflects changing prices and volatilities of the underlying asset.

Currency swap: an exchange of debt obligations in different currencies.

Futures contract: a contract to buy or sell a stated commodity (such as potatoes or oil) or financial claim (such as US Treasury Bonds) at a specified price at some future specified time. It *requires* its holder to buy or sell the asset, regardless of what happens to its value in the interim.

Futures margin: 'good faith' money the purchaser puts down to ensure that the contract is carried out.

Hedging: the protection of an open position to minimize risk; for example, to try and cover potential losses by betting that derivative prices will move the other way as well. A position where this has not been done is called unhedged, and is a riskier position to maintain.

Initial margin: the amount an investor deposits as an upfront payment.

Liquidity/Illiquidity: a market is said to be liquid when participants can rapidly execute large-volume transactions with a small impact on prices, or when a position can be reversed quickly without significant cost from the payment of a bid–ask spread. Illiquidity is seen in wider bid–ask spreads, a small transaction size for which a quoted price is good, and market-makers withdrawing from the market.

Market discipline: the market, through the price mechanism and the choice of counterparty, will reward 'good' behaviour and punish 'bad' behaviour.

Market risk: the risk brought about by changes in market conditions, for example, price, volatility, bid–ask spreads.

Moral hazard: in economic terms, moral hazard is used to define anything which encourages risky behaviour by leading financial risk takers to believe that they will benefit from risky actions, whilst being protected from the losses.

Off-balance sheet: banks' business, often fee-based, that does not generally involve booking assets and taking deposits. For example, trading of swaps, options, foreign exchange forwards, stand-by commitments and letters of credit.

Option contract: gives its owner the right – but not the obligation – to buy (a **call option**) or sell (a **put option**) a fixed number of shares or stock at a specified price over a limited time period.

Over-the-counter (OTC): transactions with customized financial instruments which are traded off-exchange.

Portfolio insurance: a form of hedging that uses Stock Index Futures contracts and index options to limit the downside risk of holding a diversified portfolio of common stocks.

Position: a market commitment.

Positive feedback: the processes that amplify price changes in a market, causing an initial price change to be followed by further changes in the same direction.

Ramping: buying a security to push up the price and then selling, hoping that there will be a time lag before investors react to the change in supply and demand.

Real interest rate: the nominal rate minus the rate of inflation. So if the interest rate is 3% and inflation is 2.2%, the 'real' interest rate is 0.8%.

Roll/Roll over: to replace an existing position or transaction with another similar position. Rolling over: the closing of a position in an expiring contract and the simultaneous opening of the same position in a later expiring contract.

Sell short: to agree to sell an asset not yet owned on the premise that its price will go down. When the time comes to hand over the asset, the trader expects to be able to buy it for less than the price at which he has agreed to sell it.

Systemic crisis: a financial disturbance which causes widespread disruptions elsewhere in the financial system.

Transparency (lack of): two principal meanings. The main one is high levels of asymmetrical information, that is, one party to a financial transaction often does not know enough about the other party to make accurate decisions. The second meaning is that derivatives are opaque because of their inherent complexity, with dynamically changing risk profiles, and because there are very few disclosure rules. For example, there is no need to disclose liabilities arising from derivatives in the balance sheet.

Value-at-risk (VaR): summarizes the expected maximum loss over a target time horizon within a given confidence interval. The time horizon will normally correspond to the longest period needed for an orderly portfolio liquidation. VaR relies on the volatilities of assets and the correlation between them; in effect, the uncertain relationships between many uncertainties. VaR is calculated assuming 'normal' market conditions. It is an educated estimate of market risk.

BIBLIOGRAPHY

Agénor, Pierre-Richard and Joshua Aizenman, *Volatility and the Welfare Costs of Financial Market Integration* (NBER Working Paper 6782; Cambridge, MA: NBER, 1998).

—'Contagion and Volatility with Imperfect Credit Markets', *IMF Staff Papers*, 45 (Washington, DC: IMF, June 1998).

Aghion, Philippe, Philippe Bacchetta and Abhijit Banerjee, *Capital Markets and the Instability of Open Economies* (CEPR Discussion Paper 2083; London: CEPR, 1999).

Argondoña, Antonio (ed.), *The Ethical Dimension of Financial Institutions and Markets* (Berlin: Springer-Verlag, 1995).

Aristotle, *Nicomachean Ethics* (trans. Martin Ostwald; London: Collier Macmillan, 1962).

Arrow, Kenneth J., 'Why Profits are Challenged', in Benjamin M. Friedman (ed.), *New Challenges to the Role of Profits* (Lexington, MA: Lexington Books, 1978).

Bank for International Settlements, *OTC Derivatives Market Statistics* (Basel: May 2005).

Barry, Norman, *Business Ethics* (Basingstoke: Macmillan, 1998).

Basel Committee on Banking Supervision, *A New Capital Adequacy Framework* (Basel: 1999).

—*Sound Practices for Banks' Interactions with Highly Leveraged Institutions* (Basel: 1999).

Beauchamp, Tom L. and Norman E. Bowie (eds.), *Ethical Theory and Business* (London: Pearson Prentice Hall, 7th edn, 2004).

Becker, Gary S., *The Economic Approach to Human Behaviour* (Chicago: University of Chicago Press, 1976).

—*A Treatise on the Family* (Cambridge, MA: Harvard University Press, 1981).

Benink, Harald A. (ed.), *Coping with Financial Fragility and Systemic Risk* (Boston: Kluwer Academic Publishers, 1995).

Benjamin, Walter, *Capitalism as Religion*, in M. Bullock and M.W. Jennings (eds.), *Selected Writings*, Vol. 1 (Cambridge, MA: The Belknap Press of Harvard University Press, 1996).

Berger, Peter, *The Capitalist Revolution: Fifty Propositions About Property, Equality and Liberty* (Aldershot: Gower, 1987).

Blaum, Lawrence, 'Community and Virtue', in Roger Crisp (ed.), *How Should One Live? Essays on the Virtues* (Oxford: Clarendon Press, 1995).

Boatright, John R., *Ethics in Finance* (Oxford: Blackwell, 1999).

Boswell, Jonathan and James Peters, *Capitalism in Contention: Business Leaders and Political Economy in Modern Britain* (Cambridge: Cambridge University Press, 1997).

Botero, Giovanni, *A Treatise Concerning the Cause of the Magnificencie and Greatnes of Cities* (trans. Robert Peterson; London: Richard Ockould & Henry Tomes, 1606).

Bowie, Norman E., and Ronald F. Duska, *Business Ethics* (New Jersey: Prentice-Hall, 2nd edn, 1990).

Boyacigiller, Nakiye Avdan and Namcy J. Adler, 'The Parochial Dinosaur: Organisational Science in a Global Context', *Academy of Management Review* 16 (1991), pp. 262–90.

Callahan, David, *The Cheating Culture: Why More Americans are Doing Wrong to Get Ahead* (Orlando: Harcourt, 2004).

Camdessus, Michel, 'Speech Opening the IMF Research Conference "Key Issues in Reform" 28 May 1999' (www.imf.org/external/np/speeches/1999/052899.htm).

Caputo, John D., *The Prayers and Tears of Jacques Derrida* (Indianapolis: Indiana University Press, 1997).

Carrier, James G., and Daniel Miller (eds.), *Virtualism: A New Political Economy* (Oxford: Berg, 1998).

Chryssides, George D. and John H. Kaler, (eds.) *An Introduction to Business Ethics* (London: International Thompson Business, 1999).

Cortright, S.A. and Michael J. Naughton (eds.), *Rethinking the Purpose of Business* (Notre Dame, IN: University of Notre Dame Press, 2002).

Cowley, Catherine, 'A Christian Reflection on Work, Culture and Society', in Anthony O'Mahony, Wulstan Peterburs and Mohammad Ali Shomali (eds.), *Catholics and Shi'a in Dialogue: Studies in Theology and Spirituality* (London: Melisende, 2004), pp. 378–91.

—'Money, Morality and Finance in a Global Economy', *New Blackfriars* 86 (March 2005), pp. 216–27.

Cox, Robert W., *Production, Power and World Order* (New York: Columbia University Press, 1987).

Daly, Kevin James, *Financial Volatility and Real Economic Activity* (Aldershot: Ashgate, 1999).

Davies, E. Philip, 'Financial Fragility in the Early 1990s – What can be Learnt from International Experience?' in C.A.E. Goodhart (ed.), *The Emerging Framework of Financial Regulations* (London: Central Banking Publications, 1998).

De George, Richard, 'Theological Ethics and Business Ethics', *Journal of Business Ethics* 5 (1986), pp. 421–32.

—*Competing with Integrity in International Business* (Oxford: Oxford University Press, 1993).

Delio, Ilia, 'Does God "Act" in Creation? A Bonaventurian Response', *Heythrop Journal* 44.3 (July 2003), pp. 328–44.

De Salins, Antoine and François Villeroy de Galhau, *The Modern Development of Financial Activities in the Light of the Ethical Demands of Christianity* (Vatican City: Pontifical Council for Justice and Peace, 1994).

Dobson, John, *Finance Ethics: The Rationality of Virtue* (Oxford: Rowman & Littlefield, 1997).

Dobson, John and Ken Reiner, 'The Rationality of Honesty in Debt Markets', in Dufrene.

Dodd, Nigel, *The Sociology of Money: Economics, Reason and Contemporary Society* (New York: Continuum, 1994).

Donaldson, Thomas and Thomas W. Dunfree, 'Towards a Unified Conception of Business Ethics: Integrative Social Contracts Theory', *Academy of Management Review* 19 (1994), pp. 252–84.

Douglas, Mary and Aaron Wildavsky, *Risk and Culture* (Berkeley, CA: University of California Press, 1982).

Dufrene, Uric (ed.), *Finance and the Ethics Debate* (Hull: Barmarick, 1996).

The Economist, 'The Good Company: A Survey of Corporate Social Responsibility', 22 January 2005.

Edwards, Franklin K., *The New Finance: Regulation and Financial Stability* (Washington, DC: AEI Press, 1996).

Eichengreen, Barry, *International Monetary Arrangements for the 21st Century* (Washington, DC: The Brookings Institute, 1994).

—*Towards a New International Financial Architecture: A Practical Post-Asia Agenda* (Washington, DC: Institute for International Economics, 1999).

Eichengreen, Barry and Ashoka Mody, *What Explains Changing Spreads on Emerging-Market Debt: Fundamentals or Market Sentiment?* (NBER Working Paper 6408; Cambridge, MA: NBER, 1998).

Ellul, Jacques, *Money and Power* (trans. LaVonne Neff; Basingstoke: Marshall Pickering, 1986).

Etzioni, Amitai, *The Moral Dimension: Toward a New Economics* (London: Collier Macmillan, 1988).

Financial Services Authority, *An Ethical Framework for Financial Services*, Discussion Paper 18, (www.fsa.gov.uk, October 2002).

—*Handbook* (www.fsa.gov.uk as at April 2005).

Financial Stability Forum, *Sound Practices for Hedge Fund Managers* (Basel, 2000).

Flannery, Austin (ed.), *Vatican Council II: The Conciliar and Post Conciliar Documents*, Vol. 1 (New York: Costello Publishing, rev. edn, 1984).

Foot, Phillipa, 'Virtues and Vices', in *Virtues and Vices and Other Essays in Moral Philosophy* (Oxford: Blackwell, 1978).

Friedman, Marilyn, 'Feminism and Modern Friendship: Dislocating the Community', in Eve Browning Cole and Susan Coultrap-McQuin (eds.), *Explorations in Feminist Ethics: Theory and Practice* (Bloomington, IN: Indiana University Press, 1992).

Friedman, Milton, *Capitalism and Freedom* (Chicago: University of Chicago Press, 1962).

—'The Social Responsibility of Business is to Increase Its Profits' (1970, reprinted in Chryssides and Kaler).

Frisby, David, *Simmel and Since: Essays on Georg Simmel's Social Theory* (London: Routledge, 1992).

Galbraith, John K., *Economics and the Public Purpose* (London: Deutsch, 1974).

—*A History of Economics* (Harmondsworth: Penguin, 1987).

Gay, Craig M., *Cash Values: The Value of Money, The Nature of Worth* (Sydney: University of New South Wales Press, 2003).

Ghorbade, Jai, 'Ethics in MBA Programs: The Rhetoric, the Reality, and a Plan of Action', *Journal of Business Ethics* 10 (1991), pp. 891–905.

Giddens, Anthony, *Central Problems in Social Theory: Action, Structure and Contradiction in Social Analysis* (London: Macmillan, 1979).

Gill, Stephen, 'European Governance and New Constitutionalism: Economic and Monetary Union and Alternatives to Disciplinary NeoLiberalism in Europe', *New Political Economy* 3.1 (1998), pp. 5–26.

Gilligan, Carol, *In a Different Voice: Psychological.Theory and Women's Development* (Cambridge, MA: Harvard University Press, 1982).

Goldberg, David J., ' "An Intelligent Person's Guide to Religion," by John Haldane', *The Independent*, 26 April 2003, p. 24.

Goodhart, Charles A.E., *Money, Information and Uncertainty* (London: Macmillan, 2nd edn, 1989).

—'Some Regulatory Concerns', in C.A.E. Goodhart (ed.), *The Emerging Framework of Financial Regulations* (London: Central Banking Publications, 1998).

Goodhart, Charles A.E., Philip Hartmann, David Llewellyn, Lilian Rojas-Suarez and Steven Weisbrod, *Financial Regulation: Why, How and Where Now?* (London: Routledge/Bank of England, 1998).

Greenspan, Alan, 'Remarks before the Independent Community Bankers of America National Convention, 11 March 2005', *BIS Review* (16/2005), www.bis.org.

Grisez, Germain, *The Way of the Lord Jesus* Vol. 1: *Christian Moral Principles* (Chicago: Franciscan Herald Press, 1983).

Gunton, Colin, *The One, the Three and the Many: God, Creation and the Culture of Modernity* (Cambridge: Cambridge University Press, 1993).

Haan, Roelf, *The Economics of Honour: Biblical Reflections on Money and Property* (Geneva: WCC Publications, 1988).

Hall, Edward T., *Beyond Culture* (New York: Doubleday, 1981).

Hammer, Michael and James Champy, *Reengineering the Corporation: A Manifesto for Business Revolution* (London: Michael Brealy, 1993).

Handy, Charles, *The Age of Paradox* (Harvard, MA: Harvard Business School Press, 1994).

Hauerwas, Stanley, *Community of Character* (Notre Dame: University of Notre Dame Press, 1981).

Hayek, Fredrick A., *The Constitution of Liberty* (London: Routledge, 1960).

—*Law, Legislation and Liberty* Vol. 3: *The Political Order of a Free People* (London: Routledge & Kegan Paul, 1979).

—*Denationalisation of Money – The Argument Refined* (London: Institute of Economic Affairs, 3rd edn, 1990).

—*Economic Freedom* (Oxford: Blackwell, 1991).

Helleiner, Eric, *States and the Reemergence of Global Finance: From Bretton Woods to the 1990s* (New York: Cornell University Press, 1994).

Hobbes, Thomas, *Leviathan* (ed. and intro. C.B. MacPherson; Harmondsworth: Penguin, 1981).

Hollenbach, David, *The Common Good and Christian Ethics* (Cambridge: Cambridge University Press, 2002).

Hood, John M., *The Heroic Enterprise: Business and the Common Good* (New York: The Free Press, 1996).

Hughes, Gerard J., 'Natural Law', in *Introduction to Christian Ethics* (London: Cassell, 1998).

The Independent, 'Priory Clinic Targets City High-Flyers who Need Drink to Cope', 5 April 2005, p. 15.

Janssens, Louis, 'Artificial Insemination: Ethical Considerations', *Louvain Studies* (1980), pp. 3–29.

Jensen, M.C. and W. Meckling, 'Theory of the Firm: Managerial Behaviour, Ownership Costs and Ownership Structure', *Journal of Financial Economics* 3 (1976), pp. 305–60.

John XXIII, *Mater et Magistra* (London: Catholic Truth Society, 1961).

John Paul II, *Sollicitudo Rei Socialis* (Vatican City: Vatican Polyglot Press, 1987).

—*Centesimus Annus* (Vatican City: Vatican Polyglot Press, 1991).

Kelly, Jonathan, 'New Products Open Banks to New Risk', *International Financial Law Review* (24 June 1998), pp. 24–25.

Kelly, Kevin, *New Directions in Moral Theology: The Challenge of Being Human* (London: Geoffrey Chapman, 1992).

Kennedy, A. and T. Deal, *Corporate Cultures* (Reading, MA: Addison-Wesley, 1982).

Keown, Arther J., John D. Martin, J. William Petty and David F. Scott Jr., *Financial Management: Principles and Applications* (London: Pearson Education, 9th edn, 2004).

Keynes, John M., 'The Consequences to Society of Changes in the Value of Money' (1922) (reprinted in *Collected Writings of John Maynard Keynes* Vol. IV: *A Tract on Monetary Reform*, London: Macmillan, 1971).

—*The End of Laissez-Faire* (London: Hogarth Press, 1926).

—*Essays in Persuasion* (London: Macmillan, 1931).

—*General Theory of Employment, Interest and Money* (New York: Harcourt Brace, 1936).

Kindleberger, Charles P., *Manias, Panics and Crashes: A History of Financial Crises* (Basingstoke: Macmillan, 3rd edn, 1996).

King, Mervyn, 'Speech at the Federal Reserve Bank, 9 Sept. 1999', *BIS Review* (95/1999), www.bis.org.

Knight, Frank H., *The Ethics of Competition and Other Essays* (London: Allen and Unwin, 1935).

—'Free Society: Its Basic Nature and Problem', in *idem, On the History and Method of Economics: Selected Essays* (Chicago: University of Chicago Press, 1956).

—*The Economic Organization* (New York: Augustus M. Kelly, 1969).

Kotva, Joseph, *The Christian Case for Virtue Ethics* (Washington, DC: Georgetown University Press, 1996).

Kuhn, Kathryn E., 'Social Values and Bureaucratic Reality', in Gerard Magill and Marie D. Hoff (eds.), *Values and Public Life: An Interdisciplinary Study* (London: University Press of America, 1995).

Lash, Nicholas, *Theology on the Road to Emmaus* (London: SCM Press, 1986).

Leeson, Nick, with Edward Whitley, *Rogue Trader* (London: Little Brown & Co., 1996).

Leo XIII, *Rerum Novarum* (1891), trans. in Michael Walsh and Brian Davies.

Lewis, Michael, *Liar's Poker: Two Cities, True Greed* (London: Coronet, 1989).

Loisel, Olivier and Philippe Martin, *Coordination, Cooperation, Contagion and Currency Crises* (CEPR Discussion Paper 2075; London: CEPR, 1999).

Long, D. Stephen, *Divine Economy: Theology and the Market* (London: Routledge, 2000).

MacIntyre, Alasdair, *After Virtue: A Study in Moral Theory* (London: Duckworth, 1981).

—'*Sophrunē*: How a Virtue Can Become Socially Disruptive', *Midwest Studies in Philosophy* Vol. XIII: *Ethical Theory: Character and Virtue* (ed. Peter A. French, Theodore E. Uehling, Jr. and Howard K. Wettsein; Notre Dame, IN: University of Notre Dame, 1988).

McCann, Dennis P. and Patrick D. Miller (eds.), *In Search of the Common Good*, (London: T&T Clark, 2005).

McCosh, Andrew M., *Financial Ethics* (London: Kluwer Academic Publishers, 1999).

Milbank, John, *Theology and Social Theory: Beyond Secular Reason* (Oxford: Blackwell, 1990).

Miller, Arthur, *Death of a Salesman* (London: Penguin, 1980).

Mishkin, Frederic S., *International Capital Movements, Financial Volatility and Financial Instability* (NBER Working Paper 6390; Cambridge, MA: NBER, 1998).

Morison, Ian, *Banking Ethics – What is Special About Banking and Finance?* (paper presented to the Finance and Ethics Group at the Von Hügel Institute, Cambridge, 1 March 1994).

Mount Jr., Eric, *Covenant, Community and the Common Good: An Interpretation of Christian Ethics* (Cleveland, OH: Pilgrim Press, 1999).

Myers, Milton L., *The Soul of Modern Economic Man: Ideas of Self-Interest: Thomas Hobbes to Adam Smith* (Chicago: University of Chicago Press, 1983).

Nairn, Agnes and Pierre Berthon, 'Creating the Customer: The Influence of Advertising on Consumer Market Segments – Evidence and Ethics', *Journal of Business Ethics* 42.1 (2003), pp. 83–99.

Nelson, Robert H., *Economics as Religion: From Samuelson to Chicago and Beyond* (University Park, PA: Pennsylvania State University Press, 2001).

Noonan, John T., *The Scholastic Analysis of Usury* (Cambridge, MA: Harvard University Press, 1957).

Novak, Michael, *The Spirit of Democratic Capitalism* (New York: Simon and Schuster, 1982).

Nozick, Robert, *Anarchy, State and Utopia* (New York: Basic Books, 1974).

Nussbaum, Martha, *The Fragility of Goodness: Luck and Ethics in Greek Tragedy and Philosophy* (Cambridge: Cambridge University Press, 1986).

—'Aristotelian Social Democracy', in Gillian Brock (ed.), *Necessary Goods: Our Responsibilities to Meet Others' Needs* (Oxford: Rowman & Littlefield, 1998).

Obstfeld, Maurice, *The Global Capital Market: Benefactor or Hindrance?* (NBER Working Paper 6782; Cambridge, MA: NBER, 1998).

Okun, Arthur M., *Equality and Efficiency: The Big Tradeoff* (Washington, DC: The Brookings Institution, 1975).

Parsons, Talcott, *Structure and Process in Modern Society* (New York: Free Press, 1960).

—*The System of Modern Societies* (Englewood Cliffs: Prentice Hall, 1971).

Partnoy, Frank, *Testimony at Hearings Before the United States Senate Committee on*

Governmental Affairs (www.senate.gov/~gov_affairs/012402partnoy.htm: January 2002).

——, *F.I.A.S.C.O.: Blood in the Water on Wall Street* (London: Profile, 1998).

Perraton, Jonathan, David Goldblatt, David Held and Andrew McGrew, 'The Globalization of Economic Activity', *New Political Economy* 2.2 (1997), pp. 257–77.

Peters, Thomas J. and Robert H. Waterman, *In Search of Excellence: Lessons from America's Best-Run Companies* (London: Harper & Row, 1982).

Petrick, Joseph A. and John F. Quinn, *Management Ethics: Integrity at Work* (London: Sage, 1997).

Phelps, Edmund S., *Altruism, Morality and Economic Theory* (New York: Russell Sage Foundation, 1975).

Pincoffs, Edmund L., *Quandaries and Virtues: Against Reductionism in Ethics* (Lawrence: University Press of Kansas, 1986).

Pius XI, *Quadragesimo Anno* (1931), trans. in Walsh and Davies.

Polanyi, Karl, *Origins of Our Times: The Great Transformation* (London: Victor Gollancz, 1945).

Popper, Karl R., *Objective Knowledge: An Evolutionary Approach* (Oxford: Clarendon Press, 1972).

Post, James E. William C. Frederick, Anne T. Lawrence and James Weber, *Business and Society: Corporate Strategy, Public Policy, Ethics* (London: McGraw-Hill, 9th edn, 1999).

Preston, Lee E., and James E. Post, *Private Management and Public Policy: The Principles of Public Responsibility* (London: Prentice-Hall, 1975).

Preston, Ronald H., *Religion and the Ambiguities of Capitalism* (London: SCM, 1991).

Prindl, Andreas R. and Bimal Prodhan (eds.), *The ACT Guide to Ethical Conflicts in Finance* (Oxford: Blackwell, 1994).

Rahner, Karl, *Theological Investigations*, Vol. 7 (trans. David Bourke; London: Darton, Longman & Todd, 1971).

——'Reflections on the Adult Christian', *Theology Digest* 31 (1984), pp. 123–26.

Ravetz, Jerome R., 'Public Perceptions of Acceptable Risks as Evidence of their Cognitive, Technical and Social Structure', in Meinolf Dierkes, Sam Edwards and Rob Coppock (eds.), *Technological Risk: Its Perception and Handling in the European Community* (Cambridge, MA: Oelgescher, Gunn and Hain, 1980).

Rawls, John, *A Theory of Justice* (Oxford: Clarendon Press, 1972).

——'Justice as Fairness: Political Not Metaphysical', *Philosophy and Public Affairs* 14.3 (Summer 1985), pp. 223–52.

Rigali, Norbert, 'Christian Morality and Universal Morality: The One and the Many', *Louvain Studies* 19 (1994), pp. 18–33.

Riordan, Patrick, *A Politics of the Common Good* (Dublin: Institute of Public Administration, 1996).

Robbins, Lionel, *An Essay of the Nature and Significance of Economic Science* (London: Macmillan, 3rd edn, 1984).

Ross, W. David, *Foundation of Ethics* (Oxford: Clarendon Press, 1939).

Rudman, Stanley, *Concepts of Person & Christian Ethics* (Cambridge: Cambridge University Press, 1997).

Sandel, Michael J., *Liberalism and the Limits of Justice* (Cambridge: Cambridge University Press, 1982).

Schein, Edgar H., *Organisational Culture and Leadership* (San Francisco: Jossey-Bass, 1985).

Schweiker, William, 'Responsibility in the World of Mammon: Theology, Justice and Transnational Corporations', in Max L. Stackhouse with Peter J. Paris (eds.), *God and Globalization* Vol. 1: *Religion and the Powers of the Common Life* (Harrisburg, PA: Trinity Press International, 2000).

Second Vatican Council, *Gaudium et Spes*, trans. in Flannery.

Selling, Joseph, 'The Human Person', in Bernard Hoose (ed.), *Christian Ethics: An Introduction* (London: Cassell, 1998).

Sen, Amartya K., 'Rational Fools: A Critique of the Behavioural Foundations of Economic Theory' (1977) (reprinted in Amartya K. Sen, *Choice, Welfare and Management*, Oxford: Blackwell, 1982).

—*On Ethics and Economics* (Oxford: Blackwell, 1987).

—*Money and Value: On the Ethics and Economics of Finance* (Rome: Editioni dell'Elefante, 1991).

Sen, Sunanda, 'On Financial Fragility and its Global Implications', in Sunanda Sen (ed.), *Financial Fragility, Debt and Economic Reforms* (London: Macmillan, 1996).

Senate Staff Report of Committee on Governmental Affairs, *Committee Staff Investigation of FERC's Oversight of Enron Corp.* (www.senate.gov/~gov_affairs/111202fercmemo.pdf 2002, accessed February 2005).

Shrader-Frechette, Kriston T., *Risk Analysis and Scientific Method* (Dordrecht: Reidel, 1985).

—— *Risk and Rationality* (Berkeley, CA: University of California Press, 1991).

Simmel, Georg, *The Philosophy of Money* (trans. Tom Bottomore and David Frisby; London: Routledge & Kegan Paul, 1978).

Simon, H.A., 'Rationality in Psychology and Economics', *Journal of Business* 59.4.2 (October 1986), pp. 209–24.

Singer, Peter, 'Rights and the Market', in Beauchamp and Bowie, pp. 72–85.

Smith, Adam, *The Theory of Moral Sentiments* (ed. D.D. Raphael and A.L. Macfie; Oxford: Clarendon Press, 1976).

—*An Inquiry into the Causes and Nature of the Wealth of Nations* (ed. R.H. Campbell and A.S. Skinner; Oxford: Clarendon Press, 1976).

Solomon, Robert C., *Ethics and Excellence: Cooperation and Integrity in Business* (Oxford: Oxford University Press, 1992).

Sternberg, Elaine, *Just Business: Business Ethics in Action* (London: Little, Brown and Co., 1994).

Sutherland, Stewart R., 'Integrity and Self-Identity', in *Ethics* (ed. A. Phillips Griffiths; Cambridge: Cambridge University Press, 1993).

Taylor, Charles, *Human Agency and Language: Philosophical Papers I* (Cambridge: Cambridge University Press, 1985).

—*Sources of the Self: The Making of Modern Identity* (Cambridge: Cambridge University Press, 1989).

—'Irreducibly Social Goods', in *idem, Philosophical Arguments* (London: Harvard University Press, 1995).

Taylor, Gabriele, *Pride, Shame and Guilt* (Oxford: Oxford University Press, 1985).

Tracy, David, 'Defending the Public Character of Theology', *Christian Century*, 1 April 1981, pp. 350–56.

Trevino, Linda K., 'A Cultural Perspective on Changing and Developing Organizational Ethics', *Research in Organizational Change and Development* 4 (1990), pp. 195–230.

Useem, Michael, *The Inner Circle: Large Corporations and the Rise of Business Political Activity in the US and UK* (Oxford: Oxford University Press, 1984).

Valasquez, Manuel G., *Business Ethics: Concepts and Cases* (London: Prentice-Hall, 5th edn, 2002).

Vallance, Elizabeth, *Business Ethics at Work* (Cambridge: Cambridge University Press, 1995).

Walsh, Michael and Brian Davies (eds.), *Proclaiming Justice and Peace* (Mystic, CT: Twenty-Third Publications, 2nd edn, 1991).

Walzer, Michael, *Thick and Thin: Moral Arguments at Home and Abroad* (Notre Dame, IN: University of Notre Dame Press, 1994).

Webb, Michael C., 'Defining the Boundaries of Legitimate State Practice: Norms, Transnational Actors and the OECD's Project on Harmful Tax Competition', *Review of International Political Economy* 11.4 (October 2004), pp. 787–827.

Welby, Julian, 'Risk Management and the Ethics of the New Financial Instruments', *Ethical Perspectives* 4.2 (1997), pp. 84–93.

Williams, Bernard, 'A Critique of Utilitarianism', in *Utilitarianism: For and Against* (ed. J.J.C. Smart and Bernard Williams; Cambridge: Cambridge University Press, 1973).

Williams, Rowan, *Resurrection* (London: Darton, Longman & Todd, 1982).

Wriston, Walter B., *The Twilight of Sovereignty* (New York: Scribner, 1992).

Young, Iris Marion, *Justice and the Politics of Difference* (Princeton: Princeton University Press, 1990).

Young, Jeffrey T., *Economics as a Moral Science: The Political Economy of Adam Smith* (Cheltenham: Edward Elgar, 1997).

Zohar, Danah, *The Quantum Self: Human Nature and Consciousness Defined by the New Physics* (London: Bloomsbury, 1990).

INDEX

Index Note: *n* following a page number refers to an author quoted but not named in the main body of the text, or to significant mention of an author or subject in footnotes.